DO'S AND TABOOS AROUND THE WORLD FOR WOMEN IN BUSINESS

Also by Roger E. Axtell

Do's and Taboos Around the World: A Guide to International Behavior, 3rd edition

Do's and Taboos of International Trade: A Small Business Primer, 2nd edition

Do's and Taboos of Hosting International Visitors

Gestures: Do's and Taboos of Body Language Around the World

Do's and Taboos of Public Speaking

Do's and Taboos of Using English Around the World

Do's and Taboos of Preparing for Your Trip Abroad, *with John P. Healy*

DO'S AND TABOOS AROUND THE WORLD FOR WOMEN IN BUSINESS

Roger E. Axtell
Tami Briggs
Margaret Corcoran
Mary Beth Lamb

John Wiley & Sons, Inc.

New York • Chichester • Weinheim • Brisbane • Singapore • Toronto

Copyright © 1997 by Roger E. Axtell, Tami Briggs, Margaret Corcoran, and Mary Beth Lamb
Published by John Wiley & Sons, Inc.

Library of Congress Cataloging-in-Publication Data

Do's and taboos around the world for women in business / Roger E.
    Axtell . . . [et al.].
        p.   cm.
    Includes index.
    ISBN 0-471-14364-2 (pbk. :   alk. paper)
      1. Business travel—Guidebooks.   2. Women in business.
    3. Business etiquette.   4. Americans—Foreign countries.
    I. Axtell, Roger E.
    G156.5.B86D67   1997
    910'.2'02—dc20   96–35911

To Mitzi—R. E. A.

To my husband, David Marshall— M. C.

To Rick—M. B. L.

And to all the inspiring international businesswomen we've worked with. Your pioneering work has strengthened international understanding and cooperation in global business.

CONTENTS

Contents

ACKNOWLEDGMENTS

The authors wish to express special thanks and appreciation to the more than 100 men and women we interviewed, surveyed, or called on for their research for this book. Quite obviously, it could not have been written without them.

In alphabetical order, we owe our thanks to the following women: Nancy Adler, Dominique Anderson, Charlene Armstrong, Maureen Quinn Aslin, Cheryl A. Baedke, Julie Baker, Charlotte Balfour, Roxanne Baumann, Dr. Claudia A. Becker, Delores M. Betti, Patricia Blankenburg, Myriam Botero, Erin Brennan, Dr. Colleen Braun, Kathy J. Bullen, Elain Buss, Teri Skluzacek Carlisano, Debra L. Casucci-Crave, Nancy J. Coune, Sue Cozine, Annick Deligny, Rosemary K. Dineen, Karen Dorian, Deborah Enix-Ross, Penny Fantacci, Barbara J. Fischer, Joanne Fischer, Joy Frederigo, Ellen Glatstein, Vivien Godfrey, Paula A. Golz, Anne Greene, Catherine C. Gryczan, Linda Hall, Jane A. Hassler, Barbara R. Hauser, Lynn Hawley-Wildmoser, Ingeborg Hegenbart, Audrey Marsh Hill, Daralynn Horner, Kate Hotchkiss, Amy Isom, Vicki Jaramillo-Solik, Maureen Johanson, Elinor L. Jackson, Anja Joswig, Susan Kadlec, Joyce L. Keehn, Dr. Jeanne Kirkpatrick, Peggy Lescrenier, Andrea Kormann Lowe, Dr. Judith Irene Knorst, Zoya Khotkina, Dr. Judith Ladinsky, Louise Laport, Tahirih V. Lee, Sheila LeGeros, Sally Little, Elizabeth Longmore, Julie Loving, Diane MacDonald, Mary C. MacDonald, Michelle Martin, Katherine McArdle, Mary McCormick, Edith C. McDonald, Lesa Mellis, Cheryl Miller, Barbara Moebius, Karen S. Moebs, Connie Okhuysen-Martinez, Kirsten Olsen, Georgia Parks, Mercedes M. Pellet, Janis L. Raskin, Mary A. Regel, Virginia Rehberg, Ann Rettie, Sharon Richardson, Charlotte Robertson, Solvig Robertson, Kate Ronan, Beatrice Rothweiler, Patricia Seago, Kathi Seifert, Catherine Tenke Teichert, Fran Theis, Mary Uppgren, Sylvia Veh, Jane Walmsley, Ann M. Wasescha, Tine Willemsen, Janet Wulf, Brenda Wyley, and Janet G. Zens.

In addition, we wish to thank the following men: Umberto Fantacci, Richard Gesteland, Steven Iverson, Dave Molnar, Robert Moran, Klavs Olson, Hugh Shankland, Fred Valentine, Shay Wyley.

All four authors want to thank Brenda Sauer, research assistant, for the intelligence, resourcefulness, common sense, and initiative she applied to this project. Also, to Barb Goodman for her help in researching Chapter 23. Thanks also to Michele McGuire of the Organization of Women in International Trade (OWIT), Tonja Berg, The Minnesota Trade Office Library, Maryse Kjerland, and Minnesota On Line.

Tami Briggs and Mary Beth Lamb would also like to thank Camille LeFevre for her insights, creativity, patience, and teamwork on this project.

The authors also wish to give special thanks to Stephanie Derderian and Martha Whitehead of The Culture Transitions Group, Lake Forest, Illinois, for their gracious permission to reprint their "Culture-Gender Awareness Quiz" found at the beginning of Part One.

INTRODUCTION

In the years ahead, more North American women will enter international business than ever before. The reason is simple: you can't stop them!

Morally, ethically, legally, no one can stop more women from moving steadily into the ranks of international management. Besides, they are needed—desperately.

In the 1960s, 1970s, and into the 1980s, male-dominated managements protested: "You can't send women out around the world on international business. It's too dangerous. Not only that, they won't be accepted." Slowly, we have learned that the attitude is an untruth, a myth—and a myth that is rapidly dissolving. Today, while the percentage of women compared to men in international business is still very low, more North American women are moving into top management positions, traveling the world, and bringing home extraordinary results.

You will read about their success stories in this book. You will learn how scores of women have broken the glass ceilings—and walls!—to enter what was solely and traditionally a male domain. You will also learn scores of tips and suggestions for becoming an effective international businesswoman.

The idea for this book sprang from a breakfast meeting in Minneapolis in 1990. Two of the authors, Margaret Corcoran and Mary Beth Lamb, sat down with Roger E. Axtell to discuss ways the two women might expand their consulting business, Transnational Strategies, Inc. Naturally, their strong suit was women in international business; for Axtell, it was his thirty-year career in international business, plus his experience in writing seven earlier books.

Over a period of four years the trio exchanged ideas and information and finally, in 1994, submitted a proposal to John Wiley & Sons, Inc., New York. There, Senior Editor PJ Dempsey agreed that a book was timely and worthy of national publication.

In any collaborative effort, it is obvious that the authors did not produce the words in unison. We apportioned the responsibilities in the following manner:

Margaret Corcoran, with the assistance of Brenda Sauer, headed the research team. Over a three-year period, Margaret surveyed and interviewed sixty-nine experienced international businesswomen. Margaret was also responsible for writing Chapters 22 and 24, for revisions to Chapters 25–32, and for assembling and writing all of Part Six (Resources).

Chapter 1, "Sex, Dating, Discrimination, and Harassment," and parts of Chapter 4, "Safety When Traveling," were a collaborative effort, with all four authors contributing ideas.

Roger E. Axtell prepared and wrote Chapters 2 through 21 plus Chapter 23. Much of the advice found in those chapters was drawn from the research material provided by Margaret and the team at Transnational Strategies, Inc.

Mary Beth Lamb and Tami Briggs were responsible for assembling the information for Parts Four and Five (Chapters 25–32), "The International Assignment," with assistance from writer Camille LeFevre.

This book attempts to offer advice about *behavior*—an often elusive and changing subject. Much of that advice comes from scores of women with impressive experience and credentials. We ask you, the reader, to recognize that these are personal observations and opinions, and not necessarily infallible declarations by the authors.

HOW THIS BOOK WILL HELP YOU

Ask a North American* businesswoman what concerns her the most about venturing overseas on business and the response you'll hear is, "How do I survive in alien lands, where males have—and still do—dominate in the ranks of business?" Accordingly, this book begins with survival techniques for women in international business. And when it comes to survival, the first burning question women ask is: "What do I do about sex, dating, harassment, and discrimination when traveling and doing business overseas? What do I do when some guy in Caracas, Calcutta, or Copenhagen suddenly starts making moves on me?" Chapter 1 offers the answers in the form of a list of "Ten Do's and Taboos of Sexual Behavior." For women living and working abroad, it also provides instructions and advice on the two "hot" words in our business culture today: harassment and discrimination.

Chapters 2 through 6 deal with different types of survival problems:

---

*A note about that term "North American." As it is used throughout this book, it means "from the United States and Canada." Literally, of course, the continent of North America includes Mexico and Central America, but few people in those areas expect—or like—to be called North Americans.

knowing the culture, protocol, safety, how to stay healthy, and even tips on luggage and packing for trips overseas.

Part Two, beginning with Chapter 7, starts you on a round-the-world journey where you will acquire country-specific information and advice. In each chapter you will learn, first, about the status and conditions of local women. Then you will be offered a variety of helpful tips and do's and taboos for business behavior in each of twenty-six major countries or regions of the world.

In Part Three, you will learn how to step up and climb onto the career ladder in international business. Chapter 23 sets the stage by describing the past, present, and future for women in international business. Of special note is an explanation of why women are especially well suited for careers in international commerce.

Then, if you are wondering how you can break into international business, Chapter 24 relates the stories of twelve women who describe how they got their first job in international business.

Chapter 25 offers an inspirational note—profiles of three fascinating international businesswomen, their stories and their successes.

Part Four deals with one of the most challenging and fascinating facets of international business: the international assignment. What should you know and do when confronted with the prospect of being posted overseas? The answers are provided in seven chapters.

Part Five provides tips for the woman who is not currently employed by an international company, but wishes to find work opportunities abroad. Part Six lists dozens of resources to help you become an international business professional.

If you are one who enjoys spotting a trend, or detecting the beginning of a business wave, we believe one is building at this very moment. That trend involves the masses of women in North America who are considering, preparing for, or are currently involved in international business. At the beginning of this introduction, we stated that this infusion of women was desperately needed. Business, particularly in the United States, demands a strong new dose of energy, creativity, and talent to move products and services into overseas markets. Frankly, the U.S. business community has not performed well in this important business sector. Proof comes from the last two decades when the United States has run substantial trade deficits, often in the $100-billion range. Simply stated, that means we, the people of the United States, are buying more goods from overseas sources than we are selling to overseas customers. That hurts the economy because it means that more and more U.S. dollars—and jobs—are going overseas.

Furthermore, the U.S. Department of Commerce estimates that there are at least 200,000 businesses in the United States capable of exporting but are not doing so now. The reason—lack of energy, combined with fear of the unknown. Managers of thousands of key medium-and small-sized businesses are reluctant to take their catalogs and samples abroad because they don't understand how they will get paid or how to ship products overseas; they also feel insecure and apprehensive about dealing with other cultures. Ironically, each of these alleged "obstacles" can be quickly and easily overcome.

What is needed is a new force, a new surge of energy and spirit. We believe having more women involved in international business will provide precisely that force.

Roger E. Axtell
Tami Briggs
Margaret Corcoran
Mary Beth Lamb

Note: If you have anecdotes, case studies, resources, or object lessons pertaining to this subject, we would like to hear about them and consider them for future editions. Please send your material to:

Roger E. Axtell
c/o General Interest Books
Professional & Trade Division
John Wiley & Sons, Inc.
605 Third Avenue
New York, NY 10158-0012

PART ONE

SURVIVAL "OVER THERE"

How does an American or Canadian businesswoman survive in the strange and often hostile arena of international business? What differences, difficulties, or dangers will you encounter? These questions are often your first concerns after leaving the safe and familiar haven of business in North America.

TEST YOUR CULTURE-GENDER AWARENESS

In the following pages, you will find a quiz in the form of six situations you might encounter in your international business career. This quiz will serve to measure your knowledge and judgment in situations that may be totally unfamiliar because the rules of etiquette and protocol change from continent to continent.

Work your way through the questions. Don't despair—if you miss some of the correct answers, then this book should prove even more important to you. In fact, after you finish reading it, return to this questionnaire and take the quiz again. We think you'll find it much easier to sort out the good from the bad solutions, and to feel confident about making the right decision when working with international colleagues.

CULTURE-GENDER AWARENESS QUIZ*

Choose one answer for each question. The correct answers, with explanations, follow the quiz.

1. You are in a Latin American country and your agent and one of his colleagues have invited you out for the evening to visit the famous local nightspots. What should you do?
    A. Join them, drink, and be merry. You're glad they view you as "one of the boys."
    B. Go, but don't drink. Agree ahead that the agent will take you back to the hotel when you are ready.
    C. Graciously decline.
    D. Invite a male colleague whom you know well and trust who will stay with you and take you home when you wish.

---

*This quiz was developed by Stephanie Derderian and Martha Whitehead of the Culture Transitions Group, Lake Forest, Illinois, and is reprinted here with their kind permission.

3

2. You're the customer-service manager at your company. An Asian client
    says he doesn't want the female who was assigned him, even though she
    does speak his language. He has more or less said that he would feel
    more comfortable with a male customer-service contact. What do you
    do?

    A. You assign a male to work as a co-contact with the original contact
        with the hope that, in the long run, the client will become used to
        dealing with the woman.
    B. You assign a male colleague to this customer. Unfortunately, the
        woman originally assigned was the only one who spoke the customer's
        language and you must now hire a male translator.
    C. You discuss with the customer the qualifications of the female
        customer-service contact and indicate that because of her language
        ability it will ultimately be advantageous to try to work with her.
    D. You very politely explain to the client that in the United States women
        assume roles of responsibility, and it would be against your principles
        and company policy to assign someone else. You ask him to please
        give it a try.

3. You are your company's Vice President of Marketing and are traveling
    with a male marketing manager who is new to international. You arrive
    at your destination, and your welcoming party greets you both at the gate.
    The potential customer walks up to your male subordinate, warmly, yet
    formally, greets him, and says, "You didn't tell us that you were bringing
    your wife!" What do you do?

    A. The two of you play along at least for a while so as not to embarrass
        the potential client.
    B. Your male colleague smiles, introduces you, and says, "Mr. Client,
        this is Mrs. Christine Lawry, our Vice President of Marketing, and I
        am Peter Smith, Marketing Manager."
    C. You and your male colleague switch roles for this client in case he
        prefers dealing with a man.
    D. You smile and say, "I'm sorry, Mr. Client, there has been a misunder-
        standing. It is my fault; I should have explained in our correspon-
        dence. I am the Vice President and Peter, here, is only our marketing
        manager."

4. You are paying a sales call to a school in a more conservative Middle
    Eastern country. You are told by the school director that you must wear
    a veil, a black head scarf, and a robe. You didn't come prepared for this.
    What do you do?

    A. Politely refuse and explain that this not your belief system.

    B. Leave, find the local *souk*, buy the appropriate garments, wear them, and call on the school later that day.

    C. Improvise by draping your multicolored, designer suit scarf over your head.

    D. Bribe the guard at the door to allow you to enter.

5. You and a male colleague have been invited to dinner at the agent's house in the Middle East. However, once there, you are put into a separate room with the host's wives and daughters where you are to be entertained with them and watch home videos. Meanwhile, your colleague is advancing his career and you don't get any business done. What do you do?

    A. Insist on being with the men since you were invited in a professional capacity.

    B. Since you realize that you will not be allowed to sit with the businessmen, return to your hotel rather than stay and be humiliated.

    C. Relax and enjoy the videos.

    D. Speak privately to your colleague and ask him to speak on your behalf so that you may sit with the men.

6. You are at a meeting in Europe with a potential joint-venture partner. He interrupts you often, repeatedly questions your information and statistics, and even takes a phone call while you are together. Although you are sure of your information, he asks you to call the home office to verify some figures. You are beginning to lose patience, and you have a strong feeling that he is testing you, sometimes bullying you, and generally not taking you seriously because you are a woman. What do you do?

    A. You explain to him that if he is interested in business, you are happy to deal with him, but if he is holding your being female against you, then you want to know now.

    B. You decide you are getting nowhere and that a change of pace is needed to proceed. You invite him to meet you later that evening for a drink and dinner to get to know each other in a more relaxed setting.

    C. You recognize that to gain credibility in his eyes, you must prove yourself. Later that night in your hotel room, you prepare yourself especially carefully for the next day's meeting. You also give yourself a pep talk on patience, perseverance, and success.

    D. You quit your job and lament that the international world is not yet ready for women in business. Besides, your children and husband will be happier to have you home more.

THE ANSWERS

1.   Women should be cautious about participating in evening entertainment anywhere in the world. In Latin America, a woman in business would not generally go out at night with two men, especially fairly new acquaintances. Analyze the situation, your colleagues, and the country you are in. Answers B or C would be correct, depending on the situation. Answer D might be good—if you have that possibility. Answer A would create the greatest potential for misunderstanding or make you vulnerable to a more personal relationship than you had in mind, especially after a few drinks. You would *not* be viewed as "one of the boys."

2.   Answer A would be best in terms of meeting the needs of the client while keeping "unnecessary" translation costs down. In the long run, the client would probably get used to dealing with the woman if there is a period of adjustment during which he can deal with the man at the same time. Of course, the woman would need to exercise great patience, ability, and quiet determination to win the client's confidence and not be seen as just another translator. Answer B would meet the needs of the client, but one could anticipate many more misunderstandings because of the language barrier. Answer C could work, depending on the individual, and answer D would be your worst choice. Your client already knows the roles that women in the United States have, and your company policy does not meet his need.

3.   You are not alone—this has happened to many women, in North America as well as abroad. Answer B is the best answer. Not only does it graciously correct the situation, but it also shows that the marketing manager respects his boss and is comfortable working for a woman. This makes a good impression on a customer who may not be accustomed to dealing with a woman. Answer D puts you in the position of telling a potential customer quite openly that he has made a mistake; it is also demeaning to the marketing manager. Answers A and C are obviously not good long-term solutions.

4.   This problem shows a lack of planning on your part. The best thing would be for you to graciously exit and choose answer B—get the right clothing and wear it. Answer C would show a lack of respect, since you're putting your need to get in there that day ahead of a tradition that is important to the director. Answers A and D would probably bar you from ever doing business there again.

5.   Answer C is really the only possibility. In the client's eyes, you have been given a privilege, since he did not need to invite you at all. He knows this is not your custom, but he must do what he feels is right and finds the only way he can to accommodate you.

6. Here is another situation that women say is common in North America. Answer C is the best answer. Answer A, confronting the situation, won't accomplish anything, and answer B is likely to be misunderstood and possibly interpreted as a "come-on." Only you can say if answer D is best for you.

How did you do? If you answered all six questions correctly, bravo! You've chosen the right career path. This book will add to your culture-gender sensitivity and hone your cross-cultural skills in dozens of other areas.

1

SEX, DATING, DISCRIMINATION, AND HARASSMENT

SEX, SEXUALITY, AND DATING

In our seminars and workshops, the most commonly asked question is: "When I'm traveling overseas on business, how do I handle flirtations, 'come-ons', or downright sexual advances?" The following list of ten do's and taboos will help you in almost any situation.

Ten Do's and Taboos of Sexual Behavior
1. *Don't do it!*   When it comes to dating, remember that this is business travel and no dating of international colleagues is appropriate. Recall the old Spanish saying: "Don't wash your feet in your drinking water."
2. *Don't be insulted if men make passes at you.*   In many countries, it is considered a compliment. And if you are young and single, advances are practically unavoidable. When it comes to deflecting passes, be calm and very firm when you say no and men will respect that. Few will be persistent.

Also, be prepared for blunt, surprising questions: "What kind of birth control do you use?" and "Would you like to have sex with me?" Respond to such questions with patience and diplomacy. Try not to take immediate offense. These questions usually stem from centuries-old, male-dominated cultures that have difficulty accepting women in business roles.

3. *Remember that you are where you are because of your capabilities, your competence, and your authority.*   If you're the boss, for example, you can personally interview and appoint your overseas distributors. This gives

8

you the advantage of being able to terminate them; they know that, so they'll behave. How you handle things initially will set the tone for the rest of your business relationship.

OK—but what happens if you're *not* the boss? One sales manager responsible for all of Latin America recounts how she dealt with a unique male move.

> At dinner one evening, this male customer repeatedly commented on how he was terribly attracted to my bushy eyebrows. I had to give him credit for a creative approach, but I realized I had to quash this whole thing quickly. So with firm seriousness I said, "Thank you for your compliment, but my company has entrusted me with this job not because of my bushy eyebrows but *because of what's behind them.*" He got the message.

4. *Don't flirt with business associates overseas.* Never, ever give off mixed signals. Always make it very clear that you are there to do business— even if you are so attracted to someone that you can barely speak. Avoid giving off any kind of vibes that could possibly be misinterpreted.

In the United States, gentle teasing and joking among male and female co-workers is considered normal and acceptable. Men and women co-workers even touch, hug, and wink at one another without meaning anything other than platonic friendship. Overseas, however, these actions may be interpreted as flirting—and that sometimes sets up expectations for things to go further.

5. *Do bear in mind that many perceptions of American women come from U.S. movies and TV shows exported abroad.* These often create the impression that American women are aggressive, sexy, glamorous—and sexually promiscuous. To counter this, you must act professionally in every aspect of your business life. That means everything from dressing conservatively (high necklines, loose-fitting dresses at a modest knee-length) to remaining cool and firm when confronted by anything with sexual connotations. Incidentally, acting professionally applies equally to men—it is not a gender characteristic.

6. *Do wear your wedding ring if you are married, and try to convey that information early in any relationship.* Where appropriate, ask your host or client about his children. You can also carry photos of your husband and children and display them when a suitable opportunity presents itself.

If you are *not* married, however, think twice before putting on a wedding ring merely to ward off unwanted advances. If you lie about your marital status or mislead clients and they find out, you'll be stuck having to cover up the original lie. This gets messy.

7. *Do give nonpersonal business gifts that are tasteful and of high qual-*

ity. Avoid personal gifts that could send the wrong message. These include very expensive or lavish gifts, designer clothes or ties, or a picture of you alone with the gift recipient. Some good gift ideas include such items as desk calendars, books about the United States or Canada or your city or state, Native American art, or quality local handiwork.

Present business gifts in a public setting and try to give a gift to every major person present—not just privately to one person. This way, your kindness will not be interpreted as amorousness.

Where appropriate, have a supply of gifts for the spouses and children of your married male associates. Some easy-to-pack gifts are: designer scarfs, quality perfumes, CDs or tape cassettes, athletic logo wear, high-quality candy, bubble gum, and kids' magazines.

(For more tips on gift giving, see Chapter 3.)

8. *Don't drink or dine alone late in the day with male business contacts.* Midday lunches in public restaurants are acceptable, but avoid evening social drinking, dining, and disco opportunities *unless* you are part of a large group. Many women claim fatigue or early morning appointments to avoid going out late.

A few words about drinking: A cocktail before dinner is safe; after dinner, it's dicey. Never get drunk. To avoid overdoing it, water down your cocktail and sip it slowly. Don't drink on an empty stomach, and be especially careful how much you drink when you are fatigued or jet-lagged.

If you do not drink, politely tell your host that you do not drink alcohol but have no objections if others do. Avoid getting into your moral views or personal history. Your host is likely to graciously accept your situation and make sure you are served bottled water, soda, or fruit juice.

9. *Don't spend long periods of time alone in public places.* These include cocktail lounges, restaurant dining rooms, hotel lobbies, or buses (on tours, for example). When you must be alone in these situations, expect sexual advances to come more frequently from strangers than from business associates. Deal with those people as you would with anyone looking for a quick pickup—give them the quick drop.

If you must spend a prolonged period of time in a public place, bury your nose in a book, a magazine, or work papers. Don't invite contact with strange, but seemingly friendly men. In a restaurant, tell the maitre d' that you wish privacy. Discourage conversation—even polite responses to questions can sometimes be interpreted as interest. Eye contact, smiles, greetings, and casual conversation with strangers can lead to unwanted attention—even while you're walking down the street.

Finally, recognize that you may unknowingly be inviting contact through your nonverbal actions. Watch your posture, eye contact, the way you cross your legs, and so on. Be yourself, of course, but err on the side of conservatism in your dress, demeanor, and carriage.

10.   *Don't succumb to temptation if both you and your business associate are* single *and there is a true mutual attraction.*   How you handle it depends, of course, on your own personal interest and ethics. Remember, there is still the issue of mixing business with pleasure and that will complicate things. If Cupid enters the picture, weigh all the risks, especially if it could be a temporary infatuation.

If a professional associate is putting pressure on you to go to bed with him, this is a bad sign. It's time to distance yourself from the personal relationship. Not only are you risking your professional and emotional situation by sleeping with a business colleague, you are also exposing yourself to the risk of sexually transmitted diseases.

If you've truly met someone special, either inside or outside your circle of business contacts, go slowly before you have sex or make other important commitments. If this person really cares about you, he'll allow you to take your time in establishing the pace and depth of intimacy.

If you meet someone outside your job whose life has nothing to do with your work, the risks are not as great. It becomes even less risky if you are living abroad.

Some final words. Although there are no "nevers" in real life, consider the risk before you act. Ask yourself: "Is there a chance my behavior could be misunderstood?" If the answer is yes, then don't say it, don't do it, don't wear it, don't go.

Finally, when it comes to sex, sexuality, and dating, despite all these warnings, try to keep certain things in perspective. One American woman stated it clearly and concisely:

> My basic strategy for doing business consists of being polite, competent, and in unfailing good humor. I never take umbrage, even when I am confused with being my husband's mistress . . . as happened in Mexico (why else would he bring me, for goodness' sake!) or when I am completely ignored, as happened during a meeting in Japan. Again, the emphasis is on business, not the ego. I do, however, recommend learning a great deal about the culture of the country and polishing up on the art of conversation. Think of your business counterparts as interesting people instead of just as "hot leads" (or hot blooded) and develop the knack of treating every person as if he or she is the most important person you are meeting that day. People invariably react positively when you treat them in a positive manner. That has worked well for me in the United States and in every country I have visited on business.

DISCRIMINATION OVERSEAS

If you are, or should become, an employee of a non–U.S. or Canadian organization based overseas, you need to make yourself aware of local employment and discrimination laws that affect you. If you think your employer is discriminating against you because you are a woman, consult a host country attorney familiar with the discrimination laws of the host country. An attorney who knows both can advise you and help you figure out your options.

If you are eligible for protection under a union or employee council, you should also consult it to determine if in fact your employer's actions are considered discriminatory and how the union or council can help you.

SEXUAL HARASSMENT OVERSEAS

Sexual harassment is a relatively new area of law in North America and Europe. The rest of the world has yet to develop any rules pertaining to sexual harassment—after all, what some of us in North America consider sexual harassment can be viewed as normal, acceptable behavior in other countries.

What do you do when you find yourself in what you consider a hostile working environment while overseas? You must first decide just how threatening the behavior is. Let's say some guy at work looks you up and down and comments, "You look great today. You should wear that dress every day." Such behavior may be outside your comfort zone. But if it's only meant as a compliment and you confront him or his supervisor claiming sexual harassment, it could be deeply embarrassing for everyone.

Let's say, however, that you perceive this comment to be part of an ongoing pattern of demeaning behavior. Now what? In that case, the second thing you must do is to weigh making a stink about this obnoxious character against potential reactions. Will it help or hurt the situation if you complain of harassment? Will you be labeled a troublemaker? Will this affect your performance review or your business relationships?

Third, if you decide to respond, do so within the norms of the host country and the company. This will increase your credibility and your chances of a positive outcome. Confide in a few trusted friends or colleagues in the host country. Try to get at least a man's and a woman's opinion. Let them advise you whether the behavior constitutes harassment in their culture and how to respond. However, remember this: if you are working for a U.S. company abroad, U.S. sexual harassment law may not apply if the harassment occurs at your place of work. Currently, U.S. harassment law only protects employees in the United States.

Let's explore some potential avenues for action, after you've tried to view the behavior through the eyes of the culture you're working in.

Strategies for Dealing with Sexual Harassment

1. Try to head off potentially offensive remarks by saying firmly, "Stop. I don't want to hear this." If the conduct continues, take the following steps:
2. Keep a written log of offensive incidents. If you believe that an individual's intent is malicious, jot down the date and a description of each incident. Describe the behavior that offends you and the actions you have taken to stop the conduct.
3. Report the conduct up the chain of command, following any rules and practices of the organization you are working with. Keep a record of your reporting activities.
4. If you are employed by an American company, consult the company's U.S. attorney. Otherwise, consult a local attorney. In either case, recognize that U.S. harassment laws will probably not apply abroad.

Note: Many of the issues discussed in this chapter are directly related to personal safety. To learn more about what you can do to stay safe while traveling abroad, refer to Chapter 4.

2

KNOW YOUR PRODUCT, KNOW THE CULTURE

Next on your list of survival essentials is the simple dictum: "Know your product, know the culture." The story of Tine Willemsen, a Danish woman who works for a jewelry firm based in Singapore, is illustrative.

On learning from a course at the Export Institute of Singapore that the three hardest markets for a woman to crack were Japan, South Korea, and Saudi Arabia, especially for a young woman just starting out, Willemsen plunged into intensive research on each of those three markets. She then scheduled trips to Tokyo, Seoul, and Riyadh. When she returned, she proudly reported success in selling her company's jewelry line in these three tough markets. And she did it on her first try.

This true story is related by veteran international businessman Richard R. Gesteland, who worked twenty-eight years for Sears, Roebuck & Co., and spent twenty-five of those years living and traveling abroad. Gesteland, who was stationed in six different major international cities and now teaches international negotiation techniques, quickly adds, "Of course, Miss Willemsen was an unusually talented marketer and salesperson. It's also true that a woman might have more success selling gold jewelry in those markets than she would with, say, machine tools or heavy construction equipment. Nonetheless, Tine's accomplishment is highly significant. It shows that today an intelligent, determined, and well-prepared woman can in fact crack some of the world's most male-dominated markets."

TIPS FOR SURVIVING—AND SUCCEEDING

1. *Know your product.* Expertise is valued everywhere, so be prepared to demonstrate your technical and commercial competence. We can-

not emphasize enough: The more you know, the less important gender becomes.

2. *Know the culture.*   Competition in the international arena is intense. Learn more about your customer than your competitor knows. Women have an advantage over men because women tend to be more sensitive to and aware of cultural differences.

The value of knowing your product is amply demonstrated in this incident related by Joyce Keehn, International Marketing Manager for Trek Bicycles.

> I was having dinner in Greece with our Greek distributor and he told me he was nervous dealing with a woman and bikes. Cycling is a very male-dominated industry, especially in Europe. He asked me if I knew anything about bikes. I smiled and said after ten years at Trek I had learned a few things. The next day when I arrived at his office for our meeting, he threw the Trek catalog at me and said, "Sell me your bikes using technical terms." I did and he placed a very large order. On the way to the airport he apologized for the way he had treated me.

As for knowing the culture, remember that this book is merely a prologue to your ongoing research. To help you, here are some key words that represent key concepts in your international business life.

KEY WORDS

Foreigner

When traveling and working abroad, you will be considered a foreigner. Interestingly, in Spanish the word for foreigner is *extranjera;* in French it is *étrangère*. For both words the English cognate is "strange." So what can you do?

Delete the word "foreigner" from your vocabulary. The reason is that the word suggests "outsider" or "alien" and connotes something unwanted. In fact, "foreigner" is actually a pejorative term. Try to avoid calling someone a foreigner and substitute the word "international," as in "international visitor" or "international host." Or simply describe someone by his or her country of origin—as Chinese, Russian, or Venezuelan. It's a small exercise in self-discipline, but a very symbolic one.

Ethnocentrism

For North Americans, "ethnocentrism" may be defined as viewing the axis of the world as extending down through North America, with the rest of the world revolving around us. Consequently, we tend to think that the way we do things is the right way. As a result, when it comes to business procedures and protocol, we like to live in our own little cuddly comfort zone. Here's an experiment for you to understand what we mean by such a comfort zone.

1.   Clap your hands together as when applauding. Note that if you are right-handed, you very likely pounded your right hand into your left palm; conversely, if you are left-handed, you struck your right palm with your left. You'll do this consistently.
2.   Now fold your hands (interlacing your fingers, as when praying). Notice the position of your thumbs. Is the right thumb on top or the left? Each of us is usually right-thumb or left-thumb oriented. Whenever we fold our hands in this manner, we'll favor one thumb over the other.
3.   Finally, fold your arms across your chest. Social scientists claim there are actually six different positions when folding our arms. Each of us has a favorite, and we become slightly uncomfortable folding our arms in any other position.

This experiment indicates that we all tend to revert to familiar comfort zones that we unconsciously regard as "ours." That's what we might call "cuddly ethnocentrism," and it's important to realize that we carry comfortable cultural habits with us wherever we go. We practice them almost unconsciously. The way we shake hands, respect punctuality, use first names liberally, dislike wasting time in social chitchat, even the clothes we wear are all examples.

Idiosyncrasy

"Idiosyncrasy" is defined by *The American Heritage Dictionary* as "a behavioral characteristic peculiar to an individual or group." These characteristics could also be called quirks, inclinations, preferences, or even eccentricities. Each group, society, or culture has its own idiosyncrasies. For example, we Americans and Canadians are taught that in business "time is money," so we like to get right down to business, wasting few minutes in useless conversation. Although this is a virtue for most of us, it is also an idiosyncrasy because not everyone adheres to this belief. Many other cultures believe there must be a breaking-in period of social conversation before talking about business; that's their idiosyncrasy.

Protocol

"Protocol" comes from the Greek and means glue—protocol therefore is the glue that binds groups of people together. More broadly, business protocol involves the customs, behavior, or rules that we have unconsciously agreed to observe and that allow us to function smoothly together: the exchange of business cards, the way we greet one another, gift-giving practices, social dining and drinking, conversational taboos, and so on. These protocols are among the first we encounter when entering a strange land.

3

PROTOCOL FOR WOMEN

Ingeborg Hegenbart, Dutch by birth, came to the United States as a young woman and is now head of the international division of SouthTrust Bank in Charlotte, North Carolina. Throughout her career, Hegenbart and her staff have developed working relationships with 450 banks in nations all around the globe, conducting business in English, Russian, Spanish, French, German, Chinese, Thai, Estonian, and, of course, Dutch. When asked for an example of international protocol for women, she responded with this story.

> I have traveled to Japan for many years, establishing banking relationships there and, in the process, learning the rules of behavior, especially for a woman. I have always been treated with politeness, in large part, I think, because I was the president of my firm. The Japanese male society respects title, position, and stature. But I knew it was difficult for them, dealing with me, a woman. Protocol dominates the Japanese business culture, and it took me ten years before, on one of my visits to Tokyo, the president of a large Japanese bank finally good-naturedly agreed to let me host him for lunch. At the conclusion of our luncheon, he patiently allowed me to pay the bill, but then as we departed the restaurant I couldn't help but notice that, in good Japanese custom, he walked several paces *in front* of me . . . as most senior Japanese men do when in the company of women. It was as though, after ten years, he would permit one deviation from Japanese dignity, but not two.

Traditions—and protocol—run strong in many countries, and Japan is perhaps the greatest diehard when it comes to preserving centuries-old customs.

We will later discuss each major region in the world and its traditions and protocol, but first let's examine some general protocols that apply equally to both men and women.

18

PROTOCOL DO'S AND TABOOS

Punctuality

If you are invited to an American or Canadian home for cocktails at, say, seven o'clock, you know automatically that this means you should arrive about a quarter past seven—certainly not before, and not a whole lot later. However, in places like Germany, Sweden, and Switzerland, an invitation for seven o'clock means you should arrive at *precisely* that hour.

In Europe, people from those countries (Germany, Sweden, Switzerland) plus Canada, Australia, the United States, England, and France are considered extremely punctual. A bromide among veteran American travelers is that when you board an airplane in Europe you can usually tell which passengers are German, Swedish, or Swiss simply by one bit of body language: at take-off, each will dutifully note the time on their wristwatches; at touchdown, each will repeat the procedure.

In Latin America, if you are invited to someone's home for cocktails at seven o'clock, you should not arrive at seven, because if you do your hosts will very likely still be in the shower. In fact, arriving at eight o'clock would not raise an eyebrow; it might even be considered borderline early. Our favorite explanation from one Latin business person is: "Why live your life in measured segments?"

In Thailand or Indonesia, too, promptness is not necessarily a virtue. Also, in almost any large metropolitan city—Tokyo, Hong Kong, Singapore, London, or New York—allowances will be made for lateness because of weather or traffic conditions.

How late can you be and still be "on time"?

Guidelines for Being on Time Around the World
- *Countries with a high regard for promptness:*   All of Northern Europe (Scandinavia, The Netherlands, Germany, Switzerland, Belgium, etc.).
- *Countries where promptness is appreciated and expected:*   Canada, Australia, United Kingdom, France, and the United States.
- *Countries with a relaxed attitude toward punctuality:*   Southern Europe (Spain, Italy, Greece, etc.) and most of the Mediterranean.
- *Countries with a lax attitude toward promptness:*   Most of Latin America and much of Asia—throw your watches away!

It should be clear that attitudes about punctuality vary widely. Wherever you plan to travel, be certain to investigate in advance their specific business practice regarding punctuality.

Business Cards

When it comes to business cards: stock up. You'll be passing them out much more liberally than in the United States and Canada. In international business, business cards are not only almost ritually exchanged, but they serve as an invaluable record of whom you encountered and how to contact them in the future.

In some cultures, however, be aware that there is a special protocol for exchanging cards (unlike in North America, where we exchange them rather informally). In Japan, where style is as important as substance, the exchange of business cards becomes almost a choreographed ballet. Here are the steps:

1. Hold the card with both hands between your thumb and forefinger. Present the card with the print facing the recipient. Dip your head in a slight bow.
2. The receiver will nod in acknowledgment, present his or her card to you in the same fashion, and then take time to carefully read the information on your card. Reason: This is your *identity;* this is who and what you are, and whom you work for—it is your persona.
3. Then, where appropriate, each player in this little ritual places the card in front of him or her for easy reference.
4. Avoid writing notes on the card.

In the Middle East and much of Southeast Asia, always present your business card with your right hand—never the left, even if you're left-handed. In these regions, the left hand is used for bodily hygiene and is therefore considered the "unclean" hand.

In any culture, don't ever stuff business cards in pockets. We have even observed a few unthinking Americans take a business card and use it in place of a toothpick! (Across the table, your customer is thinking: "Hey! That's my identity you're using.")

Bilingual Business Cards

When traveling to countries where English is not commonly spoken, the savvy traveler has business cards printed in English on one side and in the host country's language on the reverse. Make certain that the printing on both sides is of equal quality, lest one inadvertently imply the host's language is considered second rate. In many large cities, overnight printing services are available for this task. If you have arrived in Tokyo or Hong Kong without these bilingual cards, ask the concierge at your hotel for such a printing service.

Titles

In all situations, make certain your title is clearly stated. Choose a title that is understood in your host culture and that accurately reflects your position. Such American titles as "deputy," "associate," or "executive assistant" are confusing outside the United States. And the difference between a director and a manager is not comprehended in many other parts of the world. The title "vice president" is not used much outside the United States, but businesspeople in other countries have come to learn that it carries special stature. Abbreviations such as CEO, CFO, and COO are also confusing outside North America.

Among our English cousins, "chairman" in the United Kingdom is comparable to the American corporate title "president." In England, "director" is a high-level position, comparable to "vice president" in the United States; the title also indicates that the person serves on the Board of Directors.

Two American businesswomen related their experiences involving the use of business cards and titles in Japan. One was the president of her company. She reported how she was readily accepted by senior Japanese businesspeople wherever she went. The other woman, a Director of International Marketing, had the opposite reception—indifference and blank stares. Both agreed that in the Japanese business world, stature and status in a company were highly important. As a result, the Director of International Marketing received approval from her company to designate herself as president of "(her company's name) International," which was, indeed, the official name of a foreign sales corporation (FSC) that had been created for tax purposes. Since she was listed on the official corporate rolls as president of that FSC, it was an honest designation. Months later, after another trip to Japan, the redesignated "President" reported a much warmer reception.

Warning: Don't fabricate titles just for the sake of making a good impression. If your international counterpart discovers you have resorted to puffery, your credibility will be undermined, doing much more damage in the long run.

Special Tip: In male-oriented parts of the world (Latin America, Japan, South Korea, Saudi Arabia), if you are married, consider adding "Mrs."

before your name. It might serve as a deterrent to unwanted amorous advances.

Greetings

When it comes to everyday social or business greetings, most North Americans have learned since childhood to shake hands using a firm grip and direct eye contact. If, in return, we receive a limp, "dead fish" handshake and averted eyes, we think distastefully, "This person doesn't know how to shake hands." In truth, while your parents were drilling you " firm grip, direct eye contact," their parents were probably instructing, "If you must use the Western habit of shaking hands, don't grip the hand firmly, because that is rude; and don't look someone directly in the eyes, because that is impolite."

In much of Asia and some parts of Africa and Latin America, direct eye contact, especially with elders, is considered disrespectful. In our homeland also, Native American tradition teaches that direct eye contact with elders shows lack of respect.

In Japan, the traditional daily greeting is the bow. Many Americans regard bowing as an act of subservience, proclaiming loudly, "I'm not going to bow to anyone!" In Japan, however, the bow is considered an act of respect and humility. Consequently, most seasoned international businesspeople have learned the advantage of showing both respect and humility, so they have no hesitation in bowing.

In Southeast Asia, the *wai* is the greeting. In India, this same greeting is called the *namaste*. It involves placing the palms of your hands together in a prayer-like fashion, holding them about chest high, and dipping the head slightly. For Americans—both men and women—the proper response would be to politely nod the head in response. You are not expected to *wai*.

In New Zealand, the Maori tribes greet one another by rubbing noses; in parts of central Africa, friends greet each other by spitting at each other's feet; and in Tibet, a traditional greeting is to stick out your tongue. As first-time visitors, Americans or Canadians would not be expected to use any of these greetings. But on second visits, or after becoming better acquainted with your hosts, respectfully emulating the greeting will probably be appreciated.

Special Greeting Considerations for Women

Throughout Europe, women seem to shake hands more frequently than in the United States. This applies in both business and social situations, between both men and women. Don't be surprised if you encounter more and more outstretched hands. There may also be a bit more "pumping" than you are accustomed to. In the more romantic countries like France and Italy, don't be startled if at a social function a gentleman takes your outstretched hand and kisses it. However, in modern-day business settings, this occurs far less often.

When you visit places like Japan and Saudi Arabia, where businessmen are especially unaccustomed to greeting women, consider these possibilities as you move toward one another in greeting:

1. Your hosts may have done some homework and realize they should offer their hands, North American–style.
2. Your hosts may make no motion at all toward shaking hands with you. If this occurs, don't consider it a slight.
3. Get some advice in advance from North Americans who have lived in that area or who may even know the people you are meeting and will therefore know what to expect and how to react.

This last piece of advice also applies to names. If a name appears complicated, ask someone in advance how you might pronounce it. Also, in much of the Pacific Rim, a person will have three names, and the first name will be the family name. In Latin America, you will also often be presented with three names. The first name is the given name, the second is the father's family name, and the third is the mother's maiden name. (See Part Two for detailed information on specific countries.)

Gift Giving

In North American business circles, business gifts have certain distinct characteristics: (1) gifts are never lavish, lest they hint of a bribe; (2) they are usually viewed more as mementos, or bear company logos and are therefore subtle bits of advertising; and (3) they may take the form of entertainment— a dinner, a play, a sporting event, and so on. But, once you leave the United States and Canada, it's worth your time to study gift-giving practices in your destination countries.

Japan is most notable for its gift-giving customs. The Japanese are a very generous, gracious people; gift giving is ingrained in their culture. In past centuries, each prominent Japanese family retained a functionary to do nothing but determine appropriate gifts. If you are traveling to Japan, or expect to host Japanese visitors, be prepared—you will almost certainly be presented with a gift. It will usually be wrapped (pastel colored papers, but never white— white is used only at funerals). Don't open it immediately; save that for later, in private. Never give four of anything because the word "four" in Japanese is *shi*, which also means "death." (See Chapter 15 for more about gift giving in Japan.)

The Middle East, Far East, and Latin America are right below the Japanese on the gift-giving chart. In China, gift giving is appropriate and appreciated, but not necessarily required. Australia, Canada, the United States, the United Kingdom, and most of Europe are at the bottom of the chart. Business gift giving is conducted, but, if you overlook presenting a gift, you won't be deported.

Appropriate Gifts

One of the best forms of gift giving is the act of remembrance. On your first visit you might note if your hosts have any special collections—stamps, coins, or unique memorabilia—or if they have children who enjoy North American music or sports. Then, on your next trip you remember to take something to add to their collection. If you do, however, make certain whatever you choose is something of quality.

Note: For more detailed information on gift-giving practices around the world, refer to Roger E. Axtell, *Do's and Taboos Around the World,* 3rd edition (Wiley, 1993). That book devotes a complete section to region-by-region gift-giving practices, plus specific recommendations for types of gifts.

Special Tip: If you decide to carry business gifts with you, add some suitable articles for the wives or children of your male business counterparts, such as designer scarfs, perfume, toys, and so on. But be careful. In some macho-oriented lands, presenting a gift to a man may convey unintended messages. Whenever in doubt about whether a certain type of gift is acceptable, phone directory assistance for the 202 area code (Washington, D.C.) and ask for the telephone number of the embassy of the country you plan to visit. Once you reach that embassy's switchboard, request the cultural attaché or information officer; then ask your question.

Social Dining

When and How to Eat

As for when, you'll find that in many locales around the world the main meal is served at midday, with just a light snack provided in the evening. On the other hand, your business hosts might very well take you for a monstrous-sized lunch, then repeat the adventure in the evening.

Special Tip: By the second week of such high living, if your clothes are starting to feel tight around the middle, here's a suggestion. Order two appetizers—one to be served as a first course and the other as your main course. Incidentally, the word "entree" is used differently around the world. In the United States, it refers to the main course. But in Europe and many other countries, the entree is the first course, or what we call the appetizer.

As for how we eat, international observers can spot Americans at a dinner table by the way we cut our food and then flip our fork over into our right hand. In the so-called Continental style of eating, the fork remains steadfastly in the left hand. Either way is perfectly acceptable. One piece of etiquette you need to know is that in much of Europe both hands should be kept above (or on) the table. Forget what your mother told you about keeping your left hand in your lap. This European custom goes back many centuries to when diners feared that a hand under the table meant either a weapon—or some hanky-panky.

As for eating with chopsticks, no book can teach you how. Just watch others or, good-naturedly, ask for lessons. Your hosts will probably enjoy tutoring you. However, be sure to observe how and where others place their sticks. This often sends signals, such as "I'm done" or "I'd like more." And never stick the chopsticks upright in rice or other food—it's considered bad luck.

Dealing with Unfamiliar Food

Paula Golz, who is in international marketing, tells of a business luncheon she once experienced in a Hong Kong restaurant where she was encouraged to try a brown, gelatinous-looking food. Her Chinese women hosts told her it would be good for her complexion. After eating it, she learned it was congealed chicken blood. Stories like these are commonplace among veteran international business travelers.

One thing is certain: the more you travel, the more likely you'll have placed in front of you some mysterious, indescribable dish that—to your mind—belongs in an illustrated book of culinary horrors. Live fish, bear's paw soup, chocolate-covered grasshoppers, seaweed, shark's-fin soup, reindeer tongue, even cooked scorpions. But wait—it gets worse. As a guest of honor, you might also be served a sheep's eyeballs (Middle East) or even the brains of a monkey (Southeast Asia).

Your natural first reaction may be to look for help, push it aside, or, worse, let your stomach do what it demands, and empty itself. Before resorting to any of those possibilities, consider these two facts:

1. You are the guest of honor; your hosts are favoring you with what is probably a national delicacy. It could be taken as an insult to refuse.
2. People in that country have been eating this specialty for centuries, with complete impunity.

Moreover, remember that when international visitors come to North America, they encounter the same problem. For many visitors, some of our favorite dishes are as foreign as a dish of snake or grilled ants would be to you. Here are just a few North American favorites that might be regarded as disgusting by your international visitors: roast turkey, gravy, peanut butter, root beer, catsup, grits, pecan pie, pumpkin pie, rare steaks, popcorn, many fast foods, and even hot dogs. In parts of the Far East they customarily eat dog, which prompted one Far Eastern visitor to stare at an American hot dog and comment, "We eat dog . . . but not that part."

There are several ways to cope with the trauma of repulsive-looking food.

- Use transference. This means telling yourself that those cooked grasshoppers are really just like pretzels, and those ants are like breakfast cereal.
- Simply swallow—don't think about the exact nature of the beast.
- Slice it up into tiny pieces and quickly eat them.

Social Drinking

In our home society, we have a cocktail hour, usually lasting about an hour, with perhaps time for two drinks. We also take lots and lots of ice in our drinks. We drink colas, juices, water, wine, and beer, but only occasionally indulge in after-dinner liqueurs or cordials.

Our cocktail hour may be emulated overseas, but it is often abbreviated to just one drink, especially in Europe. The reason will very likely be because wine—perhaps both red and white—will be served with the meal. Many countries take special pride in their local wines, so enjoy the experience rather than requesting your favorite California vintage. After dinner, imbibing may continue with brandy or cordials. Also, ice is used sparingly. If you prefer plenty of ice, you'll probably have to request it—maybe even repeatedly.

What If You Don't Drink Alcohol?

Nondrinking won't be an issue in devout Moslem countries since the religion of Islam forbids alcoholic beverages.

Elsewhere, there are a few ways to handle this issue with grace.

- Take your host aside and quietly explain that you do not drink alcohol, but have no objection if others do. Very likely your host will see to it that you receive substitutes, such as fruit juices or colas.
- Order mineral water, tonic, or seltzer water, with a slice of lime or lemon. This has the appearance of a mixed drink and makes others around you comfortable that you have "joined" the party.
- Explain to your host that, for medical reasons, you are unable to drink alcohol. This is understandable worldwide, but it may cause your host to sympathetically inquire about your medical condition. Then you'll find yourself struggling for some benign medical malady.

Toasting

Toasting is more common outside the United States and Canada. If called upon, be prepared with a few gracious comments, an all-purpose quotation you've memorized, or some other observation appropriate for the occasion. Avoid long toasts and canned jokes, and always allow your host to toast first. If he or she does not propose a toast and you wish to take the initiative, be sure to politely ask the host's permission first. And if you don't drink alcohol, just pretend to sip your drink when the toast is made.

CONVERSATIONAL TABOOS

In this area of protocol, common sense prevails. In general, you should avoid discussing:

- Touchy political subjects
- Religious differences
- Delicate or negative historical occurrences

One recourse is to discuss these subjects only if and when your host introduces them. Then respond with discretion.

Be prepared for frank—even blunt—questions about your homeland. In the Western countries of Europe, people are more accustomed to visiting North Americans, but in less-traveled countries, people may be more openly curious. For example, don't be surprised if you are asked: Does everyone in America carry a gun? How much do you earn each year? What is your home worth? Is your company spied on by the CIA?

Special Tip: Expect questions about your marital status. One American married woman was at a business meeting in South Korea when the gentleman seated next to her turned and said, "I'm sorry about your husband." Startled, she replied, "Why?" He looked at her hand and explained, "I see you wear a wedding ring so I assume your husband is dead . . . otherwise you would be at home caring for your family."

One all-purpose piece of advice regarding diplomacy and discretion in general conversation while overseas was given to us by a longtime American expatriate in the Far East: "Try to reply to questions as though your wealthy, elderly aunt had just asked you how much you think she should leave you in her will." In other words, always converse politely, with grace, tact, and respect.

GENERAL BEHAVIOR

In all of your actions, be totally professional. That word "professional" applies to both males and females, of course, and it includes behaving in an honest and ethical manner at all times, and avoiding embarrassment to yourself, your company, or others around you.

Seven Tips for Professional Behavior

1.   Before leaving your home office, try to reach agreement with your superiors about the extent of your authority. This allows you to make decisions on the spot. In international business, your customers or clients become understandably irritated if you repeatedly reply that you "must first check with the home office." On the other hand, if you demonstrate that you have authority to make important decisions, it will not only ingratiate you but increase your stature.

2.   Avoid interpreting your international counterpart's surprise at dealing with you as disappointment or offense. Their surprise may be nothing more than that—surprise. Don't assume your counterpart is automatically prejudiced against a woman.

3.   Consider that, as a woman, you might actually have an advantage in a predominantly male society. Many years ago, in the Netherlands, the Parker Pen Company experimented by using women as sales executives to make "cold" calls on Dutch businesses. These saleswomen gained access to decision-makers much more frequently than salesmen did. Whether because of surprise, politeness, curiosity, or even chivalry, being a woman served as a distinct advantage.

4. Do absolutely nothing that would be considered flirtatious. (See Chapter 1 for more on this subject.)

5. Leave the American feminist movement at home. Other countries have not progressed as far as we have. If your male customers or clients overseas insist on opening doors or picking up the check, let them. They are just responding to decades and decades of custom.

6. Try not to take offense. See if you can work within the system since you'll get much further than if you attempt to fight it. Your job is to meet your company's objectives within the culture you're working with.

7. Observe what is going on around you in the way of protocol. In a reception line, for example, watch to see if other women are shaking hands or merely nodding heads in greeting. Better yet, talk with American and Canadian expatriates living in the country you are visiting and solicit their advice on local protocols.

Above all, the refrain "Be totally professional" should echo in your mind.

4

SAFETY WHEN TRAVELING

As a woman, never try to cut corners as far as safety. Don't take the subway because it's cheaper; take a taxi. Stay in a nice hotel and eat there. Don't be stupid. Don't come into a country at midnight. Be more circumspect. With others, be personable, but stay private. You can talk at a bar with someone, if you choose, but don't go off to a party with him. Use valet parking. No company these days has a problem with paying for safety. If you're traveling alone, you have to be concerned about it. It's not worth taking the chance.

CATHERINE TENKE TEICHERT
M & I Data Services, Milwaukee

BEFORE YOU DEPART

Here are some sensible safety steps you can take in the weeks and days before you close your office door and embark on your overseas trip:

• Keep abreast of travel advisories issued by the U.S. and Canadian governments. These may deal with natural disasters, disease outbreaks, acts of terrorism, international conflict, or civil unrest in specific countries. In the United States, advisories are provided 24 hours a day by recording when you phone (202) 647-5225.

• Take advantage of the Travel Watch advisories published by Kroll Associates of New York that may be available through travel agents using the Sabre computer reservations system. These one-page advisories on both health and safety issues cover more than 275 cities around the world and include such tips as the safest way to get from the airport to the city center and what sections to avoid in town.

30

- Make copies of all your travel documents (passport, tickets, credit cards, driver's license, traveler's checks, itinerary) and leave sets with different trusted friends whom you can easily contact if yours are lost or stolen. Include in these sets a list of the names and numbers of your attorney, physician, and insurance agent.
- Obtain copies of two valuable U.S. government publications: (1) *A Safe Trip Abroad*, a pamphlet containing tips on guarding valuables, personal and vehicle security, and protection against terrorism; it also explains the extent of assistance provided abroad by U.S. embassies and consulates; and (2) the U.S. State Department's listing of *Key Officers of Foreign Service Posts*; this pocket-size directory gives contact names, addresses, and phone numbers for all U.S. embassies, missions, and consulates abroad. Both publications are available from the U.S. Government Printing Office: (202) 783-3238.
- Visit travel stores or scan direct-mail catalogs specializing in travel products to familiarize yourself with personal safety devices: alarms, door-stops, and pouches for leg, waist, or bra to hold money and other valuables.

SAFETY ON AIRPLANES

- Keep your seat belt buckled. This is the single most important safety rule aboard an airplane and the one violated the most.
- Pay attention to the safety instructions flight attendants give before each flight.
- Know that the safest place to sit is nearest an emergency exit.
- Make sure hatches are securely fastened and avoid placing heavy objects in overhead compartments. Most accidents aboard a plane result from objects falling from compartments.

SAFETY IN HOTELS

Amy Isom, Director of Strategic Planning for a large international hotel chain, and Kate Hotchkiss, Asia Sales Manager for the Tennant Company, offer this advice for women traveling overseas.

- Never let the front desk announce your room number or even the floor you are on—you never know who may overhear. If they do, request a new room. If you ever feel unsafe or unsure, ask the hotel staff for assistance or an escort.

- Once inside your room, never open your door, even if they say "Hotel Security." Call the front desk to confirm that an actual hotel employee is standing outside your room. Err on the side of caution.
- Place all your valuables in a hotel safe-deposit box.
- Book rooms between the second and seventh floors because you can walk to the ground level in an emergency and most fire equipment cannot reach higher than that.
- Once you reach your room, go back into the hallway and take a few moments to study escape routes (both up and down) in case of fire.
- Place the "Do Not Disturb" sign outside your door and always lock the door from the inside. Some women travelers also leave on the TV or radio when they leave the room so it sounds occupied.
- Before showering or bathing, carefully check the footing in the tub or stall to avoid slipping. Also, check markings on faucets. The letter C in some countries stands for "hot" (*caldo, caliente, chaud*, etc.).
- Check to see that all sliding-glass doors leading outside or to balconies as well as other windows and connecting-room doors are securely locked.
- Always enter and exit your hotel through the main entrance.
- Ask the concierge for advice on just about anything. He or she can be especially helpful in searching for destinations, safe restaurants, and which areas of town to avoid.

DRIVING SAFETY

Many business travelers find they need to rent a car overseas to allow greater convenience and flexibility in meeting their business obligations. Depending on the country, driving can range from a pleasant experience to a safety nightmare. Consequently, before you decide to rent a car, do some research about the pros and cons of driving in your destination country and specific safety concerns for women. Also, learn as much as you can about traffic signs and rules—they differ from country to country. For example, speed prevails in Germany on the *Autobahn* (expressways); the fastest car has the right-of-way in the left-hand lane. Also, throughout Europe, drivers will flash their headlights on and off during daytime hours to get your attention.

In the United States, at stoplights, the yellow light comes on after the green and before the red. In other words, it signals "Caution: the red light is about to be lit." However, in most Latin American countries, the yellow light *also* appears after the red light and before the green. As one woman described it, "It's as though they're saying 'Get ready! It's almost time to gun the car forward!' "

In Mexico and other Latin American countries, drivers are known for being unpredictable, even dangerous. Motorists must be constantly on the lookout for such hazards as overloaded trucks, buses, and motorbikes, animals in the road, and people standing in the streets. If your defensive driving skills aren't up to snuff, you may want to think twice about renting and driving a car.

Be extra cautious about driving at night, especially alone. It can be quite risky in some countries. Additional hazards challenge you at night, and you may be putting yourself at risk for robbery and assault.

"Jane" and her female friend were driving a rental car and were involved in a highway holdup shortly after entering Guatemala. They approached a border checkpoint and were waved through without being searched by the Guatemalan police officials. A few miles later, they encountered a truck blocking the road. A man hopped out of the back, walked around to the rear of Jane's car, and fired into the rear window, striking Jane in the neck. Despite extreme pain and heavy bleeding, Jane escaped by quickly driving around the truck. She sped into Guatemala City and located a police officer. The officer refused to assist her, so she searched for and found the U.S. Embassy. Officials quickly arranged for medical treatment and helped her through her hospital stay.

Jane later learned from the Embassy staff that the robbers had meant to rob and kill her. Highway robberies are common in Guatemala, and members of the national police are often involved. The police officials at the border probably notified the robbers that tourists were approaching in a rental car— hence the Guatemala City police's refusal to help her.

This type of corruption is not necessarily widespread overseas, but it does exist.

Some Commonsense Driving Rules
- Book your rental car well in advance with a known international rental-car firm.
- Consider hiring a local driver; the concierge at your hotel is a good source for locating one.
- Make certain your U.S. or Canadian insurance policy covers you when driving overseas.
- Well before venturing on the highways, take the time to learn something about the rules of the road in that country.
- Do not stop to help at highway accidents and do not get out of your car if you are involved in an accident. Wait for local authorities to arrive.

- When possible, carry a cellular phone in case of emergency.
- Keep doors locked at all times.
- Avoid leaving your purse, camera, or any bags in plain view, even in a locked vehicle.
- Have clear directions to your location.

SAFETY ON THE STREETS

Visiting most countries overseas is like visiting most large North American cities. The same concepts apply—be cautious when walking alone, and walk quickly and confidently to your destination.

In countries with reputations for pickpockets, be sure to carry a shoulder bag and put the strap around your neck. This brings the bag up under your arm where it cannot be picked or cut loose. If you're wearing an overcoat, hold your purse inside.

More Safety Do's and Taboos
- Do take the matches from your hotel and carry them with you. They provide the hotel's name, address, and phone number and can be used to show taxi drivers where you wish to go.
- Do consider carrying a "squawk box" (alarm).
- Don't go jogging or race-walking until you determine where and when it is safe. Ask your concierge.
- Don't wear flashy jewelry.
- Do wear comfortable shoes with flat heels when possible.
- Do be alert for people bumping into you, children crowding around your feet with postcards or souvenirs, or any nearby disturbance or outburst. These distractions may be planned diversions to reduce your alertness or single you out as a target.
- Don't exchange dollars for local currency with anyone on the street offering you attractive rates.
- Don't—ever!—deal in drugs. This is the ultimate taboo. In many countries, simple possession of even minute quantities can result in long, agonizing jail sentences.

See Part Six for recommended books on the subject of safety while traveling abroad.

5

HEALTHY TRAVELING

The two basic health fears of almost everyone who journeys abroad are: (1) the fear of becoming seriously ill far from home, and (2) the fear of shoddy medical treatment. Even the slightest malady can spoil an important business trip. However, there are numerous precautions you can take to prevent or minimize illnesses, and they should begin even before you buckle your seat belt.

BEFORE YOU DEPART

1. *Learn what vaccinations are recommended or required for your destination(s).*   Do this several weeks before you are to leave. Your travel agent or personal physician can often provide this information or you can phone the U.S. Public Health Service Quarantine Station in any of these cities: Chicago, Honolulu, Los Angeles, Miami, New York, San Francisco, and Seattle. They will give you the latest information on required inoculations in various countries.

An International Certificate of Vaccinations from the World Health Organization is a valuable document because it officially records your past immunizations. (Clinics that administer vaccinations often provide these certificates.)

If you have this record in hand and up to date, you may avoid being denied entry or having to undergo inoculations on the spot. (*Note:* Take care that the dates written in this record book use the European system—with the year first, then the day, then the month. For example, in the United States, if a date is expressed as 6/5/96, that denotes June 5; in Europe, it means 6 May. We have heard of cases where health officials in overseas countries have refused admission because of this possible mixup.) The certificate will also aid your medical provider if you become sick while overseas.

35

Vaccinations for yellow fever and cholera are two common immunizations, especially when you are traveling to remote or tropical regions. However, it is equally important that you review your record of shots for tetanus, whooping cough, polio, hepatitis, measles, and mumps. Avoid getting inoculations while traveling. One experienced businesswoman received a shot for typhoid while overseas and was almost paralyzed.

2.   *Check with your medical insurance provider about the extent of your medical insurance coverage regarding overseas travel.*   Some policies have restrictions or limitations. Also, ask what type of documentation is required for you to receive reimbursement for medical costs incurred while abroad. Further, ask your employer what type of emergency response assistance they will provide in case of a serious accident or illness that could incapacitate you. Several established firms in the United States provide this special service to corporations—one is Global Emergency Medical Services. (For information, call 1-800-475-0624.) If your employer is unfamiliar with these services, ask your travel agent for a listing of firms.

3.   *Stock up on prescription medications that you regularly take.*   Also, carry the original prescription bottles with labels properly affixed; this may make it easier to get them refilled outside the United States. Because U.S. prescription drug laws are among the most rigorous in the world, it's possible you'll find your favorite prescription medication freely available over the counter in many countries abroad. But don't count on that, and be careful. Names and strengths might vary.

4.   *Contact The International Association for Medical Assistance to Travellers* (IAMAT), 736 Center St., Lewiston, NY 14092, phone (716) 754-4883 *if you worry about finding a doctor while traveling overseas.*   With a single phone call you'll receive a free booklet listing health institutions and doctors worldwide, plus information on which languages the physicians can speak. IAMAT also provides these up-to-date publications: World Immunization Chart, World Malaria Risk Chart, How to Protect Yourself Against Malaria, and World Climate Charts. The publications are free, but a donation to IAMAT would be appropriate.

Your hotel can often locate a doctor quickly, but the cost is high and you'll have no way of knowing about his or her credentials. The nearest U.S. Embassy or Consulate also maintains a list of physicians who speak English. A pamphlet titled *Health Information for International Travel* (HHS Publication CDC 91-8280) is available from the U.S. Government Printing Office, Washington, D.C. 20402: 202-783-3238. Cost is about $5.

5.   *Assemble and pack a "survival kit" containing all your favorite medications plus other essentials you might need if your luggage is*

lost. (More on this in Chapter 6.) Carry this kit with you. Include such items as: a change of underwear; prescription drugs; headache and motion-sickness remedies; sleeping aids; pain medication; tampons/sanitary napkins; a small bottle of sunscreen; adhesive bandages; antacid; diarrhea remedy; insect repellent; an all-purpose antibiotic salve; contact-lens supplies; antiperspirant; and Handi-Wipe packs.

If you happen to be one of those unfortunates who suffers from aching ears in airplanes, particularly when landing, add antihistamine tablets and a decongestant nose spray to your survival kit. The pain comes from air caught in clogged Eustachian tubes located between the ears and throat. Take the pills or spray your nose before flying and during the trip, especially before landing. This keeps your air passages open. Other remedies are to swallow frequently, chew gum, or pinch your nose with your mouth closed and blow until you feel your ears pop.

6. *Pack a supply of feminine hygiene items.* Take enough to carry you through your trip. What some countries use for sanitary supplies bears little resemblance to items we have available at home. The space this takes up in your luggage is worth the feeling of security. It is also wise to pack a small, flat supply of toilet tissue for emergencies.

JET LAG

There are as many theories about and remedies for this disorder as there are transoceanic flights. Here are our observations based on research and personal experiences.

1. Jet lag affects different people in different ways; in other words, some suffer more than others.
2. Remedies vary with the individual.
3. There is no single, simple method of eliminating jet lag.
4. With the exception of a few fortunate people, jet lag can be debilitating and can reduce your mental acuity—which translates into a lower level of business performance.

Tourists who are traveling to, say, Europe for the first time often scoff at the mention of jet lag, claiming, "I wasn't affected at all." This, however, can usually be attributed to an extra rush of adrenaline associated with a first-time visit. They literally become too excited to be fatigued. For the frequent transoceanic traveler, that excitement factor fades with each successive trip.

Helpful Remedies
1. Drink lots of water and invest in a good pair of earplugs for long plane rides. A saline nose spray also keeps nostrils moist and helps the sinuses.
2. Use an inflatable neck pillow, sleep mask, and stretch booties to make sleeping on a plane easier so you're fresh when you arrive at your destination.
3. Limit alcohol intake to one serving of wine with dinner. Alcohol can contribute to dehydration and jet lag.
4. Eat less before you travel and try to break your intake into several small snacks during the day to help your digestive system acclimate to new eating cycles.

Travel books abound with remedies. Some recommend complicated diets that must be started several days before departure. And many of these guides echo the advice quoted above: drink lots of water, go easy on alcohol, get out of your seat and walk frequently to keep blood from settling in your legs and feet, but also try to sleep on the plane.

One area for disagreement involves whether you should take a nap after arriving (assuming you arrive in the daytime following an overnight flight). Some travelers say it refreshes them; others claim it worsens their adjustment. Growing in popularity is the theory that strong light—whether artificial or natural—is important because it tricks the body into thinking it's daytime and therefore you should be awake. Followers of this school of thought recommend getting out into the light rather than staying in dark hotels or meeting rooms.

Jack Cummings's book, *The Business Travel Survival Guide* (Wiley, 1991), devotes a lengthy section to jet lag. It provides detailed recommendations on coping with it plus numerous other travel maladies such as altitude sickness, motion sickness, in-flight earaches and toothaches, diarrhea or constipation, intestinal gas, and even depression.

Because jet lag is recognized as a liability in world travel, some corporations and government bodies have adopted regulations requiring specified periods of adjustment time, depending on the number of time zones one has covered. One company reported that it actually saved money by having its travelers fly economy class (versus business or first class, which can double the cost) and then "compensating" them by encouraging as much as a two-day early departure plus accommodations at a first-class hotel or resort for relaxation and adjustment.

A final piece of advice: Don't underestimate the effects of jet lag. When you arrive in a distant country, you may be alert and peppy one moment, then suddenly feel as if you are floating in a haze two minutes behind everyone else.

STAYING HEALTHY AFTER YOU ARRIVE

•   *Wash your hands frequently*—at every opportunity. Germs are easily spread.

•   *Always drink purified bottled water.*   Try not to drink directly from bottles or cans. Examine glasses and tableware for cleanliness. In almost every country, bottled water comes either with or without carbonation. As soon as you arrive, learn the words in the local language for "water" and "with gas" or "without gas" and order accordingly, depending on your preference. Urinary tract infections are more common in women than in men because many are caused by not keeping fluid levels up (especially if you do not drink enough water, which also causes constipation—another problem when traveling).

•   *If you have any doubt about the purity of the water, use bottled water for everything, including brushing your teeth.*   Remember that ice cubes may be made from unpotable water. (*Note:* That's another good word to memorize—"potable"—because it means drinkable. On the other hand, don't believe every sign you read!)

•   *Get enough sleep.*   If you don't feel like working out one morning, it's not going to make you sick . . . but fatigue will.

•   *Make sure to go to bed warm and have enough blankets.*   If you're running short of sleep—and who doesn't on business trips—avoid getting chilled so that your resistance won't be lowered. Pack a pair of heavy cotton socks and wear them to bed if necessary to keep your feet and ankles warm. It's not glamorous, but who's looking?

•   *Dine only at the best restaurants you can find and afford.*   Resist eating anywhere that looks the least bit unsanitary, no matter how much charm and local color it has. This applies especially to roadside stands or outdoor restaurants near the beach. Ask local friends or the hotel concierge for recommendations.

•   *Avoid eating uncooked foods,* especially lettuce, tomatoes, cucumbers, watercress, and parsley. Peel fresh fruit or, at minimum, wash it thoroughly.

THE IMPORTANCE OF EXERCISE

Exercise is one proven and popular way to ward off fatigue and the risk of illness. If periodic workouts are part of your daily routine, there are no longer any excuses for not continuing while you're traveling. More and more overseas hotels provide workout or fitness rooms. Almost all quality hotels have swimming pools. However, be sure to check out local rules and customs. For example, at some hotels in Germany, certain periods of the week are set aside for nude bathing.

Some hotels also provide printed maps showing safe jogging or walking paths. Once again, your friend the concierge can often direct you to jogging areas, arrange for tennis or golf games, or send you to the nearest fitness center. Try making this a "game within a game." One of the authors, a tennis fan, decided to set the personal challenge of attempting to play tennis in as many international cities as possible. Over the years he rarely failed, playing in such diverse cities as Bogotá, Tokyo, Sydney, Johannesburg, Singapore, Buenos Aires, Copenhagen, Baden-Baden, Jakarta, London, Lima, Sao Paulo, and even Beirut. He notes, "Tennis can be played even though the players don't speak the same language . . . and packing a tennis racket in your luggage is much less conspicuous than lugging a bag of golf clubs."

One unique, efficient way of getting a concentrated workout is to pack a jump rope. You can jump for fifteen or twenty minutes each day in your hotel room while watching television. Be sure to wear good support shoes to avoid damaging your joints and muscles.

SOURCES FOR MORE INFORMATION

A physician at the University of Zurich claims that diarrhea presents the greatest risk to travelers and afflicts 40 to 50 percent of all North American tourists. Such statistics are now available on the Internet's World Wide Web, provided by the Medical College of Wisconsin's International Travelers Clinic. This on-line clinic contains a series of twenty-three documents on travel health concerns, disease, immunizations, environmental hazards, and preventative concerns. With a laptop computer, a printer, and access to the Web, you can access medical information and advice in minutes.

For books that concentrate solely on the subject of staying healthy while traveling overseas, see Part Six.

6

LUGGAGE AND PACKING

I always travel to my destination with one carry-on bag (with wheels). There is more security knowing that I will have my clothes and documents with me. I am able to fit a three-week business wardrobe into the one carry-on.

BARBARA R. HAUSER
Minneapolis Attorney

Barbara Hauser's packing is an admirable feat—three weeks of clothing in just one carry-on bag! For a specific list of exactly what Barbara places in her magical suitcase, see page 44.

In days past, business travelers usually wore dress suits, took extra clothing because they were hampered by three-day waits for hotel laundry (today it can be returned in hours—at a price) and, when they unpacked, immediately began running hot water in the bathroom to generate steam to smooth out all the wrinkles.

Today, globe-trotters are luckier. Roller-bags are better constructed and come in diverse sizes and styles. Suitbags can be looped over the rugged handles of the roller-case, and fabrics are much more resistant to wrinkles.

LUGGAGE

At the luggage industry's annual trade show in 1990, a retired Northwest Airlines pilot unveiled a suitcase that *The Wall Street Journal* called "funny-looking." It was rectangular and stood on end, with wheels on one narrow end and a retractable handle protruding from the other. This unattractive duckling eventually created waves that changed the entire American luggage industry. The pilot and inventor, Robert Plath, called his creation the "Travelpro Rollaboard" and today its progeny can be seen rolling up and down every airport concourse in North America and overseas.

While roller-bags were unanimously favored by our interviewees, opinions were mixed on soft-sided versus hard-sided luggage. Each has merit: soft-sided bags are lighter and allow for more expansion; hard-sided are better for preventing breakage.

The advantages of other preferences—tote bags, duffel bags, backpacks, attache cases, briefcases—are all in the eye of the beholder.

Luggage Tips and Tricks

•   Use name tags that either cover your name or simply show your address rather than your full name.

•   Put extra copies of your itinerary inside each bag in the event it is misplaced; the airline or hotel personnel can then track you down.

•   When purchasing luggage, pay special attention to the ruggedness of zippers, wheels, seams, and hardware. Handles should be heavy duty, corners and edges protected, and hang-up hooks should have a heavy-duty chain and a method of tucking the hook inside the bag. Locks are sometimes deterrents to theft, but never sure-fire solutions.

•   If you dislike checking luggage and prefer to carry it with you, make certain your main piece will fit comfortably in storage bins. Airlines are becoming more strict about limiting each passenger to two carry-on pieces.

•   Make certain you can carry or transport it all yourself. Don't expect porters, cabs, storage for baggage, carts, elevators, and so on, to be available wherever you go. Independence is vital.

WHAT TO PACK

The climate at your destination, of course, will strongly influence your choice of clothing. Your local library can provide data on average temperatures around the year for most major cities. Better yet, on-line computer networks now routinely offer detailed daily and weekly weather forecasts for the larger cities in each region and country.

In Venezuela, Argentina, Italy, France, Switzerland, Hong Kong, and Singapore, fashion is especially prized and respected. When doing business in those countries, women would be wise to invest in the best quality and classic styling they can afford. Elegant cuts, safe colors, fine fabrics—each will set you off as one of the cognoscenti in dress and fashion. An investment in a few high-quality outfits that give you confidence will pay off when it comes to business relationships in those places.

Tips on What to Pack
- Pack conservative mix-and-match items that wear well, launder easily, and wrinkle as little as possible.
- Select a color scheme first. For example, for a short trip, choose one base color such as navy blue, black, or gray, and two accent colors. For long trips, take two base colors that each use the same accent colors.
- Wear clothes that transcend fads in both color and style. Selecting one dark color for all the basics makes it easier to mix and match and eliminates duplication. For example, a suit jacket, one or two skirts, and one or two pairs of slacks can easily cover a one-week business trip.
- Create interesting day-to-day changes by varying blouses, stylish jewelry, and scarfs.
- Use whatever size scarfs are currently in style to do wonders for changing a dress or suit. When large ones are in vogue, you can drape one over your shoulder to change your whole look. Smaller scarfs at the neck, ascot-style under a blouse, give color and a fresh look. When visiting religious sites, custom often requires women to cover their heads, so scarfs function for that purpose, too.
- As we cautioned in Chapter 4, avoid carrying or wearing flashy jewelry. A string of pearls adds a touch of class, but if you're heading into areas that produce real pearls, leave a list of what you take with you with the U.S. or Canadian Customs office on your way overseas to avoid paying duty.
- Wear practical shoes. Women should wear high-quality, leather shoes with a moderate heel.
- If an evening dinner or gala affair is on your agenda, include a conservative but elegant cocktail dress or suit and a pair of dressy shoes.
- Avoid linen, if you can, because it wrinkles so easily. All-season wool is preferable because wrinkles will come out with hanging or steam in the shower.
- For your various airplane trips, don't wear jeans, sweats, or other dumpy looks—it's unprofessional and sets the wrong tone with colleagues accompanying you, contacts you may encounter on board, and the people who may be meeting you when you arrive. For comfort on the plane, avoid clothing that binds your abdomen.
- Consider a raincoat with a zip-out lining. It provides the double usage of protection against rain and cold.
- Remember that in parts of the Middle East and Southeast Asia, women

are often required to wear modest, long-sleeved clothing, especially when visiting religious sites.

• Unless you're going to the beach, avoid short shorts and other provocative clothing.

What does Barbara Hauser (quoted at the beginning of this chapter) pack in her suitcase for a three-week trip? Here's her answer:

> I usually pack black skirts, black pants (worn on the plane and on weekends), black shoes (one pair to double as running shoes, also worn on the plane); three white or black washable blouses, a black knit jacket (worn on the plane), two other colored jackets, and several colorful scarfs (and jewelry). Dressy evening wear can be a black blouse and black skirt and large colorful scarf/shawl. I deliberately adapt part of my clothing to styles that are familiar and/or admired in the other country: Chanel earrings in Japan, high-quality French scarfs in France, and so on.

If you'd like some more ideas about selecting a wardrobe, consult *Simple Isn't Easy*, by Olivia Goldsmith and Amy Fine Collins (HarperPaperback, New York, 1995). This book shows women how to find a style that suits them and stick to it. Its central message translates well for women packing for an international business trip: "You don't need more clothes, more colors, more combinations. You need fewer things, carefully chosen."

HOW TO PACK

For casual clothes like jeans and permanent-press items, use the sausage-roll system—roll them up into sausage shapes the size of a rolled newspaper. It saves a lot of space and the items don't wrinkle as much.

Put the heaviest items toward the bottom hinges of your suitcase. These will prevent more delicate items from being squashed when the suitcase is placed upright. The bottom layer should include shoes (stuffed with stockings and socks to use the space and help retain the shape of the shoes), handbags, toiletries, and the items you folded into sausages.

For the next layer, place skirts, blouses, jackets, dresses, and other easily wrinkled items lengthwise across the suitcase. If you must fold a piece, try to do it along a crease.

Alternate pieces like jackets and dresses. Place the neckline of one item at one end of the suitcase for a layer and then put the next item with its neckline at the opposite end. This makes the pile flatter. Place a plastic dry-cleaning bag between each layer to help keep wrinkles to a minimum.

On top of all this, place your nightclothes and other items you may want to get to first, such as your raincoat or a sweater.

Always unpack as soon as you get to your destination so your clothes won't be sitting for days, accumulating wrinkles.

When packing garment bags, try to place several items on one hanger (the rounded, plastic ones work best) and put a plastic dry-cleaning bag over each hanger. If possible, carry the garment bag onto the plane and hang it up in one of the coat compartments.

Put all liquids in plastic bottles and in separate plastic bags. One habitual traveler says she has dubbed herself "the pouch lady" because she puts different groupings of toiletries into different plastic pouches. This helps minimize spillage and is more efficient when you're searching for a particular item.

If you have a favorite perfume or cologne, keep an eye out for gift-with-purchase specials at local department stores. With these specials, when you buy a bottle of fragrance, you also receive a bag with travel-size samples of the fragrance as well as soap, deodorant, moisturizer, and bath gel.

Collect the miniature bottles of shampoo, body moisturizers, conditioners, etc., that most North American hotels now provide as free conveniences. As one woman hotel habituée states: "I haven't bought a bar of soap in years."

If you need to carry tiny items like safety pins, needle and thread, rubber bands, and paper clips, use empty 35-mm film containers or hard matchboxes.

Don't forget electrical voltage converters, which are necessary for most American-made appliances; they can be purchased at local travel and drug stores. More and more hotels, however, have hair dryers and steam irons already installed in your room. Your travel agent may be able to tell you in advance which hotels offer these amenities. However, there is also an increasingly large selection of small, portable ones available in travel specialty stores.

Finally, here is a suggested list of items to consider for your own personal "survival" kit. They will vary from person to person, but every seasoned woman traveler we contacted recommended the idea.

Passport, traveler's checks, and airline ticket
Laptop computer, adapters for local currents
Prescription medications
Valuables, such as jewelry
Reading and writing materials
Essential cosmetics
Motion-sickness and pain medications

Sleeping aids
A sleep mask, earplugs, and inflatable pillow
A small penlight, ballpoint pen
An extra pair of eyeglasses or sunglasses, contact lenses and supplies
A small tube of sunscreen
A few adhesive bandages
An antacid and diarrhea remedies
A toothbrush and toothpaste
Deodorant
Handi-wipe towelettes
A small folding umbrella
A small travel alarm clock
A change of underwear
Feminine hygiene necessities
A small calculator for figuring foreign exchange rates

Other more cautious travelers will also pack one extra change of clothes. This is an especially good idea if your luggage is lost or you are prone to motion sickness.

PART TWO

ADVICE COUNTRY BY COUNTRY

In Part Two we will travel from country to country to examine the status of local businesswomen and provide insights and tips on business behavior, customs, and protocol for each country.

7

A WORLDWIDE VIEW

If you, as an international businesswoman, are looking for the ideal country to work in, where women dominate the business ranks and rule the boardrooms, forget it. It doesn't exist—unless you can find Anatolia, where, in Greek mythology, the Amazons lived. They were a tribe of warlike women who governed and fought while men performed household tasks.

Today, the United States and Canada lead the world in the number of women occupying executive offices, but the percentage of women compared to men is still embarrassingly low. As for the rest of the world, according to McGill University professor Nancy J. Adler, "Although women represent over 50 percent of the world's population, in no country do women represent half, or even close to half, of the corporate managers."

International business executive, consultant, and trainer Richard Gesteland claims that "Despite some signs of change, most of the world's female executives today are still concentrated in a handful of countries: North America, Northern and Western Europe, plus Australia and New Zealand." Gesteland believes the chief reason women are gaining more acceptance in those regions is because they are also the so-called deal-focused cultures—individualistic societies, relatively open to outsiders, where business is somewhat impersonal.

As for the other extreme, where women are rarely seen in business roles, Gesteland calls such male-dominated societies relationship-focused cultures. These are "more group-oriented and tend to be relatively closed to outsiders," he says. Relationship-focused countries are, as North American businesswomen would expect, in the Middle East, Far East, and parts of Southeast Asia. In countries like Saudi Arabia, Korea, and Japan, for example, "group-oriented" translates into "male-oriented," where women are almost entirely excluded from the business elite. It also means businessmen will spend nights of heavy drinking and carousing in order to "get to know" one another. "Such partying is done at restaurants, bars, and massage parlors where the only women present are there to entertain men," says Gesteland.

Cross-cultural trainer James Bostain tells the story of an American businessman in Japan who, after weeks and weeks of negotiations, finally clinched a contract with a Japanese firm. After bowing and shaking hands in agreement, the head man on the Japanese side said, "Fine. Now we will all go to the brothel." Shocked, the American stammered, "But . . . but what about your wife?" Surprised, the Japanese gentleman replied matter-of-factly, "Oh, she won't want to come with us."

There is also a middle category of relationship-focused cultures where businesswomen are unlikely to encounter major gender-related obstacles. In the Philippines, for example, women have made notable advances in the business world, so much so that women there delight in claiming, "The best businessmen in the Philippines are the women." In the People's Republic of China, where equality is a mainstay of communism, women often sit side by side with men as managers of factories and heads of government offices. And in Taiwan, Hong Kong, Singapore, and many Latin American countries—where family and matriarchal-oriented societies are common—women often help run companies alongside a husband or brother in a family business.

In all relationship-focused cultures, Gesteland says, "I find many women from the United States and Canada are more adept than their male counterparts in relationship building, which is a major key to success in dealing with relationship-focused customers and business partners. (Also) relationship-focused negotiators tend to employ high-context communication, relying heavily on nonverbal signals. In my experience, women outshine most men when it comes to deciphering body language. So, female executives enjoy two important advantages in dealing with relationship-focused cultures."

In the so-called macho countries in Southern Europe and much of Latin America, the problem for visiting women is compounded because most of those businessmen are unaccustomed to encountering unescorted women in hotels, restaurants, airports, or on the street. As a result, they resort to form and assume the woman is receptive to flirtation.

The winds of change, however, are slowly shifting across many of these male-oriented nations. Young people from these countries who come to North America for college educations quickly observe the role of North American women in business and take this knowledge back with them. Also, international television, such as CNN—at this writing seen in over 200 countries—depicts the increasing responsibility given to women in our society. Even TV sitcoms that feature strong female characters (*Murphy Brown, Murder, She Wrote, The Cosby Show,* etc.) are exported and build on this new image for women.

Finally, international businessmen who visit the United States and Canada notice the presence of women in the halls of business. This fosters the realization that back home, in their predominantly male societies, they may perhaps be overlooking a valuable resource.

8

UNITED KINGDOM

The Status of Women

Margaret Thatcher was Britain's first female prime minister as well as its longest sitting one in the twentieth century, serving from 1979 to 1990. Consequently, one would think that businesswomen in the United Kingdom would also have leaped to the forefront. That has not happened. While there has been some progress for British women, they still lag far behind their North American counterparts. Women make up roughly half of Britain's workforce, but they are highly concentrated in a few traditional female fields such as health care, education, administration, and retailing. As for high-level positions, women executives are usually found in such feminine-oriented areas as fashion, cosmetics, and the arts. Women seldom hold managerial positions in manufacturing, probably the largest and most significant sector of the British economy.

In government, in 1994 women made up just 9 percent of the members in the House of Commons, even worse than in the United States where women held 11 percent of the seats in the House of Representatives and 8 percent in the Senate. The United Kingdom ranks behind such scattered countries as South Africa, Iraq, Vietnam, Slovakia, Latvia, and Estonia. In an attempt to improve this lopsided ratio, the Labour Party adopted a quota system mandating that a certain number of its candidates must be women.

Politics is not the only area in Britain where women receive short shrift. A 1992 survey by the English bar concluded that women face discrimination in the legal profession at every stage of their careers. In 1992, women accounted for 19.5 percent of barristers, the British term for lawyers who argue cases in high courts. A higher ranking barrister is called a Queen's Counsel, and out of 760 such Counsels only 41 were women. Compare this to the United States: in 1992 about 23 percent of American lawyers were

52

women; however, a significant 43 percent of those who entered the profession in that year were women.

Business Behavior

Andrea Kormann Lowe is an American fund-management marketing specialist who has lived in England for the past twelve years. She offers these observations:

• In everyday language, the British have still not become sensitized to sexist language. For example, the masculine pronoun is consistently used in speeches and literature.

• In written correspondence, the norm in Britain is to sign just your first initial and last name, disguising the sex of the writer. The term Ms. still grates on the British, and British women tend to use Mrs. or Miss. Similarly, "girl" is used frequently by British businessmen.

• In applying for a job, the British call a resume a CV (curriculum vitae), and customarily require information that would be illegal in the United States: age, marital status, and number of children.

• In British business circles, American and Canadian career women are highly visible and memorable. There is also a great deal of admiration for American and Canadian enthusiasm and management techniques.

• In first-time meetings with business counterparts, the likelihood is that they will find you somewhat intimidating as opposed to not taking you seriously.

Following are more guidelines for the international businesswoman:

Etiquette.   The British respect—and expect—proper etiquette. "Good form" is ingrained in British society; it means following long-standing conventions for politeness and propriety. The bible for good manners is called *Debrett's Etiquette and Modern Manners* (more information on this book is found at the end of this chapter), and any businesswoman planning to conduct long-term business in the United Kingdom would be wise to pick up a copy of this valuable reference.

Prejudices.   The attitude of a British businessman is likely to depend on the man's age, with a tendency toward prejudice by older men and greater acceptance by the younger generation. Indeed, the phrase "the old boy's network" is more than just an idiom. Be on the alert for this exclusive fraternity.

Proper Dress.   While men in Britain almost universally favor dark, conservative business suits (dark blue, gray, black, with or without pinstripes), women are permitted more color and slightly more informality. For cocktail parties, dinner, or any evening occasion, a woman should wear a more elegant outfit than what is worn during the day. When an invitation specifies "black tie," it signals a tuxedo for a man and a long formal dress for a woman.

Social Situations.   Jane Walmsley is an American broadcaster and journalist who lived in the United Kingdom for over ten years. In her entertaining and informative book *Brit-Think Ameri-Think, A Transatlantic Survival Guide* (Harrap, New York, 1992), she warns, "The main thing that British men will notice about American women is how much they talk. The average Yankette will probably utter 30–50% more words in a lifetime than her U.K. counterpart."

Much of British social life centers on "the local," a popular term for the local pub. American businesswomen should be aware that most British pubs are discreetly divided into two sections: the lounge and the saloon, each with separate entrances. While a woman may enter a pub unaccompanied, she should probably steer for the lounge, which is more plush and sedate; the saloon is favored by the working class. In pubs, where draft beer is the most popular drink and is served in both pint-size mugs and half-pints, it is considered more ladylike for a woman to order the half-pint size. Don't be upset if the publican (owner or bartender) or waitress calls you "Love," "Dearie," or "Darling." These are common phrases and are not considered disrespectful. If, as a visiting American or Canadian businesswoman, you are seated in a pub or cocktail lounge, it would be considered "bad form" for an Englishman to approach you and strike up a conversation. Among the younger generation, however, in places like discos and nightclubs, it might happen more easily. A general rule among polite society in England is that no man should attempt to "approach" a woman without a proper introduction.

On the other hand, if you, as a visiting businesswoman, wish to host a British businessman for a lunch, you should make it clear at the outset that you are the host. Then, to avoid any possible awkwardness, notify the maitre d' to bring you the check separately. As for an evening dinner, it would be appropriate to extend the invitation to include the man's spouse.

Do's and Taboos for Both Men and Women
  • Do watch your language. There are hundreds and hundreds of differences in word usage and meaning between the English spoken in the United Kingdom and American English. Two tips: (1) Whenever you detect a glitch

in communication, or an odd usage, stop and backtrack; and (2) visit a local bookstore and purchase one of many glossaries on the market that catalog these differences. *Note*: For more on this subject, see *Do's and Taboos of Using English Around the World* by Roger E. Axtell (Wiley, 1995).

• Do book both business and social engagements well in advance. In the eyes of Americans, the British live by their agenda books, calendars, or schedules (pronounced shed-ules).

• Don't confuse your geography. Be aware that England, Scotland, and Wales are separate entities and together constitute Great Britain. When Northern Ireland is included, the result is the United Kingdom.

• Do avoid touchy subjects in conversation, such as: the problems of the royals, the conflict in Northern Ireland, or any invasion of privacy or personal matters. (*Note:* Among the older generation, this extends even to the typical, casual query, "What do you do?," meaning "What do you do for a living?") Most British have a great love for animals, gardening, and sports (the working class is passionate about soccer, the upper classes prefer rugby, cricket, and equestrian sports), so these are safe subjects. The English tend to be very self-deprecating about personal accomplishments. For example, where an American might respond to the question "Do you play tennis?" with "I play frequently—I've won my local club championship," an Englishperson who competed in tennis tournaments at Wimbledon might reply more modestly, "Oh yes, I play a bit."

• Do respect queues. Probably more than any other culture, the British believe in queues (lines of people). When in the United Kingdom, never jump in front of anyone waiting in line.

• Don't act up. Any loud, boisterous behavior is considered both improper and impolite.

SUGGESTED RESOURCES AND READING

• If you wish to plan a group meeting in Britain, a one-stop shop for assistance is the British Tourist Authority, 551 Fifth Avenue, Suite 701, New York, NY 10176. Phone: 212-986-2266, fax: 212-986-1188.

• *Debrett's Etiquette and Modern Manners,* edited by Elsie Burch Donald (Headline Book Publishing, London, England, 1992).

• *The Economist Business Traveller's Guides—Britain* (Prentice-Hall Press, New York, 1987) is one in a series published by the respected British news magazine *The Economist.* This sourcebook provides everything from maps and lists of hotels and restaurants to detailed essays on business practices and etiquette, politics, economics, finance, sightseeing, sports, and communication services.

- *The Travelers' Guide to European Customs and Manners* by Nancy L. Braganti and Elizabeth Devine (Meadowbrook Books, Deephaven, MN, 1984). This handy book explains how to converse, dine, tip, drive, bargain, dress, and conduct business while in twenty-seven European countries, including England, Scotland, and Wales.
- *Put Your Best Foot Forward—Europe* by Mary Murray Bosrock (International Education Systems, St. Paul, MN, 1995). Similar in format to the Braganti/Devine book, this more recent work provides separate chapters on England, Scotland, Wales, and Northern Ireland. Bosrock is a former editor of *Foreign Trade* magazine and has published similar books on Asia, Russia, and Mexico/Canada.

9

FRANCE

The Status of Women

The symbol of the French Republic is Marianne, a female figure found on French coins, stamps, and as a bust on every town hall. Unfortunately, when it comes to the role of women in the higher echelons of French business, the daughters of Marianne are noticeably absent. Even though the motto of the French Republic is *Liberté, égalité, fraternité,* it apparently doesn't apply fully to French women in business.

The majority of urban French women do work outside the home, but few are found in top business positions. According to famed anthropologists Edward T. and Mildred Reed Hall, the exceptions are in such fields as advertising, cosmetics, fashion, and art. The majority of French women who are in business serve in low-level secretarial or clerical jobs.

Furthermore, many French men, especially the older generation, have difficulty accepting women in business. Not only the men, but also French women may seem uncomfortable with North American businesswomen. One American sales director recalls being quizzed by her (male) colleague's French female office manager: "She asked me who takes care of (my) kids, what do they eat, who cooks, why do you leave home if you have a family? Her idea was that it was OK to work as long as you were home when the kids were home."

Even with these prejudices and preconceptions, women visiting from overseas, especially American and Canadian women, are generally accepted and allowed in the corridors of French business. You may even encounter the occasional flirtation, but chalk it up to the fact that beauty is revered in France. So are fashion, food, and the French language.

Business Behavior

Flirtation.   Within their own offices, the French enjoy flirting with each other. They exchange glances, brush up against one another, and so on—all considered relatively harmless. French men respect women for their charm, so it's important for American women to convey charm without flirting.

Fashion.   There is strong agreement that North American women visiting France on business should dress conservatively but well. Even casual dress is dressier and classier than in North America.

French women choose their outfits very carefully, from blouse and scarf to perfectly matched earrings and bracelet, and they have a strong eye for detail. You should always look as though you have put a great deal of time and consideration into selecting your clothing and accessories. The French will be particularly pleased if you wear a beautiful French scarf or something from a French designer. For business meetings, well-tailored suits or dresses in conservative colors are appropriate. One American woman attended an important dinner hosted by her company management, a French-owned international hotel chain, and recalled that she wore probably the most expensive dress she ever owned, plus equally expensive and brand-new suede shoes. That evening, she learned something about the French as well as about behavior in international circles that she believes will serve her well for many years to come:

> This was my first contact with the management group, so naturally I wanted to make a good impression, especially since it was on their home ground in France. That's why I chose my best dress. As the soup course was being served, a waitress carrying a tureen of thick French soup approached from behind me, tripped, and spilled the soup all over me, right down to my shoes.
>
> Of course I was terribly embarrassed and angry, but I tried to exhibit poise and composure. A woman associate whisked me to her hotel room where, fortunately, we found she wore the same dress size. We managed to find a replacement outfit complete with shoes. We then returned to the party as if nothing had happened.
>
> I was certain both my expensive dress and shoes were irreparably ruined, but just tried to dismiss that. To my amazement, two hours later my dress and shoes were returned absolutely spotless. Not a trace of the soup was visible. In addition, accompanying the cleaned clothes was a gracious note of apology from my hosts and a large bouquet of flowers.

Moral: Patience and understanding are powerful assets when doing business far from home.

Food. Dining in France is comparable to visiting the Louvre for the first time: both are unforgettable experiences, and both national treasures. Elinor Jackson lived and worked in Europe as an international businesswoman. She provides this indelible memory about dining in France:

> I was in Normandy visiting clients and we went to lunch at some provincial restaurant. I ate most of the first plate. It was filling. When that was removed, the next plate arrived. I had to eat some because if you don't eat, they think you don't like it. Well, the meal lasted three hours, and at the end there were several plates with cheese and then dessert. I felt like I would explode.
>
> On the drive back to Paris, my host said we were taking a boat ride that night. It turned out to be a boat ride with a seven-course formal dinner with wine. Again, I felt I had to eat so I wouldn't insult the host. I felt like I'd eaten three Thanksgiving meals in one day.

More Dining Tips

• Remember that the word *etiquette* comes to us from the French language, so it is valued and expected—be sure to mind your manners at all times. As just one example, it's customary before starting a meal to say *bon appétit* to others at the table.

• Never eat with your fingers (even sandwiches), except for French bread served at every meal—that can be broken apart and set on the table beside your plate; bread plates are often not used. Bread is used to push food onto forks. For this reason, the French usually do not butter their bread.

• Keep your hands above the table, resting your wrists lightly on the edge.

• When in doubt, watch your host and hostess and copy them.

• Note that salad is often served after the main course. Watch carefully as the French delicately fold each piece of lettuce into a neat little packet with their knives and forks before placing it into their mouths. It's bad form to cut lettuce with your knife.

• Peel and slice fruit before eating it.

• Don't sip until your host also sips. Both white and red wines are often offered, plus mineral water.

• Conversation is a vital part of any dining occasion, but unless your French colleague initiates it, do not discuss business.

Language. Probably more than any other culture in the world, the French are proud of their language. This pride has even extended to the imposition of strict laws accompanied by language "police" who require that foreign words and phrases be omitted from legal and public documents. As a result, there is a sensitivity when visitors try to speak French. In metropolitan places like Paris, you might even be treated with cold aloofness. This is not necessarily rudeness, but instead a distaste for having their beautiful language butchered by amateurs. One of the authors once sat through an entire luncheon attended by French businessmen, surrounded by French peers and subordinates alike, and, even though he had a rudimentary ability with the language, not one of his tablemates attempted to engage him in conversation in either French or English.

French people in the countryside are generally more understanding, even appreciative, when a visitor tries to speak French. Whether in the city or the country, you should learn the phrases for politeness: thank you, please, excuse me, hello, goodbye, and so on.

As any student of French knows, it is a problematic language for two reasons: (1) pronunciation is both difficult and delicate, and (2) word meanings have many nuances in a society where the people enjoy deep, philosophical discussions. If you do practice your French, use caution and expect to make mistakes.

Hosting.   Here's a tip whenever hosting business associates for dinner at a fine restaurant: Have the chef or owner come to your table and talk with the visitors, telling them it is an honor to have them at their establishment. This goes a long way. Also, be sure to have photos taken at the dinner and send copies to your guests.

General Guidelines
•   Don't jump to a first-name basis. Use *Monsieur* (Mr.), *Madame* (Mrs.), and *Mademoiselle* (Miss) until you are invited to use first names. If you speak French, always use the formal word for you *(vous)* until you are asked to use the more familiar form.

•   Do wait until everyone has been served the wine at the dining table before sipping. Even then, your host may utter a one-word toast, *Santé* (pronounced sahn-TAY), which means "Good health." Then you can drink.

•   Do remember that the spoon and fork placed horizontally above your plate are intended for use at dessert.

•   Do be aware that cheek-kissing is usually reserved for good friends, but if you shake hands with a Frenchman and he slowly draws you forward, be prepared for an "air kiss" to the cheek, perhaps both cheeks. It's merely a custom and a sign of acceptance.

•   Do expect lots of handshaking. French businesspeople will shake hands at every greeting and every departure—and then do the same thing the very next day.

- Don't gush or overdo praise. The French do not lavish compliments. They are more likely to critique. Don't take it personally—it's just their style. And they are uncomfortable being complimented excessively. Also, avoid bragging about your own country—the French are very nationalistic and won't appreciate it. On the other hand, praising France and its culture, and asking questions about French history, art, and geography will be well received.
- Do greet each person when entering a room (unless it is a crowded room, of course). Also, when saying *bonjour* (good day), it is good form to follow with *madame, monsieur,* or *mademoiselle.*
- Don't smile excessively; the French don't smile unless there is a good reason. Also, as we mentioned earlier, flirtation is common and almost expected. Handle it with charm, but do not flirt back. It could get you into trouble if you don't know the rules of the game.
- Do bear in mind that in addition to the word *etiquette,* behavioral words like *suave, élan,* and *savoir-faire* also come to us from the French. These characteristics are important to them, so act accordingly.
- Finally, if you have heard stories about the national tendency for rudeness—especially in Paris—you can take comfort in the fact that even the French government is concerned and at this writing is staging a national campaign to encourage people to be friendlier and more polite.

SUGGESTED READING

- *Business France: A Practical Guide to Understanding French Business Culture* by Peggy Kenna and Sondra Lacy (Passport Books, a division of NTC Publishing Group, Lincolnwood, IL, 1994). This is a small, handy booklet you can easily pack in your briefcase. It covers etiquette, gestures, communication style, and negotiating techniques in France.
- *Understanding Cultural Differences* by Edward T. Hall and Mildred Reed Hall (Intercultural Press, Inc., Yarmouth, ME, 1990). This wonderfully insightful book by two of America's greatest social anthropologists provides a comparison between the French, Germans, and Americans.
- *Robert T. Moran's Cultural Guide to Doing Business in Europe,* 2nd edition, by Michael Johnson and Robert T. Moran (Butterworth-Heinemann, Linacre House, Jordan Hill, Oxford, England, 1992). Professor Moran served on the faculty of the American Graduate School of International Management (Thunderbird) in Glendale, Arizona, for many years and is regarded as one of the preeminent scholars on cross-cultural communication. He and Johnson, who was Editor-in-Chief of *Interna-*

tional Management, analyze each European country and provide both background and specific tips on how to do business there.

- *French or Foe* by Polly Platt (Distribooks, Chicago, 1995). An insightful and amusing look into the French psyche. An indispensable resource for those wanting an in-depth understanding of French culture.

10

GERMANY

The Status of Women

International consultant Dr. Judith Irene Knorst aptly describes how an American businesswoman should approach doing business in Germany: "Although more women are entering business, Germany is a male-dominated society. Therefore, it may take you a bit longer to earn the respect of your German business colleagues."

Edward T. Hall, author and anthropologist, paints the same picture: "German women have less status in the business world than American women. Few married German women work outside the home, and the percentage of German women in professions and business is far lower than in the United States."

In 1995, German women occupied fewer than 5 percent of managerial positions. Accordingly, American or Canadian women living and working in Germany find signs of resentment from both males and females in business as well as an absence of social contact and support.

In Germany's government, women occupy only a quarter of all jobs in public administration, one of the lowest ratios in Europe. And, despite a flurry of legislation, the outlook for German women is bleak.

Amid this setting, more and more North American businesswomen are finding themselves journeying to Germany because it enjoys one of the most advanced economies in Europe. Fortunately, English is widely studied and spoken, especially in the sector around Frankfurt because of its fifty-year American military presence. However, as in any country, it is a distinct advantage for you to speak the local language. Even when mistakes are made, it can build bridges of friendship, as Dr. Knorst explains.

I was traveling with two German businessmen by car from Düsseldorf to Cologne. The driver asked me to watch for the names of towns along the way. Ten minutes later I announced the town of Umleitung on a sign at the side of the road. I later learned, to my embarrassment, that this was the word for "detour." This caused us to all laugh and relax . . . and we successfully finished our business as good friends.

Business Behavior

Business behavior and etiquette are important in Germany. However, they do not necessarily involve the type of elegant or gracious deportment one finds in, say, France or Italy, but more of a respect and expectation that one should be prepared to "follow the rules." German companies pride themselves on efficiency and reliability, and it should be no surprise that they also have rather formal rules for behavior.

Dr. Claudia A. Becker, a German, is Director of the German Language and Business Program at the University of Illinois at Chicago. She advises that in business meetings you should be assertive, but not obnoxious, in order to be heard. Take, for example, the matter of seating at a meeting—older men demand and get more respect, such as a position at the end of the table. Women should not let themselves be slighted.

Other women with business experience in Germany interject that if you are too aggressive, however, it might hurt business relationships. One woman offered this tactic: Before your meeting, ask German colleagues you trust and know well where they think it appropriate for you to sit at the conference table. Then, on entering the room, politely ask those present if you can sit in the chair you've determined most appropriate. Few German businesspeople will contradict you at this point—it would be rude to do so.

Dr. Becker cautions that business relationships generally develop a bit slower than in the United States and Canada, and advises against trying to be too pushy. Male German businesspeople often do not fully accept a female businessperson, even if all other factors are equal.

What can you do to establish your credibility? Businesswomen should be firm and not self-deprecating. From the very beginning, emphasize the seriousness of your visit by stating and restating the purpose of a meeting. Be clear about your intentions, your qualifications, and, when negotiating, your bottom line. If a dispute arises, be assertive in conveying your point. However, a hyperactive businessperson is not appreciated. State your points clearly and underscore them later as needed. Also, be conscious of your decibel level. A loud female is more offensive in Germany than a loud male. Avoid flattery and lengthy statements since Germans perceive such a style as manipulative and superficial. Do not try to hurry a meeting or a project. Learn to be patient.

In Germany, great importance is placed on the proper offer and the proper completion of a job rather than on the concept that "time is money."

Dr. Becker offers this advice concerning sex, sexuality, and dating: "As almost everywhere, expect men—married or single—to offer to sleep with you. Don't do it! Also, never date the people you work with. Some of the incidents women are facing in [German] business situations from their co-workers, such as expressive flirting and sexual advances, would be considered pure sexual harassment in the United States."

In summary, Dr. Becker notes "The position of women in business in Germany is about 20 or 30 years behind the United States and Canada. Maintain a strong professional image, impress them with your credentials, titles, and intelligence. Speaking and writing German at the intermediate level is absolutely necessary to succeed."

More Guidelines

Punctuality. This is especially important and expected.

Greetings. Shaking hands is the customary greeting, with a firm grip and one or two pumps. It is done at both the beginning and end of a meeting. Ask for a business card after shaking hands and look to see if it lists any titles. Always use the title because academic and professional honors are not easily earned in Germany and are therefore a source of great pride. If there are two titles—such as "Professor" and "Doctor"—ask which title the person prefers. Similarly, if you have academic or professional titles, be certain they are shown on your business card. Never jump to a first-name basis unless or until invited. Remember that both rank and age are respected.

Dress. Dress carefully, conservatively, and neatly. Creased clothing or scruffy shoes would send the wrong messages. Jewelry should also be elegant and understated. Germans are style conscious, especially in major metropolitan areas. Make sure your clothing reflects European fashion trends. Natural fabrics and high-quality shoes and accessories are critical.

Dining. Business lunches and dinners are less common in Germany than in North America. If you are invited to a business contact's home—which is not common, especially at the beginning of a relationship—it would be appropriate to bring flowers, wine, candy, or a gift representative of your state or province such as a book or elegant calendar. (*Note:* Bring an uneven number of flowers, but not thirteen, and avoid red roses since they connote secrecy and romance.) Unwrap the flowers before presenting them. When dining at a busy informal restaurant such as a *Gasthaus,* or when drinking and eating in a pub or *Kneipe,* don't be surprised if you are seated alongside strangers. Sharing a table is quite common in Germany, Austria, and Switzerland.

Exaggeration. Avoid excessive enthusiasm. To many Germans, life is not always "great" and no product can be "the best in the world" all the time. Hyperbole is often considered distasteful, and the person who uses it can be perceived as untrustworthy. The same advice applies to gestures and body language—avoid excessive displays.

Gift Giving. Unless invited to someone's home, you do not need to present gifts. A businesswoman should not offer gifts unless some unique service was provided.

Language. German is the most frequently spoken language in Europe (after Russian), with some ninety-five million speaking it as their native tongue. While German is spoken in Germany, Austria, and parts of Switzerland, each population is proud of its own history and separateness. Each also speaks a very different German. Be careful about commenting that one country's German is "better" or "easier to understand" than another's.

Conversation. Most Germans do not like to talk about business during brunch, lunch, or dinner. Remember, part of how you establish credibility in Germany is often based on your ability to discuss topics other than business. This proves you have a well-rounded background and high-quality education. When searching for conversation starters, avoid personal inquiries typical of an American dialogue—questions about one's occupation, family or spouse, finances, education, and religion. Instead, talk about Germany's history, world geography, cultural and intellectual leaders, travel, sports, culture, or world affairs. You can, of course, always discuss politics in Germany if you really know what you're talking about. Some Germans also enjoy discussing automobiles and fine engineering. One safe rule regarding sensitive topics of conversation is that if your German host or client raises the subject, then it is OK to respond. Also, even though your counterparts may appear to speak creditable English, try to avoid slang or colloquial expressions (e.g., "a ballpark figure" or "a leg up") since they will very likely only cause confusion. In business, Germans favor the direct, matter-of-fact approach. They tend to say what they think. Combine this with the fact that, to our ears, the German language sounds both rough and aggressive and the result is that many visitors are put on edge.

Etiquette. Sometimes a German man will precede a woman when entering a public building, such as a restaurant. This is an old tradition dating back to times when men would enter first to assure the setting was safe. It is not considered rude.

Meetings. If, during a meeting or at the dinner table, two members of the group appear to be whispering to one another, do not regard it as an act of rudeness. They merely have something to say to one another that does not apply to others present.

Phones. When answering the phone in Germany, instead of saying "Hello," state your last name.

Body Language. Chewing gum, slouching, putting your feet up on a table— all are considered impolite. The OK sign (thumb and forefingers forming a circle with the other three fingers extended) is viewed as a rude gesture in Germany.

Regionalism. Northern Germans are often considered more reserved than inhabitants in the South, who tend to be more relaxed. Regionalism is very strong throughout Germany, with considerable pride present in each of the various states.

Expressways. Driving on the *Autobahn,* or expressway, in Germany is usually a memorable experience. In some areas, speed limits are nonexistent and the right-of-way goes to the most powerful automobile. The automobile is also a business status symbol: the higher the executive, the more expensive the car.

Interpreters. If it appears that you will need assistance from an interpreter, you have the burden of providing one, not your client or customer. Retain a professional; do not rely on a friend or casual acquaintance. When presenting or leaving formal written statements or proposals, have them professionally translated and prepared. (All measurements and specifications should of course use the metric system.) If you hire an interpreter, spend time with the person in advance to review technical terms and key numbers. (One American company representative was describing a "pickling" process his factory used in treating steel. The unprepared interpreter later confessed he could not understand why "cucumbers" would be used to treat metal.)

Vacations. Germans treasure their holidays, or what Americans call vacations. The month of August is customarily set aside for such holidays, so don't plan deadlines or schedule meetings then.

SUGGESTED READING

- *Update, Federal Republic of Germany* by Nessa P. Loewenthal (Intercultural Press, Inc., Yarmouth, ME, 1990). This is a comprehensive but handy book on everything from arriving in Germany to doing business there to cars, driving, and leisure.
- *Understanding Cultural Differences* by Edward T. Hall and Mildred Reed Hall (Intercultural Press, Inc., Yarmouth, ME, 1990). Previously mentioned in the section on France, this book compares three diverse cultures: German, French, and American.
- *Business Germany: A Practical Guide to Understanding German Business Culture* by Peggy Kenna and Sondra Lacy (Passport Books, a Division of NTC Publishing Group, Lincolnwood, IL, 1994). This handy little book provides just what the title promises plus helpful comparisons between the American and German styles of doing business.

11

SCANDINAVIA

Probably the best starting advice for this region is: Don't casually lump the countries of Denmark, Sweden, and Norway together into one package as we have done. Each has a separate identity and culture, which adds up to an important phrase in international business—"national pride." Many people compound the problem by including Finland along with Denmark, Sweden, and Norway. Technically speaking, the latter three are "Scandinavia" and when Finland and Iceland are added, the proper designation is "Nordic" countries. Finland is unique among the countries in this delightful Northern European region of the world. The only feature it has in common with the others is its geographic proximity. Its people speak, think, and behave differently—distinctly so. The residents of Denmark, Norway, and Sweden also have different languages, but can understand each other fairly well. Not so with the Finns. The Finnish language is more akin to Hungarian in origin and highly complex; it reads and sounds completely different from the other three.

Despite all this, many North American businesses tend to regard the Scandinavian region as a single entity that includes Finland.

The Status of Women

In Sweden, working conditions for women are among the most favorable in Europe, with perquisites more generous than in the United States. Ironically, these benefits have made it easier for Swedish businesswomen to return to traditional roles. Consider these facts:

- Some 85 percent of Swedish women work, composing half the workforce.
- They earn 77 percent of wages paid to males, a figure still higher than in most other countries.

- However, Swedish women hold only 8 percent of private-sector managerial jobs.
- Women are entitled to paid, one-year maternity leaves plus government-supplied baby-sitters. Men are provided the same parental leaves, but rarely take them.

These liberal conditions have tended to retard the advancement of women in business by encouraging them to subordinate career ambitions in favor of traditional roles of wife and mother.

In Denmark, women have equal opportunities for managerial positions in business, but their numbers are still small. Klavs Olsen owns and manages a large business in Denmark, with branches in Norway, Sweden, and Finland, and for five years served as Chairman of the Danish Chamber of Commerce. For his services to his country, he was knighted by the Queen of Denmark. Olsen offers the following observations about the role of women in Danish business:

> We will see in the near future more women in top management positions. They are not there now because they have not had adequate education and experience in business.
>
> However, we are seeing more women in public service as lawyers, judges, and in the diplomatic corps. In fact, in our law schools today the students are predominantly women. There is no overall objection or barrier for women. Being female does not hold them back.
>
> Compared to the rest of Europe, Denmark, Norway, and Sweden are a bit more advanced than, say, France and Germany. This is due to our educational system, which is mixed. In Germany and France there is still some degree of separation.

When asked about equality for women in Danish business, Olsen smiles and replies, "We will not have absolute equality in business until we have some stupid *female* managers."

In Norway, families are important and husbands and wives share authority. However, more and more Norwegian women are retaining their own last name after marriage. In business ranks, Norwegian women enjoy considerable equality; they are present at all levels of corporate life. Visiting businesswomen will find Norway a good place to conduct business.

Finland was the first European country to give women the vote, in 1906. In Finland's parliament, about 40 percent of the members are women. In the ranks of Finnish business, you will find a significant and increasing number of women in senior management positions. And, finally, social regulations are liberal: It will not be unusual if your business counterpart—male or female—breaks off a business meeting or leaves work early to pick children up at school or care for them when they are ill.

Business Behavior

Olsen offers this counsel for North American women wishing to do business in Denmark, Norway, or Sweden:

1. First and foremost, behave like your own self. Be true to yourself. Don't try to fake it. Once you are found out, you will have great troubles.

2. Expect to be treated on equal terms. Don't carry a chip on your shoulder and expect special treatment. For example, it is not necessary to imitate men's clothing to be treated as an equal.

3. This also means it is important to be ladylike. For example, in Denmark and the surrounding countries it is proper for a man to hold a door open for a lady. Treat it naturally. As for picking up luncheon or dinner checks, both men and women have the same problem—it has to be made clear who is inviting whom and that should be determined at the outset.

4. Is there an "old boy's club"? Of course, but it is not as strong as it was even five years ago. Also, your purpose is not to break into the boy's club. Your purpose is to do business, and if you are qualified and professional, the companies here will do business with you whether you are male or female. Incidentally, an American or Canadian male who thinks he can break into the "club" will have the same problem.

5. In general, an American or Canadian woman will be treated exactly the way she wants to be treated. If she wants to be treated with dignity, she will be treated that way. If she wants to go out socially and find companionship, which is perfectly acceptable, she can do that as well because Scandinavians are friendly people. Be what you are, and don't try to be the other sex. In business, the worst thing is to try to be too familiar too soon. Everyone realizes you are there to do business.

In Finland, American and Canadian businesswomen will be easily accepted, but may note a few distinct Finnish characteristics: Finns tend to be unemotional, quiet, and reserved; privacy is valued; there is less smiling and open laughter; they take great pride in the environment; and the sauna is a national tradition. As a visiting businessperson, you will very likely be invited to sauna (which is used as both a verb and a noun). The perception of mixed, nude saunas in Finland is inaccurate; they are segregated and usually taken nude, but you can wear a bathing suit or towel, if you like.

Specific Protocol Tips

- Shake hands with everyone present at a meeting or social gathering (unless dozens of people are present). At the same time, state your name. Shake hands again when leaving.
- Be on time. Punctuality is expected and respected.
- Use last names until invited to use first names.
- In Denmark, Norway, and Sweden, when meeting people, you should say, "How do you do?" instead of "How are you?" There is no equivalent greeting in their languages. When we say "How are you?," they take it literally. Furthermore, that statement or question sounds insincere to them, and, if you consider it literally, we really don't want to know if their feet hurt, their cat is lost, or their aunt is ill. The challenge is to avoid that phrase and, when meeting someone, to substitute either "How do you do?" or "It's a pleasure to meet you."
- Be reserved in almost everything you do: avoid light or insincere compliments; avoid boisterous behavior or body language; and avoid any public display of affection.
- Use the common toast throughout Denmark, Sweden, and Norway— "*Skoal.*" It is spoken while looking directly into the eyes of the person(s) you are toasting. Hosts toast first, and often the person seated to the left of the hostess is considered the honored guest. When in doubt, ask your host or hostess if and when you may propose a toast.
- In Finland, use the word *kippis* when toasting.
- Do not bring gifts; they are not expected; nor is it common to take gifts to business meetings.
- Realize that entertainment in the home has become more popular. If you are invited for dinner, send flowers to the hostess in advance, probably via your hotel concierge. An alternative is to take chocolates, wine, pastries, or liquor. The tricky part comes when you arrive. You have to be both guest and business visitor. You've been meeting with the male all day, but you must treat the husband and wife equally. Leave by 11:00 P.M., even if your hosts try to persuade you to stay longer.
- Finally, remember the admonition that opened this chapter: The four countries of Denmark, Sweden, Norway, and Finland are distinctly separate in history and culture. Each takes pride in its individual characteristics and accomplishments, and you must respect each. In your business discussions and social conversations, avoid lumping them all together.

SUGGESTED READING

For a more penetrating look at national business characteristics in these countries, read *Robert T. Moran's Cultural Guide to Doing Business in Europe,* 2nd edition (Butterworth-Heinemann Ltd., Oxford, England, 1992).

12

RUSSIA

The Status of Women

A strange thing happened when democracy and capitalism emerged in Russia—women became less than equal citizens. In the old Soviet society, full-employment was mandated; in the new Russian society, jobs are not protected. Result: Women lost out.

Zoya Khotkina, a senior (female) researcher with the Moscow Center for Gender Studies explains, "Women have turned out to constitute 70 percent of the unemployed. In other words, there are four times more unemployed women than unemployed men. [And] the main peculiarity of women's unemployment in Russia is the unemployment of women with high educational and professional qualifications."

Consequently, the social status of Russian women is qualitatively getting worse. In addition, the current Russian business society is very patriarchal, with few Russian businesswomen among its ranks. Russian women constitute about 50 percent of the workforce, but only about 5 percent of the managerial corps. However, teachers and doctors are predominantly female; so too are about 50 percent of the engineers.

Business Behavior

Rose Mary Dineen, marketing manager for a Minnesota company that does extensive business in Russia, offers some valuable suggestions.

- Know that businesswomen are referred to as "businessmen." That tells you something right at the outset.
- For gift giving, bring American T-shirts. They are Dineen's favorite choice because they pack so easily and seem universally popular.

• Be on the lookout for entrepreneurs. She notes that "They are all over Russia. As just one example, if you step into the street with one foot and happen to raise your hand six inches, don't be surprised if a plain car stops. Ordinary people will give rides for those who want a cab as a way of making a quick buck."

• Find and retain a trustworthy Russian to help you with everything you do there—translations, travel, advice.

• Be conscious of body language. There is little eye contact with people on the street, but direct eye contact is important in business. People rarely smile in public, but in the privacy of their homes they enjoy smiling and laughing. Russians say they can tell who is American or Canadian because they smile a lot.

Before you travel to Russia, try to have respected go-betweens send letters of introduction in advance. Even with these, American and Canadian businesswomen should expect some signs of distrust—Russian men have difficulty believing women in business can have the authority to make binding decisions.

More Guidelines

Names.   Russians usually have three names. The first is their Christian, or given name. The second, however, is their father's Christian name plus the sound *-evich* (or *-ovich*), which means "son of." In the case of a woman, the father's Christian name will be in the feminine form: *-evna* (or *-ovna*), meaning "daughter of." (*Example:* Petrovich becomes Petrovna in the feminine form.) The last name is the family name, which also comes in both masculine and feminine forms (*Example:* Suslov becomes, for the female, Suslovna.) Russian women sometimes retain their own family names rather than adopting their husband's last name.

Conversation.   In conversation, after you are invited to do so, refer to the man or woman using both their first names: the given name and the father's name. Thus, Ivan Petrovich Suslov is called Ivan Petrovich. Incidentally, some Russian women have adopted the Western custom of being addressed as Ms.

Greetings.   Russians shake hands every time they meet. Good men friends hug and kiss each other on the cheeks three times; so do close women friends. Men, however, won't kiss women in public unless they are lovers or relatives.

Body Language.   Men may be seen walking arm in arm; this merely means they are good friends, not necessarily male lovers. Russians may stand very close to you when conversing. And they are very demonstrative, so don't be surprised if you are on the receiving end of body hugs, backslapping, shoulder pats, and other casual contact.

Gestures.   The OK sign (thumb and forefinger in the form of a circle) so widespread in the United States is considered a rude gesture in Russia because it refers to a certain part of the body's anatomy. Also considered rude is to face forward (toward the stage), when entering theater-type seating and thus present your derriere to the people you are passing. Instead, enter with your back to the stage and walk along the aisle while facing the people you are passing. Avoid speaking or laughing loudly in public buildings and do not whistle. At sporting events where Americans boo when angry, Russians and many other Europeans will whistle.

Home Visits.   When visiting a Russian home, it is very appropriate for you to bring gifts. Pictures of your home community, good soap and books, CDs or tape cassettes of pop music, quality writing instruments, and small items of clothing are appreciated.

Social Dining.   At most meals, business or social, there will likely be many rounds of toasting. Vodka is the national drink; it is served in small glasses without ice. It's permitted (and probably wise) to sip rather than gulp.

Intermediaries.   Many resources recommend that an American or Canadian woman traveling to Russia on business engage a trustworthy Russian man or woman to act as guide, interpreter, driver, and general factotum. In Moscow, helpful contacts for foreign businesswomen may be found at the International Women's Club, the American Women's Organization, and the British Women's Club.

Black Market.   Avoid the black market. Even though it may be tempting to exchange currency at attractive rates, or buy unusual goods and souvenirs, it is against the law. Bartering is common, and don't be surprised if people offer to trade some Russian article for your jeans or running shoes.

Medications.   Take extra supplies of personal medications and arrange with your company for medical evacuation in the event of a serious illness or injury.

Crime.   The rate of street crime has skyrocketed in recent years, so be sure to use all the usual commonsense precautions to avoid theft, pickpocketing, and other forms of crime. (See Chapter 4 on safety.) The underworld has also become more active and aggressive, and many visiting Western businesspeople are taking special security precautions against robbery, abductions, and extortion.

Drinking Water.   Use only bottled water, even when brushing your teeth. Remember that ice cubes can also be made from unpurified water.

Patience.   Business is done on a much more personal basis since Russians want to become well acquainted before signing contracts or agreeing to business deals. In fact, don't be surprised at cool receptions during your first encounters. Be patient. Business transactions take longer than in the United States or Canada.

Language.   English is widely spoken. Supposedly there are more teachers of English in Russia than there are speakers of Russian in the United States. When using English, speak slowly, avoid idioms and slang, review your discussions and points of agreement frequently, and always follow up everything in writing. And never assume that people around you don't understand English.

SUGGESTED READING

- For a guide to international communication and behavior while visiting Russia, refer to *Put Your Best Foot Forward: Russia* by Mary Murray Bosrock (International Education Systems, St. Paul, MN, 1995).
- Another extremely useful book would be *From Nyet to Da,* by Yale Richmond (Intercultural Press, Inc., Yarmouth, ME, 1992). Richmond looks at the Russian political structure, culture, and national character and explains how to respond on a personal level. A final section of this book outlines how to negotiate in Russia.
- A companion book, *From Da to Yes,* also by Yale Richmond (Intercultural Press, Inc., Yarmouth, ME, 1995), deals with Eastern Europe and countries of the former Soviet bloc. Richmond provides individual chapters on the Poles, Czechs and Slovaks, Hungarians, Rumanians and Moldovans, Bulgarians, the people of the former Yugoslavia, Albanians, Balts, Belorussians, and Ukrainians.

13

ITALY

The Status of Women

It is no accident, writes cross-cultural expert Robert T. Moran, that the two most popular and common expressions in Italy—*Mamma mia!* and *Madonna*—refer to female icons. In Italy the woman is the backbone of the family. This, combined with the renowned Italian love of beauty, gives the role of women a special place in the world of relationships.

But when it comes to the world of business, alas, the man is the authoritative head, the patriarch. As a result, while Italy is the twelfth largest economy in Europe, women play a decidedly minor role in its business sector. Approximately 36 percent of the workforce is female, with very few in decision-making positions. However, Italian women managers will be found in female-oriented businesses dealing with fashion, art, and cosmetics, and those can rank among the most sophisticated, professional, and powerful women in Europe. This is especially true in family-owned businesses.

As a visiting businesswoman from North America, you will be accorded courtesy and respect. Always be aware that in Italy there are distinct roles for men as the dominant force in business. Women play decidedly lesser roles, except in the family.

It is also important to know that Italy has three fairly distinct geographic areas. The manufacturing region sits in the north, around Milan. The central part—centering on Florence and Rome—is laden with history, religion, and the arts. The south, with Naples as its unofficial capital, is in terms of resources the least endowed portion of the country.

Business Behavior

Here are some important and endearing characteristics that you may encounter among Italian businesspeople:

78

- The idea of family is important, and it often extends to business relationships. One of the authors was made "an official member" of the large Italian family that represented his company. This meant affectionate hugs, inclusion in family celebrations, gifts, and close familial-like correspondence.
- The stereotype that Italians are very demonstrative is usually accurate. Conversations are animated, the language is rich with musical sounds, and Italy has been called the "Garden of Eden for gestures and body language."
- In the business world, Italians eat well, relax well, dress well, and are astute businesspeople. And being "astute" in Italy, as Moran writes, means that "no one wants to pay full price for theater or railway tickets, no one wants to pay full taxes, and no one wants to pay the list price for a new car or suit. Only naive Italians and foreigners pay full price."
- English is widely spoken among Italians, especially among the better educated businesspeople. However, complete fluency is less common, and it would be wise to carry caution with you when communicating. Watch for potholes of misunderstanding, review major points and decisions, and always recap all discussions in writing.
- It is no surprise that the word "charm" is of Latin origin. Italians, especially well-educated businessmen, seem to have a special penchant for demonstrating it. That adds up to both an advantage and a warning for any American or Canadian businesswoman visiting Italy.

Most male-to-female overtures are more subtle than the fabled pinch on the Via Veneto: a totally ingratiating smile; a sly wink; an Old-World gesture such as kissing a woman's hand; or a truly sincere verbal compliment. Accept all of them gracefully.

However, if any of these actions—no matter how subtle—are unwanted, Italian scholar Hugh Shankland advises women to coolly ignore them, no matter how persistent or irritating. If the man absolutely refuses to get your message, a strong and vocal rejection is totally appropriate. *Basta!* is the Italian word for "Enough!" Remember that the famous Italian poet Dante wrote, "Being rude in return is good manners."

More Protocol Guidelines
- Do extend your hand first when greeting men. Handshaking as a greeting in business and social situations is both common and frequent. However, both the *abbraccio* (embrace) and cheek-kissing are reserved for longtime good friends. Direct eye contact is expected during the greeting.
- Don't be afraid to introduce yourself at a business gathering. Umberto Fantacci, Italian businessman and Yale graduate, advises that "In general, Italians often neglect to introduce themselves or say their names clearly when

meeting visitors. This is particularly true when many people are present at business or social situations. Also, they don't exchange business cards as often as other Europeans. So, when meeting someone, the only recourse is to simply request that names be repeated."

• Do use last names (preceded by *Signor* or *Signora* pronounced see-NYOR or see-NYORA) until invited to use the person's first name. Show great respect for professional or academic titles, which are more common than in the United States and Canada. Italian women frequently use their maiden names in business. Married names, or both names, may be used outside business. There is no Italian equivalent for Ms.

• Do watch for body language, but don't consider it necessary to imitate the Italian penchant for free animation. The following are examples of Italian body language.

> Italians may stand closer than you are accustomed during general conversation. Don't back away abruptly—it could be misinterpreted.
>
> If you are from Texas, you know the "Hook 'em horns" gesture—fist held upright, with the index and little fingers extended—that represents the longhorn steer, the mascot of the University of Texas. Students and alumni display that gesture frequently and with vigor. Don't use it in Italy! There the same gesture means "Your spouse is having an affair."
>
> Italians use the "fingertip kiss" to signal that something is beautiful, whether it is food, art, or a woman.
>
> If an Italian man takes his index finger and twists it into his cheek, as if making a dimple, it means "That woman is beautiful."
>
> Don't be surprised to see two women or two men walking arm in arm on public streets. In Italy this is merely a casual sign of friendship.

• When dining, don't expect the North American sequence of dishes. In Italian restaurants, pasta is often served as an early course in a multi-course dinner. Naturally, you can have pasta as your main meal, but locals will probably follow the pasta course with meat or fish.

• Don't expect the North American–style "cocktail hour," with several rounds of drinks. It is not as common in Italy since wine is usually served with every course. In Italian business circles, even mild intoxication is considered ill mannered.

• Do expect to be seated next to the host if you are the guest of honor at a dinner. A male guest of honor will be seated next to the hostess.

• Don't place your hands in your lap at the dinner table. As in most of

Europe, keep your hands above the table at all times, with wrists (not elbows) resting lightly on the edge.

•   Do consider investing in a stylish, high-quality wardrobe for business and social events. This includes elegant accessories such as shoes, purse, briefcase, and jewelry.

•   Don't be afraid to bargain in small Italian shops (but not in high-class stores). Do it politely and not aggressively.

•   Don't go to Italy in August and expect to do business unless your client or customer requests it or is agreeable in advance. As in many other parts of Europe, August is the traditional month for family vacations and it seems as if the whole business community shuts down and heads for the mountains or beaches.

•   Don't be afraid to invite an Italian man to lunch or dinner, with these provisions. First, make it clear that you wish to be the host (he will protest at length), and, second, for a dinner event be certain you extend the invitation to include his spouse. In both cases, it is much smoother if you notify the maitre d' in advance that you wish to receive the check, or possibly even explain that you wish to wait until your guests leave before settling the bill.

•   Do try to learn a few Italian phrases. It is a fairly easy language, and your hosts will appreciate your efforts because it is likely that their English will not be perfect.

SUGGESTED READING

•   *Business Italy: A Practical Guide to Understanding Italian Business Culture* by Peggy Kenna and Sondra Lacy (Passport Books, a division of NTC Publishing Group, Lincolnwood, IL, 1995).
•   *Robert T. Moran's Cultural Guide to Doing Business in Europe* 2nd edition, by Michael Johnson and Robert T. Moran (Butterworth-Heinemann, Oxford, England, 1992).
•   *Put Your Best Foot Forward: Europe* by Mary Murray Bosrock (International Education Systems, St. Paul, MN, 1995).

14

OTHER EUROPEAN COUNTRIES

AUSTRIA

Known as the gateway country in Europe, Austria had close ties with both East and West during the Cold War. Now, with trade flowing more freely in all directions, Austria serves as a wonderful pivot point for commerce. Happily, that gate is also open to visiting businesswomen, especially those from the United States and Canada.

The Status of Women

Austrian working women enjoy increasing opportunities and have made great progress in politics and industry, but parity with men in the business sector is a long way away.

Business Behavior

When you visit Austria on business, you'll find that the rules of protocol and behavior are very similar to those in Germany and Switzerland with one extremely important distinction: Never lump Germany and Austria together. Each has its own proud history and heritage. Their boundaries are contiguous and both speak German (although with differences in usage and sound), but it is an offense of the highest order to refer to them as cut from the same cloth or to call an Austrian a German, and vice versa.

Some Guidelines

Language. English is taught in the Austrian education system, so it is widely spoken. However, you will please your hosts and business contacts with your attempts to learn and speak German. Try to learn a few greetings and expressions particular to Austria.

Punctuality. Punctuality and prompt handling of all correspondence play important roles in the conduct of business.

Long-Term Goals. In business dealings, long-term goals are more important than immediate results or sales. So, extend your horizons and leave hard-sell techniques at home.

Dress. Business attire for men and women is conservative in both style and color. You will note that many Austrian women dress impeccably, so take care to dress your best.

Attitude. Austrians enjoy a happy approach to life. The concept of *Gemuetlichkeit* is present in all social situations, with much pleasure taken in wine, food, and song. Austrians are particularly proud of their classical music heritage. They also like and practice all forms of good, basic etiquette, and this extends to behavior in public, where they consider any display of loudness or extreme animation improper.

Vienna. You'll see huge signs on the facades and atop buildings with the word *Wiener*. Don't make jokes about hot dogs because *Wiener* is the German word for "Viennese." The German word for Vienna is *Wien* (pronounced VEEN).

Home Visits. If you are invited to an Austrian home, it is customary to bring flowers, but with these provisos. Don't bring red roses (they have secret, romantic symbolism); it is bad luck to bring an even number of flowers, but avoid the number thirteen; and unwrap the flowers before presenting them.

Greetings. A firm handshake is the traditional form of greeting in both business and social situations. However, a woman should offer her hand first when meeting a man. Respect all titles (doctor, professor, etc.) and use them when verbally addressing someone.

Restaurants. The following advice applies to dining in Austrian restaurants:
- As in Germany (Chapter 10), it is often the custom for a man to enter a restaurant before a woman.
- There should be no problem if a woman proposes to buy lunch, when appropriate, but such hosting and business discussions should be confined to lunch rather than dinner.

- At the dinner table, keep both hands above the table, resting the wrists lightly on top.
- Coffeehouses, rich pastries, wine and beer gardens, *wienerschnitzel* (breaded veal), dumplings, strudels—all are as revered and common as baseball, hot dogs, and apple pie in the United States.

Appointments.   Arrange all business appointments well in advance.

Social Conversation.   A short period of social chitchat usually precedes business discussions.

Gifts.   Business gifts are not expected, but it might be wise to have a few tucked away in your suitcase in case you are on the receiving end or wish to thank someone for a special favor. *Note:* In German, the word for gift is *Geschenk,* and the German word *Gift* means poison.

Bathrooms.   These are called WC's (for water closet).

Chewing Gum.   Americans have the image of being gum-chewers. Austrians as well as Germans and Swiss consider chewing gum in public improper.

Compliments.   Personal compliments—especially in excess—usually make Austrians uncomfortable.

Body Language.   Hugging and other forms of body contact (your arm around another person's shoulder) are not common, but eye contact is expected and important. In general, Austrians tend to be both reserved and formal.

Patience.   Be patient—don't expect all business decisions to be made on the spot.

BELGIUM

Visits to Belgium by businesswomen should be enjoyable experiences because so many Americans and Canadians have preceded you, either on business or as representatives of governments. The European Parliament and NATO Headquarters are both located in Brussels, and many North American companies have chosen Belgium as the center of their European operations.

In addition, in the eyes of Americans and Canadians, Belgians seem to be gourmets and wine experts, often speak excellent English, and appear to combine the *savoir-faire* of the French with the business acumen of the Dutch. A trip to Belgium is usually a happy experience. But therein lies the largest and most dangerous landmine. No Belgian likes to be compared to either neighbor, the Dutch or the French. In fact, among the Belgians, rude jokes are made about both nationalities. So, tread carefully on this territory.

Belgium is almost equally divided into two regions, characterized by two distinctly different languages. The Flemish section in the north, with 55 percent of the country's population, is Dutch in language and character, while the Walloon section in the south is French. In and around Brussels, both languages are spoken.

The Status of Women

You will not encounter many Belgian women in managerial positions. They have made great progress in the workforce since World War II but are still found mainly in support staff positions.

Business Behavior

Most of the practices involving greetings, making appointments, body language, table manners, and so on found in earlier chapters on Germany (Chapter 10) and France (Chapter 9) are followed in Belgium.

It is quite acceptable for a visiting businesswoman to invite a male business acquaintance to dinner and also to pay for it. As throughout Europe, the person who offers the invitation becomes the one to pay the bill.

GREECE

The fact that Greece follows Belgium in this catalog of countries is based solely on the alphabet. Both countries are populated by savvy, friendly businesspeople who enjoy good food—but that is where any similarity ends.

In fact, "Greek business protocol is virtually non-existent," writes Robert Moran. "The best attitude for a visitor is to leave behind all the usual rules of punctuality and tightness of the business world," he advises.

Some Guidelines
Punctuality.   This is not necessarily considered a virtue.

Dining.   Meals and drinking take precedence over any form of business. Women may dine alone in public restaurants, but it's best to choose high-class ones. In other public places you might experience some verbal attention from Greek men. Consider it a sign of admiration, not crudeness. It is not customary for a woman to invite a Greek man to lunch or dinner. To override this, invite others—or the man's wife—to accompany him. If you wish to pay the bill, you should carefully arrange for and explain this in advance.

Conversation.   Conversation at mealtimes is almost a professional pastime, and few subjects are considered taboo, with the possible exception of the politics of Cyprus and Turkey.

Values.   Greece is a male-dominated culture. However, the family is prized and honored. The word "honor" carries special—almost religious—significance to the Greeks. Business in Greece is often a case of having good "connections," which applies equally to businessmen and women. Despite the strong male orientation, Greece is a good place for visiting women to do business.

Language.   English is taught in Greek schools, so many Greeks will speak and understand English.

Body Language.   Greek men tend to be both demonstrative and affectionate—it is in their nature, and you should not regard it as harassment.

Gestures.   Here are some specific gestures you should be aware of:

- Extending the arm and hand (palm open) as if pushing something away from you is an age-old form of insult. In wars, Greeks would humiliate their prisoners by rubbing mud or fecal matter into their faces. It's called the *moutza*.
- While Americans signal OK by making a circle with thumb and forefinger, the Greeks consider this a rude gesture. On the other hand, many Greeks are acquainted with many American gestures.
- Thumbs up means OK, but thumbs down is rude.
- One special gesture—making a fist and pushing the thumb up through the index and middle fingers so that just the tip is showing—is distinctly rude. It is considered a phallic symbol. This same gesture in Brazil is called the *figa* ("the fig") and is considered a signal of good luck.

IRELAND, REPUBLIC OF

The stereotype of the Irish—gregarious, pub-loving, Catholic, family centered, with strong male chauvinism—is very accurate.

Ireland has traditionally welcomed outside business investments and, as a result, many North American companies have established ventures there. This has helped make Ireland a friendly destination for both U.S. and Canadian businessmen and women.

The Status of Women

As in Great Britain, the "old boy's network" thrives in Ireland, so who you know is important when doing business there. The older generation is less accustomed to dealing with women in business, but the younger generation is more tolerant and helping to change that attitude. The Republic of Ireland is (at this writing) one of the few countries in the world with a woman as president, Mary Robinson.

Business Behavior

• Do be patient. Business is not concluded at the pace you are probably accustomed to in the United States and Canada.

• Do be reserved, conservative, and low-key. These same adjectives apply to your choice of clothing.

• Do take the time to learn something about the history of the country. It will help you understand why the Irish are often quick-tempered, quick-witted, and critical, and sometimes ambivalent toward personal success.

• Do be genuine and sincere. "Blarney" is a social art form, but it does not extend to business dealings.

• Do expect warm hospitality and a sense of welcome. However, also be on the alert for rare occasions when you might encounter swift changes in friendliness. Don't take this personally but accept it as a characteristic of mood changes that can easily occur among the Irish.

• Don't expect language to be a problem. English is the language for business, while Irish (Gaelic) is preserved for music and storytelling.

• Don't hesitate to host an Irish businessman for a social meal, but you should probably best do it at lunch and in the company of others.

• Do be prepared to follow sacred rules when it comes to social drinking: Buy a round of drinks when it's your turn, and don't forget to offer your companions the common toast—"Cheers."

• Don't be disturbed by occasional incidents of lateness. The Irish are less punctual than Americans and Canadians.

LUXEMBOURG

Because of its modest size (smaller than the state of Rhode Island), Luxembourg has been forced to become all things to all people. Sandwiched between France, Germany, and Belgium, the people speak French, German, and their own dialect. Luxembourg has had to rely on others to fuel its economy, and its strength lies in its financial community. Visitors will find the business community to be friendly, astute, reserved, conservative, and relatively slow-paced. The family is also important, and 97 percent of the population is Roman Catholic.

Luxembourg is also noted for its strong sense of independence and national pride.

If you follow the rules of behavior and etiquette that prevail in Germany, France, and Belgium, you should not encounter many difficulties.

THE NETHERLANDS

The Dutch are widely considered among the ablest and most trusted businesspeople in the world. With few natural resources, they've been required to become astute in trade and commerce in order to survive. They are also well traveled and are excellent linguists. As one Dutch businessman explained, "Of course we've learned other languages. Who would ever want to learn Dutch?"

Skim through reference books on the Netherlands and one word repeatedly appears: egalitarian. Businesspeople tend to be worldly, hard-working, serious, and accustomed to dealing with all nationalities. During the Cold War years, a businessperson with a Dutch passport was one of the select few accepted by distrustful and wary Eastern European countries.

The Status of Women

The Netherlands are, like many "Old World" European countries, slowly adjusting to the increased role of women in business. Therefore, the older generation may be uncomfortable dealing with North American businesswomen—but nontheless accepting. The younger generation, on the other hand, will likely be much more tolerant and friendly.

Within the country, women constitute only 30 percent of the workforce, few are in managerial positions, and most leave the business world if and when they have children. The government has made equality a high priority, but progress has been slow.

Business Behavior

- Don't refer to the country as Holland. That is the name of just one region within the Netherlands.
- Do be punctual; it is expected and appreciated. In fact, the Dutch regard any incident of lateness as a sign of untrustworthiness.
- Do expect men to stand when a woman enters a room and perhaps not sit down until all women have been seated. The handshake is the traditional greeting, offered by both men and women, and more frequently than in the United States or Canada.
- Don't show strong emotions. The Dutch tend to be rather unemotional, so displays of anger or animation may be disliked, especially in business situations.
- Do dress conservatively. Business attire tends to be reserved and less elegant than, say, in France or Italy.
- Don't confuse the sound of Dutch with German even though, to the untrained ear, they may sound alike. Avoid making that comparison, especially among the older generation who may remember the German occupation during World War II.
- Do be prepared for long lunches. The business community in the Netherlands enjoys the lunch period, so two-hour luncheons, a round or two of drinks, and much conversation are the norm.
- Don't touch or be excessively animated. When it comes to body language, the Dutch are not "touchers" nor are they overly expressive. However, another form of contact—eye contact —is considered extremely important, especially during business conversations.
- Do expect frankness. Your business discussions will probably be characterized by directness, open but not offensive criticism, avoidance of superlatives and excessive compliments, and serious but friendly argument. Negotiating with the Dutch will, obviously, test all your talents and skills.
- Don't be offended by open sexuality and a permissive drug society. Amsterdam is fabled for its unique, public red-light district located in the center of the city. There, in row after row of houses and apartments, prostitutes sit in large, illuminated windows, literally displaying their wares. If you find this offensive, it might be best to remain discreet, remember that you are a guest in their country, and try to ignore it. American and Canadian women should understand that sex is dealt with more openly in countries like the

Netherlands, Germany, and Denmark, to name just a few. And when it comes to drug usage, the Dutch have adopted a very liberal attitude.

•   Don't worry about dining alone in a quality restaurant. For the most part, visiting businesswomen can dine without being disturbed. The normal precautions you would take in any large city will apply here, especially in crowded areas where there may be a danger of pickpockets.

PORTUGAL

The Status of Women

Visiting businesswomen will be met with politeness and fair treatment. More and more Portuguese women are becoming involved in business, but their ratio to men is still very small.

As a general rule you will find Portuguese men to be macho, but often charming and polite. (For an interesting definition of the "macho" concept, see the segment on Mexico in Chapter 22.)

Business Behavior

The Portuguese value personal relationships in business, so you must deal with them on less than an arm's-length basis. Always take an interest in the people you are dealing with as well as the company and the market. It may take repeated visits to accomplish your goals.

Within the Portuguese business community, much importance is placed on relationships, kinships, influence, contacts, and connections. Patience is also important in Portugal. It once took author Elizabeth Devine a week of daily visits to a travel agent to obtain a ticket from Oporto to Paris. On the other hand, she was never billed.

In your demeanor, the following qualities are most respected: restraint, conservatism, dignity, politeness, and sincerity.

More Guidelines
Greetings.   The handshake is the customary form of greeting; be sure to shake hands with everyone present. Embraces and cheek-kissing are reserved for old friends. Be respectful of and use all professional titles. Avoid using first names until you are invited to do so.

Punctuality.   There is a double standard in Portugal when it comes to punctuality. Visiting businesspeople are expected to be on time, but locals may be anywhere from fifteen to thirty minutes late.

Language. Portuguese is the national language. English and French are commonly used in the business community, but, as in all countries with a special indigenous language, it is a sign of respect to try to learn at least a few phrases that express courtesies.

Gestures. Unlike some of the other so-called Latin cultures, gestures and body language are generally restrained among the Portuguese. One body action—stretching—is regarded as inappropriate in public.

Toasting. The common phrase for toasting is "To your health" (in Portuguese *A' sua Sa'ude,* pronounced ah-sooah-sah-OOD). If you are a guest of honor, you will likely be toasted first. In this case, you should respond with a few words of thanks. Women can initiate a toast, but, as a courtesy, you should mention to the host in advance that you would like to do so.

Business Dress. Business attire for both men and women should be conservative: dresses, suits, or pantsuits.

Dining. When dining, keep both hands above the table, wrists resting lightly on top. Never pick up your food with your hands—even sandwiches and fruit are eaten with a knife and fork. If you happen to be invited into someone's home (which is not common) for dinner or other social occasions, it would be appropriate to bring a small gift (flowers, expensive chocolates, or wine), or have flowers sent the next day along with a note of thanks.

SPAIN

The Status of Women

In Spain you will find a slow, modest, but growing presence of women in business. This is due, in part, to a shortage of skilled people; women have become educated to fill the gap. Many women work, but they are still concentrated in low-level jobs and few are in the professions. A woman lawyer is a rarity, and women managers are usually found in family-owned companies.

For the visiting businesswoman, Spain presents a special challenge. Consider this rather distressing list of possible obstacles:

- Spain is a man's world, especially among the forty and older generation. Men are expected to be strong, dominant, masculine, and aggressive—their definition of "macho." Women are taught to be acquiescent, passive, and feminine.

   •   Moran writes: "To succeed in Spain, a newly arrived foreign business-person must be prepared to be completely submerged into the Spanish system. And it will be a cold shower of cultural shocks and barriers. The value of being *bien educado* (literally, "well raised" but meaning more, such as "having good breeding and good connections") is of primary importance, and success in business and in social settings will depend on one's ability to divine the proper protocol and operate confidently within it."

   •   Behavior and appearance rank very high on the list of important traits in the Spanish community.

To both men and women visitors, the Spanish are generally friendly and helpful. Keep in mind that they have a strong sense of personal pride. One's degree of affluence, social position, and personal connections are important.

Business Behavior

As a visiting businesswoman, it will be helpful if you establish your credentials and ability before you arrive and in a matter-of-fact, nonboastful way.

You will find certain Spanish male traits and mannerisms a test of your cultural flexibility. Here are some particular observations:

   •   As with most Latin cultures, the Spanish tend to stand very close in both social and business situations. They may even rest their hand lightly on your forearm or elbow.

   •   Spanish businesspeople enjoy vigorous discussion that may, to our ears, sound strongly argumentative.

   •   Where the "old boy's network" may exist in other countries, in Spain an exclusive network of leading families prevails. And it is the men who compose this special network.

   •   Pride, bordering on arrogance, is often cited as a common trait among Spanish businessmen.

   •   Spanish men tend to converse quickly and expressively. They may interrupt you, but by their standards it would be impolite for you to do the same to them.

   •   Eye contact will be a special challenge. Holding eye contact during a conversation shows sincerity; lowering the eyes signals respect. Yet, as in the United States and Canada, prolonged contact by a woman could send the wrong message.

As you may have read in earlier sections, North Americans have an image as "smilers." Other cultures claim they can spot Americans by how often they smile. In Spain, as elsewhere in Europe, one who smiles frequently is regarded as either insincere or flirtatious.

More Guidelines

Names.   The Spanish customarily have three names. *Example:* Carlos Perez Gonzalez (male), Maria Perez Gonzalez (unmarried female). In both cases, the first name is the given name; the second is the father's last name; and the third is the mother's last name. In daily use, you need only the first two names; don't jump to a first-name basis unless invited. A woman married to a man whose father's last name is Rodriguez becomes Maria Perez de Rodriguez. Spaniards may also have compound first names, such as Juan Carlos or Maria Teresa.

Titles.   Such titles as *Senor* (Mr.), *Senora* (Mrs.), and *Senorita* (Miss) are used often. If you are unsure if a woman is married, use *Senora* until corrected. For elderly or highly respected people, use the title of *Don* or *Dona.*

Language.   Although English is widely spoken, Spanish is the language of business. As in many European countries, businessmen often take pride in their English, even though it may be limited, and may insist that a translator is not required. In these cases, defer to their wishes because pride and honor are especially important in Spain. However, during all your discussions be on the alert for possible misunderstandings.

Handshaking.   Shaking hands is the traditional greeting, done at the beginning and end of a meeting. *Abrazos* (embraces) and cheek-kissing are reserved for very close friends.

Religion.   99 percent of the population is Roman Catholic, and divorce is rare in Spain.

Bullfighting.   Never make disparaging remarks about this national pastime, which is considered more an art than a sport. The most popular spectator sport is soccer.

Bathrooms.   In small towns, you might find that men and women use the same bathrooms.

Flirtation. On public walks, men may call out expressions of admiration as a woman passes. If you ignore them, the callers will probably desist. Try not to meet men's stares with direct eye contact—you may unintentionally convey interest.

Churches. When visiting churches, cover your shoulders and never wear shorts.

Dining. The evening meal occurs late, at least by American and Canadian standards. Be prepared to dine at 9 P.M. or later. Meals are a vital time in which to establish personal relationships. Business matters may or may not be discussed—let your host lead the way.

Faucets. Because *frio* means cold and *caldo* means hot, faucets are marked with an F and a C. Don't mistake the C for cold.

Patience. Business decision-making will probably not occur as quickly as you would like—prepare for delays.

SWITZERLAND

The list of national perceptions about this unique country is both lengthy and accurate: the Swiss value hard work, sobriety, thrift, and independence; they admire punctuality and value personal privacy; they live among the most picturesque scenery in the world and therefore love nature; and they take justifiable pride in being one of the oldest and most independent democracies in the world.

When you visit Switzerland, you will observe one of the world's highest standards of living. There are very few poor people in Switzerland, roads and byways are kept pristine, and automobiles are not permitted on the road if they are the least bit unkempt or rusty.

Switzerland is divided into provinces that are called cantons. Each has a unique style, history, and heritage and it would be appropriate and appreciated for you to do some research in advance about local history.

For the U.S. or Canadian businesswoman, Switzerland will be one of the more comfortable countries to visit and conduct business. While Swiss-German businessmen are renowned for being restrained, conservative, and proper, they have for centuries greeted all nationalities. Consequently, the current slow, steady incursion by businesswomen leaves them unfazed.

ration between the sexes is practiced. Men work together and are more visible; women work together and stay behind the scenes.

Business Behavior

In business, Turkey is another country where letters of introduction are extremely important. Cold calls are therefore to be avoided.

In both business and social contacts, demonstrating respect is highly important. Respect is measured by such factors as age, wealth, family contacts, academic achievements, and the position one holds in one's profession. Moreover, you show respect by not interrupting; the longer you allow the other person to speak the more respect you are awarding. In turn, you will be respected merely because you are a guest. David Shankland, an expert on the culture of Turkey, notes that this may be demonstrated in unique ways. For example, he explains that you may believe an appointment for a meeting is fixed, yet your counterparts fail to show. What has happened is that they could not be present at the stated time, but instead of refusing, which would cause embarrassment for both sides, they chose to avoid any type of confrontation.

As in the Arab world, doing business in Turkey is built on personal relationships developed over long periods. Extra patience is required, good will and friendships may involve exchanging favors, and *you* are the business you represent, while your company is some vague entity in the background.

More Guidelines
- Business cards are exchanged liberally.
- Punctuality is important.
- Business dress is conservative but fashionable.
- It is OK to invite a Turkish businessman to dinner and pay for the meal.
- It is best to travel in the company of others. At night, women should avoid walking alone—take a taxi instead. And beware of pickpockets.

SUGGESTED READING

- *Put Your Best Foot Forward: Europe* by Mary Murray Bosrock (International Education Systems, St. Paul, MN, 1995).
- *The Travelers' Guide to European Customs and Manners* by Nancy L. Braganti and Elizabeth Devine (Meadowbrook Books, Deephaven, MN, 1984).

15

JAPAN

American businesswomen cannot possibly succeed in Japan because Japanese men dominate their society and treat Japanese women as subservient.   True or false?

Dozens of women interviewed for this book responded with a resounding "False!" They quickly added, however, that to succeed in Japan you must know the rules and practice certain forms of behavior.

Mary McCormick, who represents a major maker of supercomputers, summarizes the unique role of an American woman trying to do business in Japan: "In Japan, I felt like the third sex—not a man, not a regular woman, but a businesswoman."

Before we examine what that "third sex" means and how "it" should behave, let's try to understand the male-female relationship within the Japanese business culture.

The Status of Women

In Japan, business is still a man's domain. There are few, if any, women in the complex network of power groups, associations, clubs, and cliques so characteristic of Japanese business. Males have so dominated Japanese society throughout the centuries that it wasn't until after the end of World War II that women in Japan attained the vote or were able to marry without parental approval.

Women are highly visible in Japanese business today—in fact, they represent about 40 percent of the total workforce—but they are usually young women employed in lesser staff positions. In Japan they are often referred to as "office flowers."

In recent years, Japanese women have made noticeable advances in government, the media, public relations, advertising, and publishing. They have also risen in technical fields, such as computer sciences and engineering, mainly because not enough male specialists were available to fill the high demand. But doorways to the current power structure in Japanese business are still labeled "Men Only." And in a country where tradition is almost a religion in itself, this is unlikely to change for many years.

But Japanese women do wield power by controlling the family's purse strings. It is the custom for a Japanese husband to hand over his paycheck to his wife, so she is in charge of the spending side of the partnership. In all other aspects of Japanese life, however, it's a man's world.

Japanese businessmen are viewed by the world, and correctly so, as hardworking and stress-driven, even to the point of damaging their personal health. Japanese businessmen are also known to let off steam with long, late-night drinking and carousing. Visiting Westerners with pounding morning-after hangovers can testify to that. This ritual is known variously as "after-five time" or "the water business."

Now you, as "the third sex," enter this alien world whose genders seem to occupy two neighboring planets. How do you cope? What tools should you bring to cultivate this land that has come to be such a prize to the rest of the world?

Business Behavior

There are three major ways to succeed in Japan:

1. Become aware of everything going on around you.
2. Be sure to establish your credentials and your authority to make decisions since rank and authority are important.
3. Be prepared to be patient. Whereas American and Canadian businesspeople tend to think in terms of days and months, the Japanese do so in terms of years.

Cheryl Miller spent two years studying in Japan and then returned to the United States to receive her Masters in International Business (MIB) degree at the University of South Carolina School of Business. While in Japan, Cheryl so immersed herself in Japanese society that she became an expert in the Japanese martial art of kendo and was the first woman to compete in a local kendo tournament. When asked the question, "What single piece of advice would you give to an American businesswoman traveling to Japan?," she replied:

"Be aware. Learn to watch, observe, to soak in what is happening." After she had been there a year, her sister came to visit. As they were riding on the subway, Cheryl noticed how animated her sister was and how loud she was speaking, and she became embarrassed. She knew her sister was violating Japanese custom because the Japanese never do anything to call attention to themselves in public. In fact, they have an expression for this: "The nail that sticks up gets pounded down." When Cheryl mentioned her sister's behavior to some of her friends, they said, "But you were the same way when you first came here."

Christalyn Brannen and Tracey Wilen have written an excellent book, *Doing Business with Japanese Men* (Stone Bridge Press, Berkeley, CA, 1993), subtitled *A Woman's Handbook*. Significantly, the first lines of the first chapter advise: "Establish your authority."

Do's and Taboos of Establishing Authority

• *Do pay attention to your title.*   Your title is critical. As cited earlier in Chapter 3, when two Wisconsin businesswomen traveled to Japan, the one whose business card identified her as the president of her company immediately received more attention and respect than the one with the title of marketing manager. For the rank-conscious Japanese, a "President" or "Chairman" or "Senior Director" obviously has much more authority than a "Manager."

• *Do consider hiring a "go-between,"* especially if you are new to the market. This is someone, usually a Japanese, who knows the people, the protocol, and the power centers. This person should also know how to communicate your rank and authority in the proper manner.

• *Do be especially sensitive if you are leading a group.*   Be aware of such things as where you sit at the conference table, if the others in your group defer to you, and how much you talk. Discuss this with your team in advance. Enter the room last; take the most prominent visitor's chair; alert the others in your group to look to you for leadership; and don't dominate the discussion—in Japan listening is a sign of authority. Among a group of Japanese businessmen, the one who is most silent is probably the one in charge, especially if he is also older.

• *Don't act like a low-level staff person.*   Never offer to distribute or retrieve papers, or—heaven forbid—volunteer to help serve tea or soft drinks.

• *Don't show strong emotions.*   At all costs, avoid displays of temper or anger. The Japanese are taught to stay within themselves. Anyone who pounds the table, raises his or her voice, or gesticulates wildly is considered impolite and out of control.

• *Don't ever do anything that will cause your Japanese counterparts embarrassment.* "Saving face" is sacred. And be mindful that possible embarrassment is hidden around every corner. For example, a Japanese male would find it both embarrassing and disrespectful to have a Japanese woman sent to an airport or hotel to greet him and transport him to a business meeting. Similarly, never single out one person for praise in front of a group. Japanese businesspeople are team-oriented, and positive outcomes are considered the result of team effort.

• *Do be aware of three highly treasured Japanese traits: respect, humility, and patience.* You may be the highest authority on your side of the table, but show respect for both rank and age, exhibit humility, avoid excessive boasting about your product or service, and leave hard-sell techniques at home. Don't be afraid or hesitant to apologize often, even for what might seem to be the most trivial matters or events. This show of grace and humility is important among the Japanese. Incidentally, teachers are given great respect in Japanese society and are called *sensai*. If you have teaching credentials, you should subtly make that fact known somewhere in your dealings. Finally, when it comes to attitudes toward time, be prepared to be patient.

In addition to establishing your authority, what overall image should you project while in Japan? Consider the actions of former First Lady Barbara Bush as a model. In 1992, she accompanied her husband on a visit where, as you may remember, President Bush became ill while seated on the dais at a state dinner. In fact, he upchucked on the feet of his host, the Japanese Prime Minister. Minutes after her husband was guided off to one side, the Prime Minister turned and said, "Mrs. Bush, would you like to say a few words?" The First Lady calmly took the microphone and proceeded to charm not only the audience but the whole nation. Her eloquence, serenity, and self-effacing wit gave the Japanese public an unforgettable picture of an American woman taking charge in time of need. The Japanese television media played and replayed Mrs. Bush's speech.

According to numerous women in our surveys, being a businesswoman from the United States or Canada can actually be an advantage. One observed, "It is such a shock to some Japanese businessmen to be dealing with a woman, that they don't know how to handle it. And if that woman has impressive educational credentials, or high rank in her corporation, her strangeness is even more enhanced. All this adds up to something of an advantage."

Kate Hotchkiss, a sales manager for a major U.S. company, added, "As far as doing business with Chinese, Korean, and Japanese businesswomen, they are so excited that the company has sent a woman that this is an automatic door-opener and advantage to doing business. Right or wrong, there is the start of a strong 'old girls' network' in Asia, especially in the Chinese communities."

More Guidelines

Gift Giving.   This is a deeply ingrained custom in Japan, and seems never-ending in business circles. It is not considered a form of bribery but a ritual for creating and establishing personal relationships. As a result, while gifts received from the Japanese may strike us as excessive or lavish, it is the thought and style behind the gift that are important. For example, if you present a commemorative coin, make it one with some special significance to your relationship; if you give a souvenir pen, engrave it with the recipient's name and place it in a special box. Be very careful to give the best gift to the highest ranking Japanese, and so on, down the line. When in doubt, present a single, high-quality "group" gift (i.e., from your group to their group) and, to avoid surprise, quietly notify someone on their side in advance that you will be making such a presentation.

Greetings.   In Japan, greetings can be very formal and ritualistic. They usually begin with the exchange of business cards, presented with two hands, writing toward the receiver, plus a slight bowing motion. The Japanese will take a moment or two to study your card and place it on the table in front of them for easy reference. Then more bows, and, in deference to you, a handshake. The bow is not a sign of subservience—it signifies respect and humility.

Conversation.   Be prepared for long pauses during your business conversations. This is not because of boredom, your gender, or nationality. The Japanese value periods of silence. Remember that English is a difficult and often tiring language for them. Allow these periods of silence to continue. When the Japanese nod or say "Yes," it really means "Yes, I hear you." It doesn't necessarily mean "Yes, I agree with you." The Japanese have great difficulty in saying "No" because anything that is negative is both impolite and disruptive of harmony, and harmony is all-important in Japanese life. Debate and humor are uncommon in business discussions with the Japanese, so be wary of both.

Dining.   In Japanese restaurants, sitting on the floor is common, so avoid straight, tight skirts. Women should fold their legs under their bodies and then move the weight off to one side. Some restaurants will have a recess in the floor deep enough for your legs, so you can sit almost as if you were on a chair. Western utensils are usually provided along with chopsticks, and it is perfectly acceptable to use either.

After-Hours Behavior.   Bad behavior during after-work social situations, such as drunkenness, crude comments, or aggressive touching, is usually completely forgotten the next morning; it is as if nothing had happened. Visiting businesswomen will probably not be invited on these social excursions; if you are, try to sip your drinks and go with the flow. When riding on public transportation, be prepared for groping and wandering hands. Simply move away, or, if it doesn't stop, shout "Stop!" Another solution is to try to find the special cars reserved for women and children.

Bathrooms.   Many Japanese toilets are simply a hole in the floor and sometimes the toilet door cannot be locked. The Japanese will knock gently on the door to see if the cubicle is occupied; if you are inside, just reply with a counter-knock.

Gestures.   Both loud sniffling and blowing your nose in public are regarded as bad manners. Showing a wide-open mouth is also considered rude, which helps explain why so many Japanese women cover their mouths with their hands when they laugh. Direct eye contact is also not as common as it is in the United States and Canada. The Japanese may appear to be looking at your neck or shoulder rather than directly into your eyes. Avoid slouching. By our standards, the Japanese are very formal. When seated, plant both feet squarely on the ground. When standing, it is considered impolite to have one or both hands in your pockets.

SUGGESTED READING

- *Doing Business with Japanese Men: A Woman's Handbook* by Christalyn Brannen and Tracey Wilen (Stone Bridge Press, Berkeley, CA, 1993). This book provides down-to-earth facts and advice on meeting protocol, socializing, gift-giving, wardrobe, makeup, and special health and safety concerns.
- *Japanese Etiquette and Ethics in Business* by Boye DeMente (Passport Books, Lincolnwood, IL, 1987). This is considered a classic guide for doing business with the Japanese. DeMente's books are distinguished by their clear explanations of Japanese behavior and traditions.
- *With Respect to the Japanese* by John C. Condon (Intercultural Press, Inc., Yarmouth, ME, 1984). Condon thoughtfully analyzes several cultural themes in Japanese culture, such as group orientation and saving face, and demonstrates how these themes influence business behavior and protocol.

16

PEOPLE'S REPUBLIC OF CHINA

The Status of Women

"We must struggle." With those three simple words, pioneer feminist Wang Xingjuan, former editor and (at this writing) head of the Women's Research Institute in China, summarizes the status of women in her country. This struggle is best appreciated by recalling how women were treated before the Communist takeover in 1949. Consider these facts:

- Chinese women have been subordinated since the time of Confucius (fifth century B.C.), one of the first Chinese chauvinists. "Women and servants," he is quoted as saying, "are most difficult to deal with." Under his laws, a man could divorce a wife if she failed to give birth to a son, was caught stealing, if she was jealous, if she nagged, or if she disobeyed her parents-in-law.
- As recently as the 1940s, Chinese women had to obey their fathers, husband, and sons, received no sources of income or property rights, and had almost no access to education.
- The watershed year was 1949 when the Communist regime won a bitter war. In the last four decades, life for women has improved substantially. For example, this life expectancy for women has risen from age thirty-six to seventy-two.
- Before 1949, all marriages were arranged; after 1949, women were permitted to marry and divorce at will. Now, about 80 percent of married women under age forty choose their spouses.
- The literacy rate for women is now 70 percent, up from 10 percent before Communist rule. In rural China, however, millions of girls still do not attend school because their families think only sons need to study.

With those figures as background, you can understand why only small numbers of Chinese women are today found in managerial positions. In fact, according to Chen Muhua, head of the All-China Women's Federation, in 1995 women constituted less than 10 percent of the top decision-makers in Chinese government posts.

Business Behavior

Success in business in China rests on the following several important principles.

Rank. After centuries of dominance, Chinese men may resort to form and treat you as unimportant unless you establish your rank, your authority, and your expertise. Tahirih V. Lee teaches Chinese law at the University of Minnesota Law School and travels to China frequently. Lee puts it succinctly: "Rank matters. [However] I have felt it prudent not to trumpet in a boastful way my credentials and position, but clearly my credentials and position are important to the Chinese I meet, and so to downplay them is not wise."

Guanxi. In Western terms, *guanxi* (pronounced gwan-SHEE) might be labeled "connections." In China, this is a staple in the process of conducting business. You must have relationships, contacts, influence. For example, it is much more effective—almost necessary—to have an influential intermediary introduce you to your contact than to attempt a headlong, direct contact. The phrase "to pull *guanxi*" means to get to know people, do favors, bring gifts, and spend hours and hours in small talk.

Face. This refers to a person's pride, self-respect, family honor, and reputation. Throughout the Far East, you should avoid doing anything that causes a loss of face for yourself or others. For example, when you show respect toward another person, you "give" that person face; when you embarrass another person, you cause him or her to "lose" face. A Chinese man having to do business with a woman on an equal level loses face; however, if that woman has high ranking or expertise, he gains face. Displaying impatience or anger is a way of losing face. Being patient, gracious, and generous gains face.

Age. Another important factor in interpersonal relationships in China is age. Along with rank, seniority in years gives you an extra measure of status and generates more respect. Add all this up and the result is that a youthful woman without strong credentials and connections may have a difficult time conducting business in China.

Foreign Women.   On a more positive note, visiting businesswomen will generally be treated with politeness and acceptance simply because they will be regarded as "foreign females," with the emphasis on "foreign." Being foreign guarantees special status. Being female can also be something of an advantage, according to law professor Tahirih Lee. "What's helped women I know in China is their natural demeanor—patient, soft-spoken, willing to persevere. They're not boisterous, impetuous, easy to anger. The Chinese appreciate this in all people. Adaptability is also crucial."

Humility.   In all forms of business, especially in negotiations, humility is crucial. Yet you must also recognize that too much humility can be a liability if you abandon *all* pride, dignity, or values. You have to couple humility with self-confidence and trust your judgment.

More Guidelines
•   Do try to ignore how Chinese women are treated there. Remember that you hold special status.

•   Do arrange for some type of formal introduction, or connection, before meeting face to face. As we explained earlier, this is usually done through an intermediary who is known by your counterpart. Another recommendation is to find a mentor, perhaps a retired Asian who knows your industry well.

•   Don't become offended by things that might be considered rude in your home society. For example, some Chinese men may unthinkingly blow cigarette smoke toward a woman, or let doors slam on them. These are usually not overt acts of rudeness, just ordinary behavior.

•   Do make it apparent if you are the leader of a team. Send an agenda in advance with brief biographies clearly indicating your status. Explain to your team the importance of signals and symbols—you enter the room last, take the choice seat at a table, and they defer to you at all times.

•   Don't dress extravagantly. Be conservative—avoid flashy prints, provocative styles, and lots of jewelry. Pantsuits are common and recommended. In fact, China was the first nation to clothe its agricultural workers, both men and women, in trousers.

•   Do be prepared for some curious looks, even downright staring, if you are a blond or redhead (male or female), or if you are especially tall. You will feel like a novelty, which, indeed, you are.

•   Don't drink alcohol beyond your limits. In social situations, women are expected to drink in moderation. But be prepared for frequent toasting with the national drink, *mao-tai,* a sorghum-based white lightning. Treat it with caution. The common toast *"Kampie"* is pronounced gham-BYE, which means "bottoms up." At some Chinese dinners you will notice drinkers doing just that: drink and then turn their glasses upside down, with the bottoms up, to show that they have consumed all the liquid.

SUGGESTED READING

- *Dealing with the Chinese* by Scott D. Seligman (Warner Books, New York,1989). This fine book also provides excellent information on business negotiating with the Chinese.
- *Chinese Etiquette: A Matter of Course* by Raelene Tan (Landmark Books, Singapore, 1992). Ms. Tan counsels on gift-giving, seating arrangements, communal dining, auspicious colors and numbers, foods, and dozens of other etiquette matters.
- *Chinese Etiquette and Ethics in Business* by Boye De Mente (NTC Publishing, Lincolnwood, IL, 1989). This book delves into the history, qualities, and collective traits that influence the way the Chinese do business.
- *Business China: A Practical Guide to Understanding Chinese Business Culture* by Peggy Kenna and Sondra Lacy (Passport Books, a division of NTC Publishing, Lincolnwood, IL, 1994). This pocket-size guide quickly briefs you on communication style, business etiquette, body language, decision-making processes, and negotiation with the Chinese.

17

KOREA, REPUBLIC OF

The Status of Women

If you're keeping track of which countries offer the greatest difficulties for the North American businesswoman, consider ranking South Korea near the top of your list. Korean women have been subordinated for centuries, and even though they may now smoke and drink in public and petition for divorce, they are encased in a totally male-dominated society. As a result, Korean women are found only in lower-ranking jobs.

According to information supplied by the South Korean tourist bureau, Korean women traditionally walk behind men, allow men to enter doorways first, pour drinks for men, and seldom shake hands—even with a Western woman. However, this applies to the older generation—younger Korean women are more Westernized. When addressing an audience, Koreans will very likely begin by reversing the customary salutation and say instead, "Gentlemen and ladies."

For an American or Canadian businesswoman to crack this wall of intolerance, you will need one or more of the following:

1. Rank, power, status, or—ideally—all three.
2. Expertise or outstanding academic credentials.
3. Age or seniority.

Interwoven among these factors is the extreme importance of "relationships." This translates into knowing the right people and having the right introductions. It also means spending what seems to Westerners like an inordinate amount of time developing a personal relationship with your Korean counterpart. And you may not detect a warming of a relationship until the third or fourth encounter.

Business Behavior

When it comes to personal business behavior, American and Canadian women should appear elegant, refined, and never act in what might be considered a masculine manner (e.g., engaging in loud laughter or conversation). Dress in a modest and conservative manner, and keep in mind that you may be sitting on the floor for dinner, so avoid straight, tight skirts.

More Guidelines

Names. Koreans have three names; the first is the family name. Therefore, Mr. Lee Park Sung should be addressed as "Mr. Lee." It is impolite to use the given name (Sung) unless you are expressly invited to do so.

Greetings. The bow is the traditional greeting, and males will usually follow with a handshake. You may offer your hand to a man, but make certain that you outrank him—it could be considered an insult otherwise. And don't expect a Korean woman to offer her hand in greeting.

Body Language. Never hug or embrace a Korean man unless you have a longtime relationship; even then, he should make the first move. For a woman to be that demonstrative can be insulting and embarrassing for the man, especially if he is in the company of other Korean men. Direct eye contact is very limited; avoid any form of casual touching, such as brushing the forearm, or linking arms. Avoid sniffling or blowing your nose in public—retreat to a hallway or bathroom. Proper posture is important: stand straight; when seated, don't slouch, and sit with both feet on the floor. Pass and receive objects with your right hand, or with two hands.

Business Cards. When meeting for the first time, exchange business cards using both hands to present and receive the card. Also, make certain that your title is clear and as impressive as possible.

Laughter. Along with several other cultures in Asia (e.g., those of Thailand, Indonesia, and the Philippines), Koreans may laugh at seemingly odd times. It is a way to cover up embarrassment, anger, or surprise. Since it is considered impolite for women to display a wide-open mouth, cover yours when laughing or yawning. The Korean business community enjoys hosting visitors at elaborate dinners with much singing and gaiety, so be sure to remember these customs.

Dining. Meals are an important part of Korean social life and Koreans take pride in their cuisine. You will quickly learn that Korean food is usually heavily laced with garlic. Conversation is sometimes limited, so don't be bothered by periods of silence. If in doubt about table manners, watch what others are doing. Meals are usually followed by singing, and, if you are invited to perform, try not to refuse—even if you have to sing "Mary Had a Little Lamb."

Gifts.   Gift giving is fairly common between business contacts, especially at the first meeting. When presenting or receiving a gift, use both hands. Defer opening the gift until later. And try to make it sound as if your gift is a mere trifle. See Chapter 3 for more tips on gift giving.

Values.   Remember that expressions and acts of humility are an integral part of Korean behavior. Also, "face" is extremely important, so try to avoid any action—no matter how trivial—that might cause embarrassment. The worst insult is to confuse anything Japanese or Chinese with something Korean. Koreans are very proud of their culture and their country.

SUGGESTED READING

- *Business Korea* by Peggy Kenna and Sondra Lacy (Passport Books, a division of NTC Publishing Group, Lincolnwood, IL, 1995). This is a concise guide to such areas as communication style, business etiquette, body language, decision-making, and negotiation.
- *Looking at Each Other* by Marion E. Current and Choi Dong-ho (Seoul International Tourist Publishing Co., 1983). This heavily illustrated handbook provides excellent insights into the differences between American and Korean lifestyles and behavior.
- *Put Your Best Foot Forward: Asia* by Mary Murray Bosrock (International Education Systems, St. Paul, MN, 1994). Billed as "A Fearless Guide to International Communication and Behavior," this comprehensive guidebook covers all the Asian countries.
- *Culture Shock: Korea* by Sonja Vegdahl Hur and Ben Seunghwa Hur (Times Books International, Singapore, 1988). This book is part of a series of comprehensive guidebooks on countries in the Pacific Rim. It is filled with detailed and helpful information on the Korean society.

18

HONG KONG, SINGAPORE, AND TAIWAN

The common denominator among these three important destinations is a simple one: American and Canadian businesswomen will find an easy, comfortable acceptance in all three.

Hong Kong, Taiwan, and Singapore have each become major trading junctions in the Pacific Rim. Each has achieved success by different paths, but their very existence depends on a free flow of commerce. That means cultural differences—and gender—are usually not serious obstacles.

The Status of Women

The attitude toward women in business is best summarized by one American woman who lives and works in Hong Kong: "It doesn't make any difference if you are blue, green, purple, or a frog. If you have the best product at the best price, they'll buy."

Hong Kong and Singapore have mixed cultures, but are accustomed to hosting and conducting business with every other culture in the world. Hong Kong is a combination of Chinese and British influence. Singapore has been heavily influenced by both plus strong strains of Indian and Malay. English is spoken freely, and businesswomen will have little or no difficulty being accepted.

As for Taiwan, it is important to know and understand its political history. After World War II, China engaged in a fierce civil war between the Communists led by Mao Tse-tung and the Nationalists headed by Chiang Kai-shek. By 1949, the Communists had prevailed and the Nationalists were forced to withdraw to the island of Formosa, now called Taiwan. Over the past four decades, the Taiwanese created a democratic, capitalistic system. It, in turn, generated a highly efficient manufacturing sector that has exported products—mainly electronics, textiles, chemicals, clothing, and food processing—to customers throughout the world.

The culture in Taiwan is Chinese and based on the Confucian ethic: hard work, with high moral standards and a strong emphasis on the family unit. Because of its extensive trade activity, Taiwanese hotels are constantly filled with buyers and sellers from around the world, and English is widely spoken.

Business Behavior

As for general protocol and etiquette, be mindful of many of the Chinese customs and then mix in an easy familiarity with Western ways. Remember the Chinese traditions of respect for the elderly, patience in business dealings, and humility in personal relationships.

In Hong Kong, a visitor will find two distinct cultures: British and Chinese. Therefore you would be wise to have a fundamental acquaintance with the social practices of both. The same is true of Singapore, and knowing something of the Malay tradition there would also be helpful.

Because of large doses of publicity and world attention, Singapore has also become known for its strict enforcement of laws concerning cleanliness and personal behavior. For example, littering of any kind is punished with huge fines. When Albert Kiong, manager of the Singapore Ritz Carlton Hotel, was asked "Do Americans, and particularly American businesswomen, have problems doing business in Singapore?" he replied, "Absolutely not. Yet they should observe certain protocols. For example, people in Singapore exchange business cards with a touch of ceremony—they take the card respectfully, and read it carefully. Americans tend to toss their card on the table, or stuff it into a briefcase. Little things like that are important."

SUGGESTED READING

- For books on these three markets, refer to the earlier section on China for information on Chinese etiquette.
- As for Singapore, for your next visit purchase *Culture Shock: Singapore and Malaysia* by JoAnn Craig (Times Books International, Singapore, 1979).
- Another valuable guide has been mentioned earlier: *Put Your Best Foot Forward: Asia* by Mary Murray Bosrock (International Education Sys-

tems, St. Paul, MN, 1994). This book also contains excellent detailed information on India, Indonesia, Malaysia, Philippines, and Thailand.

- *The Economist Business Traveller's Guides: South-East Asia* (Prentice-Hall Press, New York, 1988) covers Hong Kong, Indonesia, Malaysia, Philippines, Singapore, South Korea, Taiwan, and Thailand. For each, useful information is provided on politics, economics, the business framework, finances, and cultural awareness. This comprehensive handbook also contains maps of major cities in Southeast Asia as well as lists of hotels and restaurants.

19

AUSTRALIA

The Status of Women

Although Australians shun class distinctions, some North American women assigned to a post in Australia have found difficulties in being accepted because male chauvinism is still rather strong. American and Canadian women working in Australia are often confronted with blunt, earthy male associates who are uncomfortable with women.

Despite Australian feminists like Germaine Greer and singer Helen Reddy, Australian women seem to enjoy that their major responsibilities are home and family. Many Australian women are part of the business world, yet the proportion of women to men in business is smaller than in the United States and Canada. The net result is that while the male Australian business community will respect a visiting North American businesswoman, especially if she has expertise plus decision-making authority, traces of discomfort may exist. Australians have been called "Chicagoans with an accent." That's because they tend to be friendly, unpretentious, easygoing, and egalitarian—all desirable qualities. With a few notable exceptions, this adds up to an atmosphere of general acceptance for the visiting businesswoman.

Business Behavior

Generally, Americans and Canadians—both male and female—who visit Australia on business find it a thoroughly enjoyable experience. Australians are informal and direct, and usually won't waste time in convoluted negotiations or haggling.

In your business dealings with Australians, you would be wise to be well prepared in two areas. The first deals with language differences, and the second involves an important attitudinal difference.

114

Language. For Americans, Australian English can sometimes be difficult to comprehend. In fact, it has been said that two Australians could carry on a conversation that most Americans or Canadians would find totally confusing. For example, "Can I bot a chewie" translates into "Can I borrow a piece of chewing gum."

"Strine," as Australian-English is called, is a rich stew filled with words derived from the Aborigines and the British and combined with the inventiveness of a pioneering people who settled a huge island continent. The Australian Tourist Commission, 489 Fifth Avenue, New York, NY 10017, phone (212) 687-6300, publishes an entertaining and informative glossary of unique Australian words and phrases. If you're planning a business trip to "Ozzie" land (translation: Australian land), it's worth obtaining a copy beforehand.

Attitude. The attitudinal difference hinges on one word: boasting. Australians dislike anyone who lays claim to being the best, the largest, the greatest, and so on. This sometimes presents a problem for Americans—just consider the high-flying claims in many of our national advertising campaigns. In Australia, egalitarianism prevails, so it's best to leave self-promotion and puffery at home.

More Guidelines
•   Australians are proud of their heritage. They don't like to be lumped with either the British, or—worse—New Zealanders. (Among New Zealanders, incidentally, the feeling is mutual.)

•   You won't usually find a man winking at a woman. It is considered especially impolite.

•   If, after a large meal, you happen to say "Oh, I'm stuffed," Australians think that you are really announcing that you're pregnant.

•   In Australian English, the word "randy" means to be "horny." So, beware if a man approaches you and says, "Hi, I'm randy." That's *not* his name.

•   The thumbs-up gesture, especially if done with an upward jerking motion, is considered rude.

•   As in England, the V for Victory or peace gesture (forefinger and middle finger forming a V) is known and understood—as long as the palm faces outward. If it is reversed, with the palm facing inward, you are signaling "Up yours!"

•   Since January is the peak of the summer season in Australia, when most everyone goes on holiday, it is obviously the most inopportune time to consider a business visit.

•   Business attire is very similar to that in the United States and Canada, but Australian businesswomen tend to wear dresses more than slacks.

- Australians enjoy social drinking sessions, usually at a friendly pub. Beer is almost the national drink and tends to have a higher alcoholic content than North American beers. Be aware that when it's your "shout" (your time to buy a round of drinks), it is important that you do so.
- Plan on hearing the statement "All the best." That seems to be the customary, universal way Australians say good-bye, whether in person or on the telephone.

SUGGESTED READING

- Cross-cultural communications expert George Renwick has written a valuable reference book on interactions between Australians and Americans, titled *A Fair Go for All* (Intercultural Press, Inc., Yarmouth, ME, 1991). If you are planning to do business in Australia, this book is highly recommended.
- For a general reference book on Australia and many other countries in the Asia-Pacific Rim, turn to *The Travelers' Guide to Asian Customs and Manners* by Kevin Chambers (Meadowbrook, Deephaven, MN, 1988).
- As for dealing with American/Australian language differences, Roger E. Axtell's *Do's and Taboos of Using English Around the World* (Wiley, New York, 1995) might be helpful.

20

THE LANDS OF ISLAM

As you consider a career in international business, you have probably envisioned distant lands filled with exotic people and customs. If so, on your first visit to the Lands of Islam, particularly the Middle East, your dreams will very likely be fulfilled. Perhaps in no other region of the world will you feel so foreign, so alien, or so far from home.

First, it is important to realize that since Islam was born in Saudi Arabia, people tend to think that Islam is synonymous with the terms "Arab" and "Middle East." However, the Islamic religion can be found throughout the world and, in fact, only about one-third of its followers are found in the Middle East.

Second, there is no Arab race or nationality. The term "Arab" comes from "Arabia," the land peninsula between the Red Sea and Arabian Gulf that contains Saudi Arabia, the two states of Yemen, and the United Arab Emirates. The term "Arab world" applies to a large and diverse crescent from Morocco on the western tip to Iraq in the east. Those countries are bound together not by race—although many of the people are descended from the ancient Semites—but by three disparate elements: language, religion, and oil.

Of those three, the dominant one is religion—the religion of Islam—and people who embrace the Islamic religion are called Moslems. (*Note:* Moslem is the form used most commonly in American journalism, but Muslim is preferred by scholars, English-speaking adherents of Islam, and members of the Nation of Islam.)

Before doing business in the Islamic world, it is important to know some fundamentals about the faith. The prophet and founder of Islam was Mohammed, but it is incorrect to refer to the religion as "Mohammedanism." The teachings of Mohammed are preserved in the Koran, a much-revered book considered to contain the words of God as revealed to Mohammed that provide the followers of Islam with rules for ethics and behavior. The cradle of Islam is in the holy city of Mecca, in Saudi Arabia.

117

Moslems believe Christ was holy and one of several important prophets; they also accept the teachings of the Bible. However, they base their religion on the biblical prediction that there would be one more prophet after Christ who would be the true prophet, and they believe that person was Mohammed, who lived approximately 600 years after Christ.

The Islamic religion extends geographically into countries such as Afghanistan, Pakistan, and other parts of the Asian subcontinent. Indonesia has the largest concentration of Moslems as a percent of its population. In fact, Islam is found in most parts of the world—in the United States there are an estimated two to six million followers.

For this chapter, however, we will concentrate on doing business in the Middle East exclusive of Israel. (For Israel, see Chapter 21.) Politically and religiously, the countries of the Middle East range from liberal to highly conservative or fundamentalist. Egypt and Jordan are considered liberal in terms of both politics and religion; consequently, Westerners are more comfortable visiting there. At the other end of the political/religious spectrum are countries like Syria, Iraq, and Libya that are characterized by strong anti-American sentiments and equally strong religious practices. Saudi Arabia is, of course, closely allied with Western politics, but is the most devout and adheres to the teachings of the Koran with great fervor.

The United Arab Emirates are linked to the Western world because of rich oil deposits, are ruled by wealthy monarchs and their families, and emulate Saudi Arabia's religious adherence.

Before the war in Kuwait in 1991, that tiny country was little known to most Americans, but it was, and still is, a pivotal point for commerce throughout the Middle East. It tends to be liberal in both camps—politics and religion.

Within the Arab world, Iran fits into a slightly different category. The state religion there is Islam, but the people are descended from the Persians and speak their own language, Farsi.

The Status of Women

By North American standards, the status of women in these Arab countries ranges from tolerable to shameful. In many, women are forbidden to vote, cannot divorce, and have limited rights to testify in court. In Kuwait, for example, where more women work outside the home than any other Arab country, women still have not been granted the right to vote. In any Islamic country, polygamy is accepted, and a man can marry up to four wives if he can support them.

Despite these conditions, Arab women are respected: They are protected and are not considered inferior. Men love their mothers with great emotion, and mothers of sons are given additional status. However—and here is the critical difference—the conservative countries believe that women should be kept *separate*—separate from the strain and stress, the temptations, and the competition of the rest of their society.

Western women are currently visiting and doing business in the liberal countries such as Jordan, Egypt, Morocco, the United Arab Emirates (UAE), and Kuwait. However, because of anti-American policies in Iraq, Syria, Iran, Libya, and Yemen, it is unlikely that you will be traveling to those countries on business.

In the conservative parts of the Arab World, a visiting businesswoman may be regarded as a "third sex." She will be greeted with courtesy, especially if she has strong credentials such as a special expertise, academic honors, or is the chief executive of her company. Yet she will not be fully accepted into the society of males.

Dr. Jeane J. Kirkpatrick, former U.S. Ambassador to the United Nations and the first woman to hold that position, told one of the authors about her first visit to the United Arab Emirates. She noted that her male counterparts were respectful and polite, but clearly uncomfortable having to deal on an equal basis with a woman. Kirkpatrick recalls, "One of the monarchs even went so far as to suggest he could make me an 'honorary male,' but I just laughed it off and said 'No thanks.' "

In Saudi Arabia, local women are entering the workforce and today represent an estimated 10 percent of the total. They have slowly been permitted to take up professions in medicine and education, but they rarely work alongside men because of the belief that women must be kept separate.

Business Behavior

In this segment on behavior, we will emphasize Saudi Arabia because behavior there is representative of behavior throughout the conservative countries in the Middle East.

Western businesswomen going to Saudi Arabia on business will be met with respect and courtesy. However, there are many rules you must know and observe. For example, it is essential to have a Saudi sponsor, established in advance, who will pave the way and perhaps even accompany you. Women are not permitted to travel in a car alone, so the sponsor would provide a car and driver. Also, be prepared for what you might consider blunt questions—"Are you married?" and "Do you have sons?"

In the devout Moslem countries, where the teachings of the Koran are closely observed, daily behavior—especially for women—is a matter deserving close attention.

More Guidelines

Public Displays of Affection.   In Saudi Arabia, such displays are considered a serious breach of behavior. A Western woman was once observed entering an auto driven by a Western man, who then reached over and kissed her. Local police who watched this scene immediately detained the couple to determine if they were married. When it was learned that they were not, the man was deported from the country.

Hospitality.   Gracious hospitality is a trademark of people in the Arab World. It descends from the desert nomad tradition of the Bedouin people who believe guests must be received openly and without question, even though they may be enemies. On the other hand, don't be offended if, during social situations, you find yourself separated from the males and grouped with the wives of your hosts.

Alcohol.   Alcohol is forbidden in devout Moslem countries, so be prepared for cup after cup of thick, strong coffee or tea, plus plenty of colas and fruit drinks. If you don't want more coffee, shake your cup—a signal that you've had enough.

Business Meetings.   Your business meetings may sometimes be held in one large room where other small groups of people will be spaced around the perimeter. It is then customary for Saudi business hosts to move around the room, conducting different and private meetings with each group. Don't be offended.

Prayers.   If your host suddenly excuses himself and disappears for twenty or thirty minutes, he very likely has gone to say his prayers, a religious requirement that occurs five times daily, beginning at sunrise and concluding at sunset.

Fridays.   Throughout the Middle East, Friday is the equivalent of the Christian Sunday, so don't expect to conduct business on that day. At the same time, prepare to continue working on Saturday and Sunday, which are viewed as ordinary workdays. Many Americans schedule their itineraries so that they travel from one country to another on Fridays.

Language.   English will be spoken liberally. Many of the younger Saudi businesspeople have been educated in the United States and Canada; they will also have a better understanding of the roles women play in our societies. If you hear a younger Saudi speaking colloquial American English, you may have found an understanding friend. Nonetheless, he will have at least one foot planted firmly in his traditional land, so don't expect miracles. Arabic is a language filled with what we Westerners would consider flowery emotion. Don't be surprised to receive letters in English that appear gushy and overdone. Also, while in Saudi Arabia, be certain to refer to the Gulf as the Arabian Gulf. Some maps and the Iranians label it the Persian Gulf, but Saudis are very sensitive about this and may consider it offensive.

Punctuality.   Try not to be irritated by the apparent disregard for punctuality. Most Arab businessmen do not view lateness as disrespect.

Gifts.   People throughout the Arab world are very generous, and gifts—sometimes lavish ones—are often presented to visitors. Therefore, be cautious about casually admiring a tea set, a painting, or any nearby object—you just might be the on-the-spot recipient of it. How do you reciprocate? It is difficult. One recourse is to respond with thoughtfulness and kindness—extending a special favor or concession in your business dealings, or assisting the children of your counterpart who may be studying in American schools. (Refer to Chapter 3 for more tips on gift giving.)

Personal Relationships.   Saudi and other Arab businessmen like to do business on a personal basis. That is, they like to spend time getting to know people who have come to conduct business with them. For a Saudi, it won't matter how good your business proposal is if he doesn't know you well and trust you. This translates into long "breaking-in" periods of conversation when you are being tested. Saudis are also vexed by the American practice of frequently transferring or rotating executives—they want to deal with the same person on a long-term basis.

Decision-Making.   Prepare for interruptions during your meetings, and for extended periods of time for decision-making.

Respect.   As in the other male-dominated cultures reviewed in this book, visiting businesswomen with strong credentials and expertise in their field will have the best chances of success. Saudi businessmen respect those who are well organized, well prepared, and thoroughly knowledgeable about their product or service. For example, shuffling papers in search of an answer will be viewed as lack of competence.

Touching.   Among men throughout the Middle East, touching is more common than in the United States or Canada. Men also stand what we consider to be very close to one another when conversing, resting a hand on the other person's elbow, or touching the other's shoulder. This will not be a problem for women visitors, however, since the concept of separateness will apply.

Dress.   In all the conservative countries, the dress of local women is best described with one word: modesty. The safest clothing choices would include the following: hemlines falling below the knees, arms covered, loose-fitting rather than form-fitting. Avoid any attire with low necklines and open backs. In places like Pakistan and Afghanistan, the dress for women is particularly severe, with the full body draped in various combinations of scarfs, shawls, veils, and cloaks.

In the liberal Arab countries, dress is very Western oriented: suits, dresses, even pantsuits. However, in the conservative countries like Saudi Arabia, it is best to be ultracautious: hemlines of dresses and skirts should fall below the knee, provocative necklines should be avoided, and sleeves should cover the elbows.

A special note about veils. They come in many forms and send many complicated messages. Turkish veils range from the discreet headscarf to the full-bodied sort of black balloon. A Pakistani woman may wear a seductive *dupatta* around her neck or she may prefer total coverage with an Afghan *chadri,* a sacklike garment with a small eyehole covered in mesh. Another type of veil is the *hejab,* always in black. There is some disagreement over the purpose of a veil—are they tokens of purity or badges of oppression? Do they cover just the hair or the whole body? Are they intended to turn men away or attract them? The answers depend on the country and the culture. Should a visiting American or Canadian businesswoman plan to wear a veil? No, it is not expected, but in the strict religious countries, very conservative clothing is expected. Make inquiries of your sponsor or the United States or Canadian embassy in the country you are visiting about the current state of protocol regarding all forms of attire.

Shopping.   Shopping can be a special adventure in Saudi Arabia and throughout the Middle East, especially where the traditional Arab marketplaces—called *souks*—are found. Handmade carpets, jewelry, exotic brass and copper pieces, locally woven fabrics, and a host of other unusual articles can be found there. However, it would be best if you were accompanied by an Arabic-speaking male if for no other reason than that haggling is both expected and enjoyed.

The Future.   Avoid putting too much emphasis on the future. For a Moslem, it is bad luck to talk about the future because the future is in God's hands. Thus, among many Arabs, if you should mention something like, "So, you will be coming to North America next year," the response will probably be

Inshalla, meaning "If God wills it." Obviously, they make plans for the future, but it is best to not dwell on that subject.

Worry Beads. Throughout the Arab world, you will observe men fondling strings of beads similar in appearance to a rosary. These have no religious significance and are colloquially called worry beads. They serve merely as stress relievers.

General Behavior. In your general demeanor, politeness, respect, and graciousness should prevail at all times wherever you visit in the Middle East. Avoid public criticism that might embarrass your counterpart as well as displays of emotion. And avoid hard-sell techniques. Most Arab businesspeople are good negotiators and very honorable and loyal. Once a mutual feeling of respect and comfort is achieved, doing business can be both enjoyable and rewarding.

SUGGESTED READING

- *Understanding Arabs: A Guide for Westerners* by Margaret K. Nydell (Intercultural Press, Inc., Yarmouth, ME, 1987). Nydell is an Arabic linguist as well as a trainer in dealing with the Arabs for the U.S. State Department.
- *Update: Saudi Arabia* by Joy McGregor and Margaret Nydell (Intercultural Press, Inc., Yarmouth, ME, 1990). Whether you will be visiting Saudi Arabia for three days, three weeks, or three years, this is a handy, information-packed book on working and living there.
- *The Economist Business Traveller's Guides: Arabian Peninsula* (Prentice-Hall Press, New York, 1987). This is one volume in a series of books about key business locales in the world. This book not only provides detailed maps and charts for the area, but also covers the following topics: business practices, etiquette, finance, politics, economics, hotels, restaurants, shopping, communications, and local business services and resources.
- *Working in the Persian Gulf: Survival Secrets for Men and Women* by Blythe Camenson (Desert Diamond Books, Deerfield Beach, FL, 1992). This useful book gives women the advice they need to operate properly and comfortably in the Gulf.

21

ISRAEL

The Hebrew word *sabra* means "native-born Israeli," either male or female, but according to Professor Ido Oren at the University of Minnesota, it also serves as a metaphor for the Israeli character. "A *sabra* is actually a fruit that grows on a cactus," he explains. "That particular fruit is tough on the outside but sweet on the inside and so, in that regard, many people believe it represents the Israeli character."

In spite of that label of toughness, American and Canadian businesswomen visiting Israel should have little or no difficulty doing business there.

The official languages are Hebrew and Arabic, but English is widely used as a second language and Russian has become commonplace. Also, distances are not a problem. To say Israel is compact is an understatement. The country's total population is just over 5.5 million in a territory approximately the size of the state of New Jersey.

You will probably find yourself heading for the coastal city of Tel Aviv because it is the business center of the country. Tel Aviv is described as a combination of Mediterranean and Western in nature; it is cosmopolitan, outward-looking, and more secular than the rest of the country. Jerusalem, on the other hand, is the center of government and has a large Orthodox religious population. It also is home to a large concentration of Arabs in the eastern part of the city.

The Status of Women

According to Lucy Shahar and David Kurz, authors of *Border Crossings: American Interactions with Israelis* (Intercultural Press, Inc., Yarmouth, ME, 1995), women comprise only about 15 percent of managers in the Israeli economy, and the proportion gets smaller as the levels get higher. And at the very top, the proportion of women is only 1 to 3 percent, whereas in the United

States an estimated 40 percent of executives, managers, and administrators are women. Professor Oren believes the status of Israeli women in business can be compared to that of women in business in the United States fifteen years ago.

Business Behavior

Visiting businesswomen should be aware of the following:

- There still may be traces of male chauvinism in the business community. The best advice is to not expect the same degree of political correctness that has swept across North America. You might even be prepared for a touch of teasing from Israeli businessmen who are still adjusting to having women in the ranks of commerce. Ignore it.
- The Midwest Consul for Economic Affairs, Oded Boneh, explains that Israeli businessmen tend to be less formal and more frank than American businessmen. "Israeli businessmen are friendly, open, well-traveled, and accustomed to working with Americans, but don't be surprised if you are asked what may seem to be blunt questions—such things as how old you are, or if you have a boyfriend. They mean this in a friendly way, and do not intend to be rude," he explains.
- Handshaking is the customary greeting, but if an Israeli or Arab businessman does not offer his hand, or seems reluctant, it is not an insult; it could be for religious reasons or merely because he doesn't consider it an important formality.
- Punctuality is expected, with allowances for delays due to traffic or inclement weather.
- Business cards are exchanged in the same manner as in North America, but, with Arab and Orthodox Jewish men, avoid touching. It is not necessary to have your cards printed on the reverse side in Hebrew or Arabic.
- Religion is important in Israel. Judaism has four major branches: Orthodox, Conservative, Reform, and Reconstructionist. They differ in both philosophy and practice. Many Orthodox women wear hats and wigs, dresses with high necklines, sleeves below the elbows, and skirts that reach about mid-calf. Also, many Arab Israeli women wear the traditional Arab dress described in Chapter 20. It is important to be sensitive to these differences. If you visit religious sites or traverse Orthodox neighborhoods, for example, you should dress modestly, with hems below the knees—no slacks—or at least be prepared with a long skirt that you can put on over your clothes as

needed. Also, some beaches are separated for Orthodox followers, and you should respect their privacy.

•   As for business attire, Israeli businesspeople appear to dress a notch more casually than in North American business circles. During the hot summer months in particular, business suits are rarely seen and short sleeves are appropriate. In Jerusalem, however, where Orthodox religious views are more prominent, it is best to dress conservatively.

•   All businesses are closed from sundown Friday through sundown Saturday in observance of the Jewish Sabbath. Sunday is a work day. If you are doing business with Arab Israelis, keep in mind that Friday is the Islamic day of rest.

•   Most Israeli business associates will be fluent, or nearly fluent, in both English and American English. Even so, be sensitive to possible misunderstandings as a result of American idioms, slang, and jargon.

•   Many Israeli Arabs wear modern Western attire and are indistinguishable in appearance from Israelis of other backgrounds.

•   In Tel Aviv, be prepared for a high level of cosmopolitan living with considerable nightlife (it has been dubbed "the city that never sleeps"), good restaurants, and one of the highest densities of cellular phones in the world.

•   Most common American gestures are known and recognized in Israel. Consul Boneh offers one word of caution, however, for visiting American women:

> Americans in general are known for their custom of smiling when in public. Even when a women offers a slight smile, as a woman might do in, say, a U.S. supermarket, some Israeli men find this unusual and it could be misinterpreted. Therefore, American women visiting Israel on business should be cautious about excessive smiling. The same is true of any casual, friendly touching.

•   Business entertainment is common in Tel Aviv, but, as a matter of pride, most businessmen there would feel obliged to host their business guest first, before the guest hosted them.

In conclusion, Boneh advises that visiting American businesswomen should expect to encounter a high degree of national pride in Israeli professional accomplishments. "Israel has more engineers, more scientists, more lawyers, more physicians, and more musicians per capita than any other country," he explains.

22

LATIN AMERICA

Just when you think you know the land called Latin America, and you are celebrating because you think you know the people and how to conduct business there, that's when some surprise jumps up and spoils your party. So, the best way to approach this collection of countries is to, first, know the similarities between them, but then to also know the differences.

The words above, from a businessperson who managed the Latin American area for four years, describe our approach in this chapter. We begin by listing important generalizations, or similarities, about doing business throughout Latin America and then we shift to the important differences between the major countries.

A word about geographic terminology. Throughout we have used the term "North America" to denote the United States and Canada. Obviously, the North American continent also includes Mexico and Central America. However, in general usage, the area of Latin America begins at the Rio Grande River, which separates the United States from Mexico.

The Status of Women

Among Latins, the term *macho* is defined differently than it is in the United States and Canada. We consider *macho* to mean overtly masculine, overbearing, even boorish; the Latins regard it as being chivalrous, gallant, protective, and virile. In Latin America, women are admired, respected, and loved, especially mothers. Their primary role is to care for home and family—not participate in business.

Common Characteristics Among Latin American Countries

Politeness.   Wherever you go in Latin America, you will usually be greeted politely and, especially if you have seniority in age or title, will be treated with respect. But beware: Male dominance is rooted throughout the continent.

Religion and Language.   The continent (plus Central America) is bonded by a common religion, Roman Catholicism, and a common language, Spanish, except for Brazil where Portuguese is the national language.

Colonization.   Almost every country in Latin America was colonized by Europeans, mostly Spanish and Portuguese. This invasion from the East, usually brutal and very bloody, overran and subjugated the indigenous ancient civilizations: Aztecs, Mayans, Incans. The invaders brought their languages and their religion and, unlike the North American continent where settlers came in search of freedom and democracy, they installed autocracies and feudalism in Latin America.

Social Structure.   Almost everywhere in Latin America you will quickly discern a polarized social structure—the "haves" and the "have-nots." A middle class does exist, thrives, and is perhaps growing in some countries, but it is a thin stratum of society throughout the region. Most first-time visitors are struck by the stark contrast in living conditions between the very rich and the very poor.

Personal Relationships.   Business is built on personal relationships. Latins like to really know the people they are dealing with. For this reason, visitors—especially Americans—become impatient with what seems to be a slow, circuitous path in business negotiations and agreement. The use of personal contacts and intermediaries is also important. Consequently, in all your business dealings, remember that personal friendships and the building of mutual trust are essential to success. Remember, too, that Latins are generally eager to do business with North Americans because we are considered rich and successful. However, envy may also enter the picture, plus an apprehension that we may take advantage of them because of our power.

Social Life.   Socially, Latins enjoy good food, music, and laughter. They are also extremely family oriented, and family celebrations such as birthdays, weddings, and holidays are especially joyous occasions.

Punctuality.   One of the most frustrating Latin customs for U.S. and Canadian businesspeople is the Latin concept of time. North Americans tend to be both punctual and time conscious. Not so south of the Rio Grande. The Latin view is "Life is a flow, not a series of starts and stops." When you head south, be sure to pack a good dose of patience; maybe even plan your itinerary to stay longer than you think is necessary under normal conditions. When you must set a time of day for a meeting or to be picked up at your hotel and after you get to know your Latin associates well, if your Latin colleague says he will pick you up at 9 A.M. (which, in truth, will probably be between 10 and 11), ask, with a smile, *la hora ingles* or *la hora espanol?* (the English hour or the Spanish hour). Many Latins accustomed to dealing with North Americans will smile back and remember our penchant for punctuality.

Indian Populations. In almost every Latin country (except Argentina), you will perceive the bloodlines and descendents of the original settlers of the continent, the Indians. In Brazil, because of the slave trade from Africa, the population is one of many colors.

These are some of the more important generalizations. Now let's consider the differences. Each Latin country prides itself on its own particular historical path: its origins, patriots, struggles, resources. Therefore, before each visit it is important for you to learn something of the individual culture and demographics of your destination.

Differences Among Latin American Countries

Argentina. Visit Buenos Aires and you will think you are in a European capital. Fashion, architecture, nightlife, cuisine—all are reminiscent of Paris, Naples, or Madrid. Heavy emigration from Italy and Spain at the turn of the century, and later by the British and Germans, has left a deep imprint. The business community is sophisticated, gracious, and efficient. Many North American businesspeople find Argentina among the most alluring countries in Latin America.

Bolivia. Bolovia is as different from Argentina as East is from West. The population is over 50 percent Indian, 25 percent *mestizo* (mixed Indian and European), and the rest mixed nationalities. As the highest country in Latin America, it seems like one huge mountain range. Mining is its principal economic force.

Brazil. This is the continent's largest country, with a population of about 150 million. After Mexico, it is usually the next destination for Americans and Canadians seeking business opportunities. In business, you will learn something about the term "hyperinflation," an insidious cancer in finance and pricing that in past decades has caused inflation to grow at annual rates of 500 percent—or more—each year. Although this has ameliorated in recent years, cash flow is still the name of the business game in Brazil. Nonetheless, the lure of a country blessed with every natural resource and a large, vibrant, life-loving population draws many North Americans to invest time and money in search of business opportunities.

Chile.   Stretching like a long, wandering piece of rope on the lower Western coast of the continent, Chile is marked by a business community of English, German, and Spanish descent. Visiting businesswomen will usually find a comfortable and gracious reception and will note less of the blatant *machismo* found in many of the other Latin countries. (See the section on Mexico for a definition of *machismo.*)

Colombia.   Colombia, and its business center Bogotá, greet most North American visitors with an air of sophistication, rich culture, and reserve. However, these enviable traits are disturbed by an ever-present undercurrent of tension caused by the notorious drug trade (more prevalent on the northern coast), occasional revolutionary violence, and pods of homeless children who wander the streets of the big cities. In the business sector, "courtliness" is a word often used to describe Colombian businesspeople. American business-women will be received politely and respected, especially if they have rank and expertise and avoid aggressiveness.

Mexico.   Our nearest Latin neighbor to the South has one of the fastest-grow-ing populations in Latin America, and on your first visit to crowded Mexico City it will seem as if you have been thrust smack in the middle of the entire population. The result is smog, endless lines of traffic, and still more smog. Some 37 percent of the workforce is female, but only a few Mexican women head businesses or hold meaningful positions in the corporate world. This is the land of *machismo* that, to North Americans suggests a pistol-carrying, mustached, leering man proudly displaying his mistress. But, as explained earlier, in Mexico and all of Latin America, being macho signifies strength, self-confidence, courage, and masculinity—all positive traits. As a result, Mexican men are often chivalrous and attentive toward women. Be prepared, however, for an air of superiority on their part when it comes to dealing with *Norteamericano* women in business.

Panama.   Mention Panama and most Americans instantly think of the Panama Canal. For the visiting businesswoman, however, the historic U.S. involve-ment in the Canal Zone has had mixed blessings. On the one hand, the Pana-manian business community speaks English and is aware of the advancement of women in American business. On the other, there is also a strain of anti-Americanism. Another concern for visiting women is the high rate of crime in both major cities, Panama City and Colón.

Peru.   In Peru you will very likely be struck by the strong Indian influences. More than in most Latin countries, Peru's population is visibly Indian. The business center is Lima, an arid and dusty city painted in every shade of brown, situated on the edge of an entire ocean stretching to the west. Visitors are graciously welcomed, but the economy is relatively poor compared to other markets, and commerce centers on only the essential commodities. Under the leadership of its president, Alberto Fujimora, Peruvian born but of Japanese descent, Peru has emerged from a dark period of revolution and strife and at this writing is enjoying relative stability and progress.

Venezuela.   For most North Americans, a visit to Venezuela on business means a visit to Caracas. As you cross over the coastal mountain range from the airport into the huge valley occupied by Caracas, you will think you are viewing a large metropolitan city in the United States or Canada. Caracas teems with people, tall buildings, and traffic, traffic, traffic. Venezuela enjoys one of the more prosperous economies in Latin America, and North American businesses have thronged there. English is widely spoken, many Venezuelan businessmen have been educated in the North, and Latin politeness will prevail. But—once again—remember that the traditional role for women in Latin America is in the home with the family, so maleness predominates.

Business Behavior

If you speak some Spanish or Portuguese, it will certainly be useful in everyday practical ways. Unless you are fluent, however, it is unwise to try to conduct complex business discussions. Many Spanish words and phrases have different meanings depending on the country. You would do better to retain an interpreter or rely on a trusted and fluent business associate.

Each Latin country also has a slight but individual Spanish accent. Cuban Spanish, for example, sounds very slurred, with many syllables omitted; to the untrained ear it is one of the most difficult to understand. On the other hand, the Spanish spoken in Colombia is regarded by many as the purest and most precise of the entire region.

More Guidelines
Harassment.   Many businesswomen surveyed for this book reported that when traveling in Latin business circles they did not encounter any more harassment than in, say, U.S. business society. However, in other situations—hotels, restaurants, airports, and especially on the streets—be alert for overt and annoying advances. (Refer to Chapter 1 for more on this subject.) Mercedes

M. Pellet, co-founder of a Maryland computer software company, suggests the following: "In Latin America, you will greatly enhance your personal safety if you maintain a distant and firm demeanor with all the people you encounter on your way to your hotel. This means that you do not smile needlessly nor advertise your inability to understand the language or the currency." Also, if you are married but traveling alone, be certain to wear your wedding ring.

Business Attire.   Dress conservatively yet elegantly. Avoid provocative styles and flashy, expensive jewelry. Do nothing that might be considered flirtatious.

Maleness.   The fraternity among Latin men is strong and difficult to broach. Remember that it stems from centuries of learned behavior that women are to be respected as mothers and homemakers, not as businesspeople. An insight on the Latin male's view of women in business was provided by businesswoman Barbara J. Fischer of Cedar Falls, Iowa:

> I was meeting with two gentlemen from a company that wanted to be a possible distributor for U.S. products. Since everything was going through the interpreter, they assumed I spoke no Spanish and started throwing in side comments about my looks. I had to almost bite my tongue off to keep from reacting when one said: "How can she be in business? She's too pretty." I found out later that in most Latin countries, traditionally the only women in business are the members of the wealthy families that have not been able to attract husbands. Therefore, by definition, a woman in business may be intelligent, but she has to be ugly.

SUGGESTED READING

- *The Travelers' Guide to Latin American Customs and Manners* by Elizabeth Devine and Nancy L. Braganti (St. Martin's Press, New York, 1981). This book answers hundreds of questions about everyday life and behavior in fifteen Latin American countries.
- *Business Mexico: A Practical Guide to Understanding Mexican Business Culture* by Peggy Kenna and Sondra Lacy (Passport Books, Lincolnwood, IL, 1994). This book provides a concise comparison of business styles and practices between the United States and Mexico. It deals with communication style, business etiquette, body language, decision-making processes, and negotiation and contracting.
- *Good Neighbors: Communicating with the Mexicans* by John C. Condon (Intercultural Press, Inc., Yarmouth, ME, 1985). This book describes how

to bridge the gap that exists between North Americans and Mexicans. Dr. Condon has lived in Mexico and teaches at the University of New Mexico.

- *Inside Mexico: Living, Traveling, and Doing Business in a Changing Society* by Paula Heusinkveld, Ph.D. (Wiley, New York, 1994). An insightful book. Dr. Heusinkveld explains the roles of the family, language, religion, men and women, work, business, dress and appearance, time, manners, meals, leisure, holidays, art, and music in the Mexican culture.
- *The Spanish Speaking World: An Anthology of Cross-Cultural Perspectives* by Louise Figer Luce (National Textbook Co., Chicago, 1992). This anthology of twenty readings will help readers understand Hispanic cultures.
- *The Hispanic Way* by Judith Noble and Jaime Lacasa (Passport Books, Chicago, 1991). This brief guide provides an overview of how the Spanish-speaking world thinks, acts, and does business.

PART THREE

WOMEN IN THE WORLD OF WORK

Part Three contains advice and real-life examples to guide you as you place your foot on the first rung of the international career ladder.

23

WOMEN IN INTERNATIONAL BUSINESS: PAST, PRESENT, AND FUTURE

THE PAST AND THE PRESENT

Let's begin with the bad news. According to the United Nation's Fourth World Conference on Women held in China in 1995, women throughout the world are woefully behind on any type of economic or social parity with men. Women hold only 14 percent of the top managerial positions in business and only 10 percent of national legislative seats.

Not only are women in a shameful minority when it comes to their numbers in business, but they are paid far less than men. If they received wages equal to their male counterparts, and were compensated for their millions of hours of unpaid labor, women of the world would be $11 trillion richer.

Now, some good news. Women in North America have probably advanced farther and faster than women in any other region of the world. Nancy Adler, a professor at McGill University, is one of the world's authorities on women in international business. According to her research, women's participation rate in U.S. management has risen slowly but steadily in the twentieth century from 14 percent of all managers in 1950 to 42 percent in 1992. Finally, the UN's study reports that, compared to the rest of the world, American women do much better than other women around the world in business, health, and education.

THE FUTURE: BUSINESSWOMEN
ARE GOING GLOBAL

After losing worldwide competitive advantage in many industries over the last twenty years, North American companies are finally lifting their heads out of the "domestic" sand and confronting the new global business reality. Firms are widening the sphere in which they do business—they're going global. This means searching worldwide for the best resources at the best cost and linking these resources with worldwide markets at a profit. Consequently, globalization affects every aspect of business from sourcing, staffing, product/service development, and manufacturing to sales, customer service, finance, and communications.

Smart firms are now focusing on suppliers and markets outside the "developed" world. Nancy Birdsall, executive vice president of Inter-American Development Bank in Washington, D.C., says, "It's important for North American workers to know what's going on in the rest of the world because in the next decade most of the market growth will occur in developing countries." In her opinion, the fastest growth for North American products is going to be in Latin America.

All this means exciting change for American and Canadian businesswomen. More and more women are seeing global dimensions added to their jobs and international career opportunities they never before thought possible. Jobs for the internationally skilled will continue to increase at a faster rate than domestic positions and lead to more recognition and better rewards. Women are recognizing this trend and positioning themselves to forge into international commerce.

Consider the following facts:

- In the early 1980s, a handful of women in Chicago founded the first chapter of the Organization of Women in International Trade (OWIT). At this writing, there are over 2500 members in twenty individual chapters across the United States, one in Mexico, and more chapters being formed. (See Part Six for OWIT contacts.)
- More internationally oriented U.S. companies are taking steps to move women into line positions and ultimately top management. Examples include American Airlines, DuPont, Arthur Andersen & Company, and Procter & Gamble.
- *U.S. News & World Report* recently declared that the best graduate school for international business is the American Graduate School for International Management, Glendale, Arizona, also known as "Thunderbird." To

date, it has trained over 6000 women graduates. Women represent 38 percent of its current 1458 student enrollment; enrollment is at an all-time high, and there is a waiting period.

In the past, North American management believed that women were ill suited for international business assignments because it was too dangerous or they wouldn't be accepted. Was that attitude correct? Experts say no. In the 1980s, Professor Adler surveyed sixty-one women expatriates working in the Pacific Rim countries. Forty-two percent said being female actually gave them a competitive advantage.

Clearly, opportunities for women in the global marketplace are proliferating, but there's also plenty of room for improvement. Women represent less than 10 percent of all corporate employees sent overseas by their U.S. companies. On the positive side, traditional barriers toward women are steadily easing around the globe. In addition, interest in international opportunities is growing among North American women, and management can no longer afford to ignore the positive impact they can make.

IT WON'T BE EASY

The road to an international career isn't always smooth. You'll meet resistance at many turns. And, unfortunately, many of your detractors reside on North American shores.

Kate Hotchkiss, of the Tennant Company in Minneapolis, offers this observation about American management:

> In my experience doing international business for the past ten years, by far the biggest challenge as a woman is the misperceptions and often sexist attitudes of managers in the United States. This is a very important point. Women are succeeding internationally despite setbacks and barriers put up back home, not setbacks or barriers put up when we are actually doing international business.

Are you among the doubters? Do you wonder how you can be effective working with business cultures unaccustomed to or uncomfortable with women? This is a legitimate concern, but don't let it keep you from following your dream. In truth, international business tends to be uncomfortable for most North American managers—men as well as women. Many have yet to develop cross-cultural experience, skills, perspective, and confidence.

You can allay your doubts by taking action. To overcome negative attitudes toward women in international business you must assume the initiative and thoroughly prepare yourself. The information found in Parts One and Two will help you gain access to broader international career opportunities and enhance your chances of success on the job.

PREPARE YOURSELF

First, seek professional training: an advanced degree, professional certification, foreign language(s), cross-cultural training. Then formulate a self-study plan to bring yourself up to speed on international business trends affecting your industry, current events, history, economics, literature, art, wine tasting, and so on. No matter what your professional situation is, you will need to be intellectually and culturally well-rounded to work effectively in the international arena.

Next, get to work on building your network of international contacts and resources and stay active in that network. At the same time, look for opportunities in your current job or company to expand your international experience. In the next chapter, you'll read how twelve women followed diverse pathways into international jobs.

Recognize that getting along in the global marketplace will be a lifelong learning process filled with challenges that can range from the very basic (how to avoid ordering animal intestines for lunch in a restaurant in France), to the very complex (how to get a global team to put aside its cultural differences and work together toward a common objective).

Everyone has had embarrassing mistakes and setbacks in international business because there's no way of knowing everything about every culture. One experienced female executive made the mistake of inviting her Australian male host to lunch in front of his colleagues. He acted coolly during lunch. She later learned she had embarrassed him deeply by singling him out in front of his "mates" (close friends and colleagues). She could have blown a major deal for her company. Did she throw in the towel? No, she analyzed the situation and vowed to learn from her mistake. She formulated some strategies for smoothing things over and a few more for avoiding similar problems with Australian men in the future.

Be aware that as a woman in international business, you will find yourself in the minority. You may encounter few or no businesswomen in many of the countries you'll work with. And you may not be treated the same as your male colleagues from North America. It's possible that they'll receive more respect and attention from overseas counterparts—at least initially. It's also possible that you will face discrimination and harassment.

Should all this make you feel uncomfortable? Absolutely! Should it stop you from taking part? No way!

One way to overcome the obstacles is to recognize that you may already have the seeds of success planted within you. Many North American women are crossing cultures successfully and perhaps unknowingly each day.

Like it or not, business in North America is still dominated by men. The unwritten rules we play by in the workplace are masculine rules about how to communicate, compete, prioritize, and so on. Adaptation to the masculine world of work can be difficult and painful for many women, but it is excellent training for crossing international cultural borders.

Many women have also received some invaluable training for international business from two unlikely sources—their families and communities. They've been raised to maintain harmony in interpersonal relationships. As a result, female styles of thinking, empathizing, communicating, and cooperating have evolved. All of these coping mechanisms are essential for international business.

Barbara Fischer, an international attorney from Minneapolis, says, "American women have an advantage over American men doing business in Japan. Japanese men's style of communicating—indirect, hesitant, ambiguous speech—is the way women have been socialized. It's what we in the United States had to unlearn, the being deferential and patient."

ELEVEN BASIC RULES FOR CROSSING CULTURES

1. *Be culturally aware.* Look for similarities and differences. Use them to understand behaviors of your international counterparts.

2. *Don't expect equality.* If you expect men and women to be treated equally everywhere you go, you're in for a big disappointment. Be honest— it doesn't even happen in North America. Recognize that women of other nations contribute to society in many valuable ways—even though they may not be active in business.

3. *Respect and honor cultural norms.* Remember, just because your culture is more familiar than another doesn't make it better. Always be thinking of ways you can do your business *within* your host country's system.

4. *Prepare.* Develop your knowledge of the cultures and businesses

you're working with. Study their history, heroes, languages, literature, food, economies, and so on. This knowledge will give you a context for understanding cultures and deepen your appreciation of them.

5. *Build a personal network of international contacts, experts, and resources.*   Find a mentor, male or female, with international business experience. This person will be the "backboard" you need for bouncing off your ideas and problems. Your mentor may also be able to open doors and give you an occasional credibility boost.

6. *Be professional.*   Develop your competency to the highest level possible so your international colleagues will know they are dealing with the best person for the job. Never fail to act with tact and diplomacy, and always exercise self-confidence and self-control. Take the "win-win," not the "win-lose," approach. Don't take your mistakes personally; learn from them.

7. *Be compassionate, patient, tolerant, and flexible.*   International success hinges first and foremost on personal relationships.

8. *Keep your sense of humor.*   Learn to laugh at yourself. In your international career, there will be plenty to laugh about, because you are human and you will make mistakes.

9. *Recognize that success lies in humility.*   Admit that there's a lot you don't know. Tahirih Lee, professor of Chinese law at the University of Minnesota, insists, "Humility is a key to overcoming obstacles. Don't ever believe you are better than anyone else because of your job or your education. This always makes communication and trust-building more difficult. Know what you don't know—never stop learning."

10. *Learn to distinguish between gender differences and cultural differences.*   As a woman, your first reflex may be to conclude that gender differences are the culprit when you and your international male colleague can't work together. The problem could be a result of cultural, gender, or personal differences—or all three. It's your job to analyze the situation, keeping all these factors in mind.

24

HOW I GOT MY FIRST JOB IN INTERNATIONAL BUSINESS

How does an ambitious American or Canadian woman shed her college cap and gown or current job and stride over the career threshold into her first job in international business? One way, of course, is to be fortunate enough to be recruited directly from college into either an international training program or a specific job opening that fits like the proverbial glove. While this may be occurring more frequently than in the past, it is not the path of most currently successful women.

The route between "aspiration" and "acquisition" of a high-quality job in international can sometimes be long and bumpy, filled with twists and turns, and may even contain several detours along the way.

Some women have mentors to guide them; others just happen to be in the right place at the right time; and still others wait and try, and then try and wait some more until they finally succeed. The common denominator in the following case studies is a combination of top-notch professional skills, plus a venturesome spirit and plain old perseverance.

PORTRAITS OF TWELVE WOMEN

Right Place, Right Time

Roxanne Baumann, Manager, Parts & Accessories, Europe and the Pacific, for a major U.S. manufacturer of motorcycles, got her first job because she was in the right place at the right time; she also had a boss who became a mentor.

143

She joined her company's administration department directly out of college where her education had been in foreign languages with education credits. In the mid-1970s, when the company landed a huge $80 million contract for a three-year supply project in Algeria, she was assigned to the team as a French/English translation secretary. "I really didn't discover that exporting was my niche until I got involved with all the international exporters on the Algerian project," she says. "I knew immediately this was exactly what I wanted to do."

Her boss served as her mentor; she says he "totally encouraged me and helped me determine what additional education background I would need to be successful. He was very progressive for the mid-'70s. He provided opportunities for me to network with other exporters in my local World Trade Association and advised me on additional coursework. My gender was completely irrelevant to him—he was only interested in my abilities."

Serendipity

In Dr. Colleen Braun's case, she stepped out of the surf on a beach in Tahiti and "fell into" an opportunity to enter international business. "I had attended an international diabetes federation meeting in Melbourne, Australia, and stopped over in Tahiti en route home," she explains. "A German man on the beach asked me the time, and we engaged in conversation. I talked about a small business I had started in Cincinnati. He asked if I had considered taking my idea international. I explained I welcomed the possibility but hadn't the resources." Six months later she joined his German group.

Active Pursuit + Patience

Barbara J. Fischer, executive vice president of International Business Associates, Cedar Falls, Iowa, actively pursued an international job. She had developed an interest in international business in her teenage years. But even with a carefully plotted education track, when she graduated from the prestigious Wharton Graduate School with an M.B.A. she was unable to find a job in international business. Fischer recalls, "After graduation, what I initially wanted was a position in international finance at a bank. But, one after another of the banks said a woman simply would not be accepted by their international clients. They offered me positions on currency trading desks or in domestic banking, but not the international department." Corporations said the same thing. She finally went to work at a large multinational company

and spent two and a half years in various domestic market positions. Throughout this period she remained eager to get into international.

Fischer's father, meanwhile, was serving as executive director of the Soy-
bean Council in Iowa. He wrote his daughter seeking her help in writing an
advertisement for someone to help market agricultural equipment worldwide.
Fischer says, "I asked what he would think if I applied, and he replied, 'What
airplane will you be on?' "

Promotion from Within

Jane A. Hassler works for a manufacturer of accessories for audio and video
equipment. She had been working as a domestic sales coordinator and was
promoted to administrative assistant to the president of the company. The
president's office also handled international sales activities. Shortly after,
Hassler was promoted to the job of international sales coordinator, and then
to account executive. She credits her success to the following traits that helped
her assume responsibilities in international business:

- Knowledge of world geography and history and of current geopolitical
  climates.
- Awareness that most American attitudes in dealing with foreigners are
  ineffective.
- Willingness to learn and be open to any awkward situation in which you
  may find yourself.

Networking

Susan Kadlec was interviewed for this book as she was finishing her Ph.D.
dissertation and teaching international business and business strategy at the
University of Illinois. Her pathway was not only uphill; it also twisted in
discouraging directions.

As a youngster, Kadlec always wanted to travel and see the world.
While working on her M.B.A., she realized that she could not only travel but
work abroad as well. She also had a job in a company where she supervised
several people with diverse nationalities. "I jokingly referred to them as my
United Nations staff. They reinforced my desire to work abroad."

In her studies, she concentrated on international business and sought to
learn languages. She developed a familiarity with the major European languages, including some of the less common ones, such as Czech. Then, in the

mid-1980s, she found a job with a corporation where she oversaw the financial operations of its foreign subsidiaries. Even with her extensive credentials in international business, she was not encouraged to visit those operations. "I was told point-blank that they preferred not to send women into overseas positions. They justified this by explaining that the attitudes abroad toward women were not as advanced as in the United States. I perceived this attitudinal problem as part of the 'old boys' network' because now, almost a decade later, women are holding highly responsible international jobs."

Perseverance

For Elinor Jackson, perseverance is what did the trick. At the time of this writing she was an international sales manager for a company that manufactures and sells medical devices and electrical stimulators for physical therapy.

Jackson knew she wanted a career in international at an early age and began her quest while still in high school. She was an AFS (American Field Service) exchange student and lived in France when she was sixteen. In college, she received a degree with honors in international relations, and she later studied in Argentina. Even with those qualifications, after graduation she spent nine years in jobs with two global corporations, but without responsibilities in the international side.

"I just never felt like giving up," Jackson says. "This is what I wanted to do. I couldn't see myself doing something I wasn't interested in. Finally, after searching and searching, I found a guy who hired me on a leap of faith."

Follow the Boss

When Joanne Fischer's boss, who was her mentor, was promoted from vice president, sales and marketing to vice president, international sales and new business development, she followed him. Fischer says the transition was both a challenge and an opportunity "because I enjoy customer contact and the challenge of dealing with them. I was able to grow into my current position as export administrator."

Fischer helped pave the way by taking product knowledge classes and studying Spanish. She also actively participates in programs at her state trade office.

The Carefully Plotted Path

At the time of our research, Teri Skluzacek Carlisano was the European marketing manager for an upper-Midwest import company and worked with European craftsmen to develop and market nutcrackers and Christmas ornaments in the United States. Her territory was Europe—primarily Germany, the Czech and Slovak Republics, Poland, Italy, Portugal, and Ukraine.

Carlisano carefully plotted her course into international business starting in high school and continuing in college. With a solid background in languages plus experience living and working in Europe, she found that "jobs came to her" rather than the other way around.

The desire to be involved in international business has been one of the strongest driving ambitions in her life. "I've always managed to find ways around obstacles," she says, "because I kept at it. I didn't accept common wisdom about whether a woman should be traveling, or whether or not a language was needed. Actually, I landed my last two jobs because of my languages."

Throughout high school and college, people told her she would need five to ten years of experience with a company before being able to work in international. As a college senior, she decided that anything she did overseas would be international, so she set to work on getting a job in Europe.

By age twenty-three she was traveling to Europe bimonthly for a Minneapolis trading company. Visiting Italian businessmen for the first time, she noticed the questions in their eyes. But after they learned that she'd lived in Europe, studied and worked there, spoke several languages, and was competent in her business, they respected her and her company for sending someone who wasn't "a typical American," and who understood that things are different in Europe. "It pays to establish yourself early on so that you gain the respect you deserve," she says. "It's tremendously helpful to be well-prepared and good at what you do—especially for a woman."

Internships

Tahirih Lee's use of internships in her academic career helped her acquire the skills and credibility she needed to become associate professor of law at the University of Minnesota. She is one of the few law professors in the United States who teaches Chinese law.

At Stanford University she majored in history with a focus on China and completed a master's degree in East Asian studies. This required the study of

Mandarin Chinese, history, economics, anthropology, and the politics of China. Lee advises anyone pursuing an international career to study in more than one discipline in order to gain a variety of skills and perspectives.

While completing her undergraduate degree, Lee took full advantage of summer study programs and internships in China. Internships gave her international work experience, a chance to learn Chinese, and first-hand contact with the culture of the People's Republic of China. Lee had three opportunities to study and work in China as an undergraduate and spent two summers there.

Mount Holyoke College set up her internship with *Newsweek* magazine in Beijing. "Internships are a way to pay your expenses in another country," she explains. "However, be sure to avoid internships that saddle you with grunt work. At *Newsweek,* I wrote my own articles. This was essential in helping me develop my research and writing skills." Lee's contact with American lawyers for one of her writing assignments sparked her interest in Chinese law.

The following summer, she took part in a second internship in Beijing, this time in Chinese law. Her first internship helped her develop personal connections that paved the way for housing and other daily necessities on her second visit.

Lee got her J.D. degree from Yale Law School, her Ph.D. in Chinese history from Yale University, and was a scholar-in-residence at Harvard University's Academy for International and Area Studies, where she researched nineteenth- and early twentieth-century Chinese law. She also clerked for a U.S. Court of Appeals judge in Washington, D.C.

Lee urges aspiring women, *"Jia you"*—"Add grease" in Chinese. On a deeper level, it means "Hang in there" and "Go for it!"

Learn the Basics and Network

Mary Regel, director of the Division of International Development for the State of Wisconsin, helps companies develop export opportunities.

Regel didn't start her career in international. During her first eight years with Wisconsin's Department of Agriculture she provided consulting expertise and organized trade shows for food and agricultural supply companies. This allowed her to develop expertise in domestic manufacturing, distribution, and promotion. Her expertise transferred beautifully to the international positions she was promoted to. "You have to get to know the basics of exporting and know a product or industry prior to jumping into selling products internationally," insists Regel.

She also relied on networking to launch her international career and advance it. Regel became active in local international organizations and served on the Governor's advisory committee on international trade. Regel eventually was elected to the board of directors of several Wisconsin international trade organizations. "The more you network," she says, "the more you learn, and people begin to recognize your interest and involvement."

Starting at the Bottom

Kathy J. Bullen, an international banking officer at a large Chicago bank, began her international career by working her way through the ranks. In her first job, Bullen did the operations for the bank's international department—she issued letters of credit, processed collections, facilitated foreign exchange trades, and did bookkeeping.

For Bullen, the best way of learning international banking operations was starting in a purely clerical function. "I learned a lot in that position," she says, "because I was willing to do work that many people may feel is beneath them because they have a college degree."

Opportunity Knocked

Edith C. McDonald, president of a software company in Oswego, Illinois, never pursued a course into international business—it just happened. In her case, overseas orders for her software products began arriving in the mail. McDonald had to quickly call in outside consultants (in her case, she turned to SCORE, the "Senior Corps of Retired Executives" sponsored by the U.S. Small Business Administration). They advised her to enroll in an international marketing course, and she shipped her first products abroad after the second class.

WHAT THESE TWELVE WOMEN TELL US

From these real-life case studies, we can observe at least a dozen different trails leading toward that first job in international business.

Your best preparation is to first acquire a sound and attractive educational foundation. Then, focus on the skills you need to succeed in your chosen profession, whether finance, marketing, or engineering. Acquire these skills in school, internships, and entry-level positions, domestic or international. Use your college or university placement office to seek interviews with firms that are offering positions in, or leading to, international careers. Banks, large consumer-goods manufacturers, and advertising agencies are just three possibilities that may offer training programs leading to international jobs.

Realize that it may be necessary to begin your career in the domestic operation of a large company. Many firms believe that it is essential to first acquire a grounding or basic understanding of the company along with professional experience and credibility before you receive international job responsibilities or are sent on overseas assignments. Be certain in your job interviews to receive assurances that it will be possible for you to at least be considered for movement through the company toward your ultimate goal.

If you are among the majority who are or have been unable to step directly into that office marked "Director—International," then, like the pioneering women profiled here, you must try other pathways.

TEN PATHWAYS TOWARD A CAREER IN INTERNATIONAL BUSINESS

1. *Develop skills, credentials, and experience in the business or profession you have targeted.* International is a territory, not a career, therefore you need concrete skills and experience in a recognized area: marketing, finance, law, engineering, and so on. A love for international and a few language courses are insufficient qualifications for an international job.

2. *Learn to speak one or more foreign languages.* Strive for fluency, not just familiarity. While you're learning a language, find out everything you can about the business culture and protocol of the country or countries that use that language. (See Part Six for suggested reading.)

3. *Pursue a job that will give you solid work experience in some specialty of international business.* Examples are: freight forwarding, export shipping and documentation, international insurance, any aspect of international banking and finance, and so on.

4. *Get work experience in marketing, sales, or customer service.* If and when your current employer expands into international sales, you'll be positioned just outside the doorway waiting to be admitted.

5. *Search out international internships and volunteer opportunities.* These can provide the skills, experience, and contacts necessary for initiating an international job search. (See Part Six for suggested reading on internships.)

6. *Internationalize yourself.* Cultivate traits that make you attractive to employers—knowledge of world geography and economics; experience living abroad; and demonstrated work experience with people from other cultures. Travel overseas at every opportunity, including AFS as a high school student and college year-abroad programs.

7. *Lower your expectations for an entry-level job in international.* Clerical positions or translation work often are the best places to learn about international business. Prove that you have value and potential and then encourage your employer to reward and motivate you through increased international responsibility.

8. *Join trade clubs and international associations in your area.* Attend seminars at community colleges or universities. This will bring two benefits: It will add to your present store of information and knowledge; it will also allow you to do valuable networking.

9. *Make your current employer aware of your interest in expanding your responsibilities and your career directions into international.* Make certain your employer knows why you are interested and why you are qualified.

A note of caution: Avoid giving the impression that the chief reason you are interested in international business is that you are anxious to be posted overseas to live and work. Most employers are extremely wary of people who spent one year abroad on a student-exchange program, fell in love with a certain country, and are merely looking for a cheap return ticket.

10. *Strive to exemplify the following qualities.* They are essential for a successful track record in international business.

- The three "p's"—patience, persistence, and perseverance
- Flexibility
- An open mind
- Team-player mentality
- Creativity
- Self-confidence
- Superb communication skills
- Energy
- Enthusiasm
- Determination

25

PROFILES OF THREE SUCCESSFUL WOMEN

Whatever women do they must do twice as well as men to be thought half as good. Luckily, that is not difficult.

CHARLOTTE WHITTON
Late Mayor of Ottawa

To demonstrate the truth of the statement above, we offer the following profiles of three successful women.

Deborah Enix-Ross

Director of International Litigation for Price Waterhouse

In 1988, two months after starting her job as the director of legal affairs for the U.S. Council for International Business in New York City, Enix-Ross flew to Paris to attend her first overseas meeting. Six years of job experience and networking were about to pay off. With her position at the U.S. Council, she was fulfilling her lifelong dream of working in an international job that would take her around the world.

When she checked in at the private club where she had prearranged to meet a group of American attorneys based in Paris, the concierge told her she could not use the front staircase to the meeting room. She repeated, in French, that she was expected for a meeting, but once more was told not to take the front staircase. "Is this because I'm black or because I'm a woman?" she thought. Enix-Ross pondered her dilemma. "Do I refuse to go to the meeting, having spent the last six years trying to get into international law, or do I go forward?" She allowed herself to be escorted through the kitchen and up the back staircase.

152

Her male colleagues were embarrassed and apologetic when they learned what had happened. Women are not allowed to use the front staircase because the club's management feared the portraits of nude females on the staircase walls would offend them. As a gesture of solidarity at the end of the meeting, her colleagues took the back way with Enix-Ross and vowed never to use the club again.

Enix-Ross admits her route to international law was unusual and circuitous. Since childhood, she was interested in travel and cultures. "I had a knack for getting along with people," she explains. "You'll find most people involved in international law have an affinity for or easiness with people in other cultures. For me, speaking a foreign language was part of this interest."

After her first year in law school at the University of Miami, she took electives in international law. She seized the chance to study at the London School of Economics and backpack through Europe during a summer break. "I highly recommend studying abroad and travel. It looks good on your resume, especially with limited international work experience." Enix-Ross says study-abroad programs call attention to you just as degrees from Ivy League schools, internships with prestigious law firms, and law review honors do.

With her law degree in hand, Enix-Ross set out to find a job in Florida—ideally, in international law. She immediately ran into barricades. Everywhere she turned, she received the subtle message: "You're a woman, you're not law review, and you're black, so you can't be in international law." She explains, "People never came right out and said this, but their actions spoke louder than their words. They suggested civil rights law, criminal law, and legal services."

She returned home to New York and took a job at legal services because she believed in legal counsel for the poor and because she wanted litigation experience. "All the while," she says, "I kept looking for opportunities in international law."

While at legal services, Enix-Ross volunteered to serve on union/management negotiation and became involved in mediation. This gave her the critical experience that qualified her for her next job as an attorney with the National Advertising Division (NAD) of the Better Business Bureau. There she mediated disputes between companies over advertising. "I agonized over accepting the job because it wasn't international in scope," she says, "but I liked mediation and it gave me a chance to work with corporate counsel. I thought maybe it would lead to something."

Two and a half years passed and, one day, she saw an opening for a position at the U.S. Council for International Business. The advertisement called for someone who had experience in mediation, arbitration, and advertising and an interest in international. Enix-Ross says triumphantly, "I called the woman who became my boss and said, 'I hope you haven't hired anyone for this position, because I'm the perfect person for the job.' "

"You don't break into this field in just one way," advises Enix-Ross. "I took the circular route and it worked. I am now involved strictly in international arbitration and litigation. Things are connected and we don't always know why. If you're really good at what you do, your skills will transfer, but you must have the skills."

"I know so many top-notch women who should be further in their international careers," she continues. "You can't be bitter and you can't give up. Make a new way. Never be envious of what other people have. Prepare yourself and when the opportunity comes up, you'll be ready to recognize it and to take advantage of it."

"Be patient," she counsels. "It took me seven long years to build a reputation in international arbitration. I became involved in the American Bar Association. It's important to choose organizations and get involved in order to establish yourself."

Enix-Ross believes women are particularly well suited for international mediation. "We have experience with the spirit of cooperation and with conflict resolution. We know how to compromise without capitulation."

Her self-proclaimed greatest moment in international law is a situation in which she took full advantage of all her aptitudes. Representing the U.S. Council, she was able to move a proposal forward through the sixty national committees around the world for important changes in international business conciliation and arbitration. Enix-Ross explains, "The key to moving the proposal forward was to get the French national committee to agree with the proposed changes. I was able to talk about the changes the United States thought were necessary and to present them in a way so we could reach consensus. A series of telephone calls ended in an invitation to attend a French meeting and explain the U.S. position—in French. I was one of two women and the only black person at the meeting. After debating the pros and cons of the U.S. proposal, the French agreed with our position."

"Speaking French was part of the success," she continues, "but it boiled down to an appreciation of their culture. I knew not only what needed to be said, but how to approach them."

Her success and reputation in international arbitration caused Price Waterhouse, a big-six accounting and consulting firm, to create a position just for her. She is the national coordinator of international arbitration practice in the company's Dispute Analysis and Corporate Recovery Group in New York.

"The economy really is global," says Enix-Ross when sizing up the opportunities for women in international business. "While I was at the U.S. Council, I received calls from small companies all over the country entering the international market for the first time because their domestic market is saturated. Everyone has the opportunity to do business internationally and they need professionals to help them."

She emphasizes that "if you are really interested in international, you'll find a way to do it. Don't be discouraged. How you overcome the obstacles is more important than the fact that they are there. If you don't have control, don't let it make you angry or bitter. Go forward, through, or around the obstacles."

Catherine Tenke Teichert

Assistant Vice President of New Business Development, M & I Data Services, a division of Marshall and Ilsley Corporation

Arab countries are widely perceived as the most difficult places for women in international business, yet Catherine Tenke Teichert enjoyed enormous success there. As a new product development director for the Gulf Bank in Kuwait in the 1980s, Teichert held the most senior job of any Western woman in an Arab country.

"The challenge is to convince a Western white guy that you're seen as an American first, and second as a woman," says Teichert. "To convince white males, you just do it. Then they accept it." She adds, "I knew I was being considered with the rest of the boys, when my Arab counterparts came after me with as much vim and vigor as the American men."

In deference to Arab clients, Teichert strictly followed cultural rules. She states, "I always made client calls with a male account officer—it was more form than substance. It would have been bad manners to be unaccompanied. I was paying attention to cultural form. It was not a question of competency."

This respected executive attributes her success to her finely honed business skills and her cultural instincts, which, she thinks, come naturally to women. "Women have the skills by nature or by culture or whatever it is," states Teichert when talking about women's potential in the global marketplace. "They have more of the skill set that's needed and important in international. Women are better at networking, empathy, and ambiguity. Consequently, my Arab friends and co-workers were more comfortable with me. I had the technical skills *and* I could deal more on a cultural level."

"What makes you good in America," says Teichert, "gives you difficulty overseas. In the United States, things are clear-cut, black and white. We have a tendency to lack tolerance for diversity and we have the concept of group think—that we all have to believe the same thing. If you bring up something that's questioning (and this is very female), it's not good. But in many cultures, that's how people think."

One of her greatest multicultural moments involved a high-level meeting when she was director of business development with Talal Abu Ghazalah, the largest accounting, auditing, and consulting firm in the Middle East. She conducted a meeting where Arabic, English, French, and German were being spoken at the same time. Conversations switched from one language to the other during the meeting, and she thought to herself, "This is so incredible. This is what I wanted to do my whole life. It's so complex. And I'm the only American at this meeting and the only Westerner in the entire company. I'm functioning and productive in this environment." Teichert looks back on that day with great pride. "I will always remember that feeling," she recalls. "Here I am sitting in a boardroom in Kuwait with heads of government and bankers and technocrats and I'm from Waukesha, Wisconsin."

So how did this young woman from Waukesha secure the career opportunities that would be the envy of international businessmen around the world? She did it by applying the strategies successful males have secretly guarded: (1) develop top-notch professional skills, (2) remain fiercely loyal to your network, and (3) embrace ambiguity.

The professional skills Teichert has developed throughout her successful career include cross-cultural communications and new product market development. She maximized her expertise in cross-cultural communications through a combination of formal education, overseas travel, and work experience. She studied psycholinguistics at Marquette University and the University of Utah, focusing on the semantic development of children learning to speak in bicultural, bilingual families. While completing research for her M.A., Teichert applied her expertise on linguistic development to help create bilingual training programs for adults. After receiving her master's degree, she was invited by a Japanese friend to spend six months with his family in Tokyo. They lived in a suburb that was unaccustomed to Westerners at the time. During her stay, she studied conversational Japanese at a local community college and learned ten new Japanese words every day from her friend's father. In a short time, she was able to communicate comfortably in Japanese.

Thanks to her hosts' cosmopolitan lifestyle, says Teichert, "I had exposure to many Japanese businessmen who did business with the United States. They came to me for unstructured coaching on how to make presentations to Americans. In Japan, presentations give lots of detail, but not so in the United States. And they had to look at how Americans make decisions."

Teichert used this cross-cultural coaching experience as a basis for starting a consulting and training business in southern California. She created sales and marketing training for organizations with multicultural workforces, and taught her clients how to motivate their diverse employees.

In an effort to sharpen her professional skills while running her company, Teichert applied simultaneously to a Ph.D. program in communications and an M.B.A. program. During her application process, her boyfriend received an untimely job offer in Kuwait with Getty Oil. She found herself at a "fork in the road." She had to decide whether to stay in California and continue her education and communications consulting or take a risk and accompany her boyfriend to Kuwait.

Teichert is by nature a risk-taker, so her direction was obvious. She left for Kuwait. After two years as a business editor of the Arab newspaper, *Dar Al Seyassa* in Kuwait, she made a bold, vertical career move. She became director of business development for Talal Abu Ghazalah, where she gained a reputation for knowing how to turn market plans into reality. She reported directly to the company chairman, an Arab, and worked as a liaison between Arabs and Western groups, such as bankers and consultants. "I focused on communication issues—reading between the lines," she says. "I would listen to one side and then say, 'Here's what they really want, here's how you should present to them.' "

Throughout her career, Teichert has leveraged her professional skills in market and product development and cross-cultural communication to climb the ladder in international business. "My main strategy for working up the ladder is having a specific expertise to offer," she says. "In corporate America, it's often how you get along in the organization. In international, you have to hit the ground running. You have to be productive right away."

The next rung up the international career ladder took Teichert to the Gulf Bank in Kuwait where she directed new product development and managed a balance sheet. She credits her loyalty to her network for helping her maximize her effectiveness on the job. "I had a Mitsubishi client I met with ten times before closing a deal to be sure we could work together. They would say of me, 'She is known to us.' This means they could trust my character and we could work through any differences rather than go to court."

Teichert's networking helped her find increasingly more interesting positions throughout her career. "Networking is part of your job," she stresses.

"Women focus too much on competence. Keep up your contacts. Your loyalty is to your network," she continues, "not your employer (especially when you work for an overseas organization). Your employment contract is usually for two years, so you always keep your eye open for where you'll work next."

Her network in Kuwait included people who could help her with difficult acculturation to Arab culture. She joined the American Women's League in Kuwait and eventually became a member of its board. Active membership in the Kuwait Business Council helped her navigate in the Arab business world. "Whether it's a business group or a tennis club," she concludes, "you'll meet people from different walks of life. There's always someone who can help you solve a problem or knows someone who can."

Mentors have also played a strong role in Teichert's network, helping her with her business judgment and problem-solving. "At the bank, I had a strong mentor," she says. "He was very supportive. He was American. He told me which battles to fight and helped me with issues where I had one foot in the United States and the other foot in another country. You're torn between what you know is right in one culture and wrong in another."

"It's not a straight shot into international," she warns. "You have to be the type of person who can live with ambiguity and be a risk-taker. You have to be willing to come back and start again because people forget about you." After eight years abroad, the twists and turns in her career pathway have now brought her back to Wisconsin.

Her current job as assistant vice president of new business development for M & I Data Services in Milwaukee has her looking for strategic business opportunities for the company's financial software in both domestic and international financial communities. "It took longer to fit back in here," says Teichert of her repatriation. "I think differently and have had different experiences than my colleagues." Judging from her impressive rise in international, these differences are what have helped to make her such an asset to her employers.

Because international has been ignored by so many companies, Teichert believes there are a lot of opportunities for women with strong business skills. She says, "If you can create something for yourself, you have some opportunities."

Teichert would love to have more professional women with whom to share issues and aspirations. Women should strongly consider careers in international business, she says, "because it's so much fun—it's so interesting and it's constantly changing." She concludes, "The world has really changed. No company is domestic any more. It's so interesting to work in America now."

Kathi Seifert

Group President, North American Personal Care Products, Kimberly-Clark Corporation

When Chinese officials representing Kimberly-Clark's first manufacturer in China paid their inaugural visit to the company's Neenah, Wisconsin, headquarters, they were given their choice of whom to meet first. They said that in addition to meeting the CEO, they wanted to meet "Kathi Kotex."

After dedicating eleven years of her career to Kimberly-Clark's feminine care products, Seifert has moved on to manage all consumer personal care products for the company, and she oversees the Kotex line plus a half-dozen other equally famous brands. Nevertheless, her nickname endures. Kimberly-Clark personnel around the world know her as "Kathi Kotex."

"When you think of the business I used to represent (feminine care products), it's only appropriate that a woman represent it," she says. "Starting off in feminine care gave me instant credibility because I am a woman."

Unlike most women in international business, Seifert has never encountered any gender-related challenges with overseas counterparts. "I don't have to deal with many obstacles because of my status. I represent the success of Kimberly-Clark to overseas operations."

Indeed, she does. At forty-seven, Seifert is the highest ranking woman at Kimberly-Clark, a $14-billion corporation that's made it big with such brands as Huggies Disposable Diapers, Pullups Training Pants, Depends incontinence products, Kotex and New Freedom feminine care products, Kleenex tissues, and Scott products.

As president of North American Personal Care Products, she reports directly to the CEO. She heads up four of the company's consumer product sectors—infant care, child care, feminine care, and adult care. In concert with the four sector presidents who report to her, Seifert oversees the research, development, marketing, sales engineering, and manufacturing of consumer products in North America and supports worldwide product development.

Seifert joined Kimberly-Clark in 1978. Before that she received her undergraduate degree in marketing management from Valparaiso University in Indiana. After two and one-half years in marketing research at Procter & Gamble, she worked in distribution at a division of Beatrice Foods in Madison, Wisconsin. After that, she went out looking for brand management experience and found it at Fort Howard Paper Co. in Green Bay. All the while, she watched for something to open up for her at Kimberly-Clark. Seifert eventually landed a position in Kimberly-Clark's Service and Industrial Products

Division, and since then has worked her way up the corporate ladder through marketing.

"I do not have an M.B.A.," she explains when talking about her academic credentials. "That's somewhat unusual for someone in my position." Nevertheless, she has compensated for her lack of an advanced degree by consistently producing bottom-line results. In 1991, she became president of Kimberly-Clark's feminine care sector. That's when she started working to help develop products for international markets.

Kimberly-Clark places high value on the personal characteristics Seifert brings to her international work. "I have a lot of energy and enthusiasm. I try to inspire and motivate people around the world. I share stories about how ten years ago we were number three in the U.S. feminine care market and now we're number one. I tell them, 'You can do it also.' "

"Another strength," continues Seifert, "is that I love to brainstorm with teams to build businesses. I try to be one of the team and understand the environment and provide as many ideas and as much encouragement as possible. I make sure I understand before I recommend. I never assume what works in the United States works around the world. In essence, I try to transfer good creative ideas and business development ideas around the world in a team fashion."

Seifert regularly visits Kimberly-Clark's worldwide operations. "I do a lot of observing and listening," she says, "and therefore spend time in manufacturing operations and the marketplace. In the retail outlets, I'm looking to see what our products look like on the shelf, how they're priced, and how they're positioned versus the competition."

She thinks going global is making Kimberly-Clark stronger competitors in North America "because we're opening our eyes to product enhancements not thought of before. We say 'If it works overseas, let's try it here.' "

In addition to product enhancements, Seifert looks to her international personnel for product, advertising, packaging, and cost-saving ideas. "In emerging markets, consumers don't have much disposable income," she says, "so we need to get costs down as low as possible so consumers can afford our products. Product and advertising ideas around the world can be applicable in North America. As the population of North America shifts—more Hispanics, Asians, African Americans, and elderly—our learning from around the world is more and more beneficial to the U.S. market."

One might think that a woman with Seifert's clout doesn't need to pay attention to cultural protocol, but she's fastidious about it. She never fails to prepare herself for each new country she visits. "We have the World Support Group at Kimberly-Clark which supports communication between business groups and international partners," she says. "We always touch base with them before getting involved with a new country. They give us extensive cultural information and background on how the country is doing from a business standpoint. It is important to get their perspective about opportunities in these countries."

In more socially reserved countries, Seifert tones down her naturally expressive style. "I'm very outgoing; I pat people on the back to show support and naturally shake hands. When I'm in another country, however, I observe local customs, realizing that some cultures prefer a more low-key style." Honoring a country's protocol, Seifert believes, is a way to ensure long-lasting business relationships. "Relationships are so important," she insists. "You have to build up trust. It is imperative to let them lead with their cultural practices. But at the same time, I have to convey leadership from North America."

Seifert leads in a highly personable and motivational fashion. She recalls a successful meeting she held a few years ago in Panama City, Panama, which was attended by all of Kimberly-Clark's Latin American managers. Her success was due in part to the human touch she added to her presentation. "I used transparencies with drawings of palm trees on them and in the middle of the meeting some of my colleagues walked in with Panama hats for everyone. Then we went outside and took a picture of the whole group. It was a gesture to say we're all one and seemed to demonstrate teamwork, partnership, and international linkage."

On the humanitarian side, Seifert is helping Kimberly-Clark design outreach programs to show its international subsidiaries and partners that it is interested in more than just profits. "I think we can make an impact on the health and well-being of young girls around the world on the health issues of hygiene and possibly AIDS," she says. "It's a long-term goal of mine. When I explain this to our teams around the world, their eyes light up. They feel good that Kimberly-Clark has the potential to reach out and help in more ways than providing superior products."

Seifert has encouraged Kimberly-Clark to take advantage of emerging global opportunities for personal care products, particularly in markets experiencing significant population growth, such as Latin America, China, and India. The opening of Eastern European markets also offers great business potential for personal care products.

Women can play a key role in the vast array of global opportunities, contends Seifert, because the taboo of women in business has declined significantly around the world. "I have been accepted everywhere I've gone. In countries such as Saudi Arabia, it's more challenging, but in 80 percent of the world there are strong opportunities for women."

Seifert adds her voice to the throng of cross-cultural experts and experienced international executives who say women are naturally suited for international business. "Women are naturally more caring, nurturing, and better listeners," she says. "They like to help and to respond to people's needs. This is consistent with most business cultures around the world because everything is based on relationships. This works in favor of women."

To prepare for a job with global responsibilities, Seifert recommends that women analyze growth opportunities and decide where they can make the greatest impact with their business skills and ideas. "Learn as much as you can about a country, its culture, and business situation ahead of time," she advises. "Do whatever you can to help the country build its business. Then take your learning and implement it in other business opportunities in North America or elsewhere."

PART FOUR

THE INTERNATIONAL ASSIGNMENT

The number of North American women working overseas is on the rise. Currently, U.S. women, for example, make up about 10 percent of the American international workforce—up from only 3 percent in 1988. As companies continue to realize that women are an undertapped resource, more and more North American businesswomen will be facing the exciting possibility of an overseas post.

In Chapters 26 to 32 you will learn to:

- Prepare for living and working abroad.
- Prepare your family for life overseas.
- Evaluate on-the-job challenges.
- Identify the signals and remedies for culture shock.
- Learn about repatriation and reverse culture shock.
- Choose appropriate language and cross-cultural training.

26

TO GO OR NOT TO GO

I felt I was really ready for change. I was feeling tapped out at that stage of my career. I was ready to take a risk and do something new.

ANNE GREENE
Marketing executive, Pillsbury

Anne Greene was sent on an international assignment to Tokyo in 1990. Not only was she one of her company's first women executives to be transferred overseas, but she was also a single mother with two children.

EVALUATING THE ASSIGNMENT

If you're considering your employer's offer of an international assignment, start your decision-making process by coolly and objectively evaluating the assignment. You need to get an accurate picture of the job and your responsibilities. Be sure to clarify these points with your employer:

- What are the objectives of the assignment?
- How long is the assignment?
- To whom will I report and who will report to me?
- What will the company gain?
- What skills do I possess that make me a good candidate?
- What professional skills will I need to develop during the assignment?
- Where will I fit into the home organization after I return?
- How long is the typical workday? Typical work week?
- How much travel does the job require?

- Will I be required to participate in and plan business-related social activities? How often?

Pay special attention to the job responsibilities by asking yourself:

- How comfortable am I working without direction? (Many overseas posts require extensive self-direction and initiative.) What's my style in working with colleagues or supervising others?
- How do I handle failure? (The initial failure rate can be high as you get up to speed on your new job.)
- How well do I handle cultural and communication differences with host nationals?
- What potential complications might arise in the host country? How might I handle them?

Ask how much cross-cultural and language training your company will provide prior to and after your transfer. Both are critical to successful living and working abroad. Seek out training on your own if your company won't offer it. (See Part Six for more on cross-cultural and language training.)

Also consider how the assignment fits into your career goals. In many companies, an overseas transfer can mean time spent "out of the loop" and "away from the action." Greene remembers deliberating over whether "going out of the mainstream was a good move. There was a danger my career could get sidetracked."

While you can keep in touch with colleagues and supervisors through mail, phone, fax, and computer e-mail, you need to feel that the assignment will benefit you as much as if you'd stayed at the home office. Or more. Greene's superiors, for instance, assured her the international assignment would jump-start her career and put her head and shoulders above her peers because of the experience, knowledge, and growth she would gain.

Is This the Right Job for Me Personally?

Certain personal characteristics go a long way in smoothing the often rocky path of international assignments. Consider what sort of personality you are before accepting. Liz Longmore, a British business development manager who transferred to the United States from England, says, "I knew I was flexible and that I could adapt rather than just rely on importing my own culture."

Ask yourself the following questions to determine if you possess the traits needed to thrive in a new environment:

- Am I emotionally stable? This is important in managing difficult situations with dignity and respect. Am I the kind of person who could actually flourish—not just get by—in a different culture? Do I like new experiences? How many people do I know from different cultural backgrounds? Vivien Godfrey, vice president of international marketing for a food company, has the right idea when she says, "Diversity is the norm. There isn't one flavor of doing things; the world is made up of many different flavors."
- Am I genuinely curious about or interested in other cultures? What past experiences have I had that indicate my genuine interest in learning about other cultures? Do I enjoy eating in ethnic restaurants, watching foreign films, participating in cultural events from other countries, or learning a new language? If you have a healthy curiosity, you're probably willing to broaden your thinking and problem-solving skills as necessary in a foreign country. Such skills, in social and business settings, also help set host nationals at ease.
- Am I flexible, adaptable, and resourceful? When have I had to make my way in unfamiliar surroundings? How did I do? Did I enjoy it? These attitudes will help you meet the daily challenges of living and working in another country.
- Do I have a sense of humor? This trait will always help you put awkward situations into perspective.

Is This the Right Time for My Family?

Some women have only to evaluate their own readiness for an overseas relocation. Others must take into account the needs of a spouse and children. All research shows that if your kids and your spouse aren't happy about the transfer, your assignment will probably fail. "There's no denying it," says an international transferee. "If your family or spouse really doesn't want to go, you probably shouldn't either. Your life will be miserable and the assignment could even endanger your marriage." Hundreds of businessmen and businesswomen will attest to the additional difficulties presented by a suffering family member or unsupportive spouse who cannot adapt to living in another culture. The personal costs to families can be severe and range from stress to alcoholism to divorce. For these reasons, carefully consider the implications of moving your family abroad.

Special Considerations for Families
- Custody of young or school-age children if you're divorced or separated. Will it be legally possible to take your children out of the country?
- Recent stress (a separation, relocation, illness, or death) in the fam-

ily. An international move could compound the stress and pain your family may be experiencing.

• Relationships with extended family. Do you have close ties to your extended family? Could you and your family thrive away from your relatives?

• Care of a child or spouse with special physical, mental, or medical needs. Can he or she tolerate such a dramatic change in daily life and routine? Can you find comparable care and schooling in your destination country?

• Schooling. Are the educational options for your children sufficient to meet their needs?

• Personal safety (if you are moving to a culture with special safety concerns). Will this cause you to be fearful and overprotective to the point that it negatively affects your family life?

• The availability of cross-cultural and language training for children and spouses. Will your family have the support it needs to adapt successfully to the new culture?

For a more in-depth discussion of family issues, see Chapter 28.

What About My Husband's Career?

Some husbands are fortunate enough to accompany their businesswomen-wives on an assignment of their own. Others plan on finding work in the host country. Still others are unable to secure work and must find ways to fill an area of their life that was once taken up with career.

Ask your spouse to consider the following to help put the situation in perspective when judging the pros and cons of an international move.

Evaluating the Situation
• Does the host country allow both spouses to work, or only the one on an international assignment?
• What work options are available for him in the host country?
• How will his long-term career goals be affected if he takes an extended leave from his job?
• How will the potential loss of his income affect family finances?
• How might the assignment change your relationship with each other or his relationship with the children?
• What other opportunities does he have for creating a meaningful life (educational opportunities, volunteer work, caring for the children) if he's not employed?

Some husbands manage to turn their wives' international assignments into opportunities for personal growth or career enhancement. By accompanying his wife to the United States, Myriam Botero's husband was able to earn a master's degree in international management to boost his marketability. When he returns home to Colombia, he is convinced he'll secure a better job than the one he left. Mary Uppgren's husband, Fred, knew the job market in England precluded him from finding work as a hotel manager. So he occupied himself managing the house, enhancing his son's education, and acting as family tour director.

THE "LOOK-SEE" TRIP

Your company will probably offer you a "look-see" or decision-making trip to the host country designed to help you decide whether or not to accept the assignment. As such, it will often include a whirlwind of business orientation activities, including company meetings, facility tours, and dinner parties with future bosses and colleagues.

A look-see trip also serves other purposes. You can meet with relocation specialists; learn about housing, schools, shopping, customs, and entertainment; familiarize yourself with the city and transportation; and learn more about the country.

The look-see trip is truly the time to ask yourself, "Will I ever regret doing this?" "Will I ever regret *not* doing it?" This is your opportunity to do the legwork necessary to clinch your decision. Consider all the angles of every question or concern you have. Make lists of pros and cons. Face up to all the tough questions you haven't had the information for—or the heart enough—to ask yourself.

If you have already accepted the assignment, a look-see trip can serve as the opportunity to take care of the necessary logistics for ensuring a smooth move to the new country. The next chapter will examine those logistics in detail.

Look-See Trip Activities
•   Explore school options for your children. A relocation services company can put you in touch with local schools. Your options might include public, private, or international schools. International schools enroll primarily children of expatriates, and classes are often taught in English. Make appointments with the schools' headmasters so you can see the school facilities and ask about teaching methods, curricula, after-school activities, and so on.

• If you have a child with special needs, be sure to make time to find the right school and therapy providers. If necessary, also make arrangements for managing such special medical needs as allergies or asthma, physical therapy, medication, counseling, or psychotherapy overseas.

• Identify your housing options. Whether to buy or rent, or how to find a realtor are high-priority items (see Chapter 27 for more on housing). You'll also want to check out the availability and types of furnishings and appliances. And get the lowdown on neighborhoods. If you're a single woman on an international assignment, you may be interested in apartment buildings or complexes close to work, with security systems or personnel. Such living arrangements provide some built-in possibilities for socializing—and for help, should the water shut off one morning, or you wake up to below-zero temperatures and ten feet of new snow.

• Find out about health-care professionals and facilities. Your proximity to these facilities may be especially important if your assignment takes you to a rural area. Brenda Wyley says of her family's decision to relocate from California to rural Mexico, "Our first priority was deciding whether we could live with the consequences if one of our kids got sick. Would we be able to evacuate if need be? The company said they'd send a plane for us but sometimes you can't fly if you're sick. We knew in a situation like that our children would be at risk without proper medical care."

FINANCIAL CONSIDERATIONS

The glory days of the golden carrot for international assignments are over. As one expatriate services director states, "Many companies no longer provide an international-assignment premium to entice an employee, because they consider the assignment part of a natural path of career enhancement."

Since financial security is no longer a given, you must "do the numbers" as part of your decision-making process. This will help you determine whether the assignment meets your financial objectives. Here's some consolation. Many companies take careful steps—through pre-assignment interviews, written documents, and helpful networking—to ensure that you understand the financial challenges of living overseas before accepting the assignment.

Assignment Letter

Corporations commonly use the assignment letter to address financial and other issues related to the international assignment. Whether or not you receive an assignment letter, the points below are essential for you to consider and discuss with your employer prior to accepting their offer.

- Assignment start date
- Length of assignment
- Compensation
    Base salary (including date performance and salary review)
    Profit sharing
    Bonuses
    Continuation of benefits
    Medical/dental/vision insurance
    Disability insurance
    Pension-plan participation
    Vacations/holidays/maternity and family leave
    Tax equalization
- Availability of cross-cultural and language training before and after the transfer
- Allowances (discretionary depending on company, job, and host country)
    Goods and services allowances (to cover cost-of-living differences)
    Foreign housing allowance
    Hardship allowance
    Property management (if you rent your home while on assignment)
    Car allowance
    Education allowance (for children)
    Relocation allowance (to set up your new household)
    Emergency leave
    Dependent family member visits
    Home leave
    Tax planning (to cover taxes incurred on income from dividends and interest, spousal income, stock-option income, and sale of U.S. residence and purchase of foreign residence)
- Relocation
    House-hunting trips
    Moving-expense reimbursement (to/from)
    Temporary-living expenses
    On-site orientation assistance (to acclimate your family to daily life in the host country)
- Repatriation
    Services, allowances, and assistance available to help you and your family readjust to life in your home country

Job security (to ensure your return to a position of equal or greater standing)

(*Source:* Genevieve M. Deich and Robert B. Klein, Ernst & Young, LLP, "Personnel and Tax Challenges for Companies Going International," *Journal of Corporate Accounting and Finance,* Summer 1990.)

Compensation

Let's zero in on the financial components of the assignment letter.

- *Salary.* According to Lesa Mellis, director of expatriate services for a major accounting firm, "Most companies will keep your overseas salary equal to your salary at home. The base salary should reflect merit pay or promotional increases, if applicable."
- *Cost Equalizers.* They may be added to your base salary, if they'll help you maintain your standard of living. Compensation may also include a goods-and-services allowance to cover excess costs of living overseas as well as a housing allowance for excess housing costs in a host country.
- *Tax Equalization.* Overseas you'll probably be liable for tax in both your home and host countries. Tax equalization is therefore a must, which means you will pay no more or no less income and social-security tax than you would have paid had you remained in the home country earning your normal compensation package and personal income. Tax-equalization policy should accompany your assignment letter (with sample, hypothetical tax calculations for your review).
- *Additional Tax Liability.* Tax rates vary among countries, with stiff penalties for nonpayment. Your employer will probably assume responsibility for payment of any additional tax liability (foreign and home income, state and social-security taxes) you'll incur. All taxes you'll pay are based on a hypothetical stay-at-home tax. The difference between the actual and stay-at-home tax is borne by the company. In most cases, however, filing tax returns in both countries (home and host) is your responsibility, not your company's.
- *State Tax Considerations.* Your company may insist that you terminate state residency while on the assignment, so you're not subject to actual state taxes. However, many companies continue to charge hypothetical state tax as part of tax equalization to help offset host-country taxes. Conversely, some states are becoming more assertive in defining criteria necessary to break state residency and escape liability for state taxes.

- *Spousal Allowances.* Investigate whether your employer will make up for the loss of your spouse's earnings. Frequently, employers will not cover this, so consider the financial impact of losing that income. Also, find out whether your company will provide tax equalization for your spouse if he finds employment in the host country.
- *Benefits.* Make sure the company has structured your employment arrangement so that you can continue to participate in 401K, profit-sharing, and pension plans while overseas. Review vacation and holiday time. And ask about maternity and family leave in case you become pregnant and have a child while on assignment or a family member becomes seriously ill.
- *Treaties.* When possible, your company should utilize social security tax treaties between your home and host countries so you and your employer can continue to pay home social security tax instead of the host equivalent.
- *Other Reimbursements.* Check whether your compensation package includes a relocation allowance (a lump sum to cover the miscellaneous costs you'll accrue on the way to the host country and once you've arrived) and financial assistance with school tuition.

SUGGESTED READING

- *Accounting firms* like Arthur Andersen & Co., Deloitte & Touche, Price Waterhouse, and other large firms offer detailed guidebooks on taxation and working abroad. These publications are usually free.
- *The Adventure of Working Abroad: Hero Tales from the Global Frontier* by Joyce Sautters Osland (Jossey-Bass Publishers, San Francisco, 1995). Sautters Osland, who spent fourteen years abroad, recounts the stories of the courageous expatriates who are exploring today's global frontier. The book describes the highs and lows of the overseas experience as well as the personal growth that expatriates enjoy. The book also gives insights and tips for adjustment to a new culture, a new work environment, and difficulties of repatriation.
- *Americans Abroad: A Handbook for Living and Working Overseas* by John Z. Kepler, et al. (Greenwood Praeger Publishers, Westport, CT, 1983). Moving, housing, health, children, adaptation, legal, departure, and readjustment are all addressed, along with profiles of seven major world cities. The authors are two couples with extensive overseas experience.

- *Craighead's International Business, Travel, and Relocation Guide to 71 Countries*, 7th edition (Gale, Detroit, 1994–95). Offers general tips on travel, relocation, and safety, with country-specific sections.
- *Moving Abroad: A Guide to International Living* by Virginia L. McKay, 2nd edition (Intercultural Press, Inc., Yarmouth, ME, 1992).
- *Moving and Living Abroad* by Sandra Albright, Alice Chu, and Lori Austin (Hippocrene, New York, 1986).
- *Moving Your Family Overseas* by Rosalind Kalb and Penelope Welch (Intercultural Press, Inc., Yarmouth, ME, 1992). Advice on informing your children of the move, look-see trips, living quarters, servants, social life, and reverse culture shock when repatriating.
- "Personnel and Tax Challenges for Companies Going International" by Genevieve M. Deich and Robert B. Klein, *Journal of Corporate Accounting and Finance,* Summer 1990.
- *Updates* series (Intercultural Press, Inc., Yarmouth, ME). Examples of countries offered in this book series include Belgium, France, Saudi Arabia, Japan, Hong Kong, and Germany. The books give a thorough coverage of the needs and issues of families relocating overseas.
- *Women's Guide to Overseas Living* by Nancy J. Piet-Pelon and Barbara Hornby (Intercultural Press, Inc., Yarmouth, ME, 1992). Addresses important relocation issues for women and their families—culture shock, stress, loneliness, and staying healthy.

27

PREPARING FOR YOUR
LIFE ABROAD

As you contemplate your transfer to a new life of work and play abroad—
whether you're alone or going with your family—fear, at times paralyzing
fear, is often a big factor. You can deal with it and overcome it—the key is to
be prepared.

From the moment you accept your company's international job offer, you
must begin to manage a wide variety of preparations. Most transferees agree
that there is never enough time to get it all done before the move, especially
when you, and probably your spouse, are working full time until your move.
The key is organizing yourself and your family and then getting started on
moving arrangements as quickly as possible.

This chapter provides an overview of the preparations to consider as you
move your family, your life, and your household overseas:

- Securing overseas housing
- Making school arrangements for your children
- Completing the necessary paperwork
- Making financial and legal arrangements
- Sorting and packing your belongings
- Getting to know your host country
- Mobilizing a professional support system

If you're a list maker, the overseas assignment is your dream come true. If
you're not, now is a good time to start learning to love lists. Numerous publications on moving domestically and overseas, available at bookstores and
libraries, will supply you with detailed information on making complete "to-
do" lists and time lines. One is *Moving: A Complete Checklist and Guide for
Relocation* by Karen G. Adams (Silvercat Publications, San Diego, CA, 1994).

175

Adams believes the frustration of international moves can be reduced through careful organization. Her book is a collection of to-do lists, schedules, forms, and pointers that cover the complete range of tasks required for moving. Moving and storage companies, as well as relocation companies, also provide helpful lists of reminders.

HOUSING

"Should I sell my home or rent it?" This is a tough call. You'll probably deliberate at length before making your final decision. It's a difficult decision but a good one to get off the list because so many other arrangements will hinge on it.

Take a hard look at your family's needs over the course of the assignment. Before moving to Germany, one executive and her husband sold their house. "My family was growing, so my husband and I knew our house would need to be totally different when we got back," she says. "Also, we had just redone it and it was in beautiful condition and we weren't eager to rent."

Very few people are eager to become absentee landlords, so be sure to examine the responsibilities and risks carefully before you choose this option. Because returning home after an assignment to the same house can be a source of stability and comfort for some families, many employers will accommodate this desire by paying for a property-management firm to handle your house as a rental property while you are on assignment. *Note:* If you decide to rent your house, upgrade and update your homeowner's insurance.

If you decide to sell your house, be sure to consider company policy and tax rules regarding that sale. You potentially have four years (while on assignment the regular two-year period is suspended for up to two additional years) to purchase and occupy a new home that costs at least as much as the old house or you risk being subject to a capital-gains tax.

In the meantime, if you've sold your home, you need to think about investing the proceeds in a low-risk investment to make sure you don't lose the principal. Do this immediately after selling and before leaving the country. And keep that money in the United States. If you invest in another country, the value of foreign currency could shift during your assignment, causing you to lose your principal. You could also increase tax-equalization costs for your employer if you invest in a host country.

Finding the perfect accommodations in your host country may be simple, if you're very lucky, or it may take a lot of work. One woman's employer worked through a real estate company to find her housing in Tokyo, meeting nearly all of her faxed specifications, which included a single-family house in a neighborhood within biking distance of her childrens' schools. On the other hand, another woman's husband had to drive the Johannesburg neighborhoods of South Africa on his own, scouting out real estate signs, contacting agents, and viewing houses himself.

SCHOOL ARRANGEMENTS

If you did not make school selections on your look-see trip prior to accepting your transfer, you may wish to consider working with a relocation-services company or an organization that specializes in finding schools for international transferees. One is SchoolMatch of Westerville, Ohio (614-890-1573). It offers information and counseling services to expatriate families searching for the ideal community and school(s) for their children.

Once you've made your school choice, you need to begin making arrangements for such things as:

- Uniforms
- Transportation
- After-school care or activities
- Tutoring (to bring your children up to speed in certain subjects, especially language, if necessary)
- School supplies or other required equipment
- Medical exams and forms

If possible, during the look-see visit, try to make a videotape of your children's school(s), both inside and out. Include some shots of the school uniform, recreation facilities, and the surrounding neighborhood. Let your children see the video well before the move since it will help them feel more prepared for their new school environment.

PAPERWORK AND DOCUMENTS

- Forward mail—The U.S. Post Office forwards all first-class mail free of charge for one year; notify creditors of your address change; fill out a form at the post office; and cancel any magazine subscriptions that you don't want forwarded.

- Get required inoculations and shots for all members of the family and obtain written records to take with you.
- Send out a change-of-address postcard to family and friends so you can receive mail from them as soon as possible after your transfer.
- Assemble all pertinent documents and keep them in a safe place away from movers so they aren't packed by mistake. Hand-carry these documents with you on the plane:

> Passports, visas, and work permits
> Birth certificates and certificates of citizenship
> Adoption papers
> Marriage certificates, divorce papers, child-custody papers
> Wills
> Driver's licenses
> Income tax records (for the past five years)
> Medical and dental records (including vaccination records)
> Personal and moving company inventory lists with insurance documents
> Medical and eyeglass prescriptions

FINANCIAL AND LEGAL ARRANGEMENTS

Confirm financial and legal considerations with your banker, broker, accountant, and lawyer to ensure that you're prepared for any situation. Here are some things they likely will advise you to do:

- Update your will. An attorney familiar with the laws in your host country can make sure your exposure to estate tax in the host country is minimized.
- Secure a power of attorney who can sign legal documents on your behalf while you're overseas.
- Consult with your broker about handling overseas transactions if you want to continue buying and selling stocks and bonds.
- Insure any valuables (jewelry, musical instruments, furniture, art) you plan to take with you.

SORTING AND PACKING

Deciding what to take along is a time consuming, often emotional process. You have to separate all your belongings, itemize for insurance, and decide what goes into storage and what gets shipped overseas. You will have to figure out what you need to live for the next week, the next three weeks, the next month, the next two years.

One savvy transferee advises videotaping the inside of the house you will live in during your look-see trip—this is tremendously helpful for deciding what to take and what to put in storage.

Some transferees choose emotional and personal things to help them feel at home in an unknown environment. These might include furniture, books, china, and pictures. Others decide to rent furniture abroad, or live in furnished housing. Unfortunately, you may have no choice but to ship your furniture if you can't locate a store or agency in your host country that rents furniture. Think carefully about taking anything of financial or sentimental value because of security issues. And family heirlooms are safest when left at home.

Other families take a more comprehensive approach to moving overseas. "When we move we pretend we're moving forever," says one experienced transferee from Ireland. "We don't believe in putting anything into storage, because that's putting your life on hold. It's important that we have everything with us." There are risks to this approach. When the 1989 earthquake hit California, she and her family were living three miles from its epicenter. All of her Waterford crystal, and many wedding gifts, were destroyed.

KNOW YOUR HOST COUNTRY

Your look-see trip provides you with a first-hand opportunity to explore many of the details you need to know about your host country before you make the final decision to move abroad. Nevertheless, you should also prepare yourself for recognizing and dealing with culture shock—an inevitable by-product of international assignments. Optimally, your company will provide your family and you with cross-cultural training, known as pre-departure or relocation training, well in advance of your moving date. Pre-departure training helps familiarize you with your host country's culture, lifestyle, and business protocol and the challenges of moving abroad. (See Chapter 30 for more information on culture shock and Chapter 32 for more on cross-cultural training.)

Cross-cultural training can also provide answers to questions like these:

Money and Banking.   Are you familiar with the country's bills and coins? Do you know how to make change? Where to get the best exchange rate? How to wire money? How to select a reliable bank? How to use your checking and savings accounts as well as debit and credit cards? Where to get the best interest rates?

Laws.   What are key laws that will apply to you and how do they differ from those in your home country?

Electricity.   Is the voltage of electric current different? Do you have the right adaptors and will your personal care appliances (hairdryer, contact-lens sterilizer) work with adaptors?

Transportation.   Does your host country rely on trains, subways, buses, bikes/mopeds, taxis? Will you be willing and able to use public transportation? How easy, safe, and reliable is it? Also, check on the availability of a car. The expense of having a car overseas is generally three times greater than in North America. If your company doesn't provide a car, they should compensate you for the cost of operating one you've bought or leased on your own. Make sure you know how to purchase gas, get your driver's license, interpret traffic signals, park, and deal with an accident.

Shopping.   What are business hours? Do people shop everyday? Where are the stores? What is shopping protocol? (For example, is it okay to sample food or haggle prices? What can you touch? What's the best time of day to buy specific food items?) What is the availability of goods and seasonal produce?

Health Care.   Will you be using public or private hospitals? How do you choose a doctor and dentist? Where are the pharmacies and will they fill your prescriptions? Are there any twenty-four-hour pharmacies? Do doctors make house calls? Who is paying for your health care? How do you call an ambulance and where will they take you? Who can give you reliable ob/gyn and pediatrician referrals?

Tipping.   When, and how much, do you tip waiters, hotel porters and chambermaids, taxi drivers, customs officers, parking attendants, and hair stylists?

Food/Water.   Is the water safe to drink? What foods should you avoid or prepare in special ways for safety reasons? When do people eat their meals, and what do they eat? What are the specialties of the host country? Are there specific meal traditions? When is cocktail hour? Are there special ways of preparing beverages like coffee and tea? Do table manners differ from those in your home country? Are there conversational taboos while eating? What is the local restaurant protocol? Are reservations necessary? Who seats you? Do you pay at the table or at the door?

Personal Appearance.   When and to whom is personal appearance important? How often do people bathe? What is the appropriate attire for business, dinner, and social engagements? Can women wear shorts, jeans, or tennis shoes in public? Is there special significance for various colors? What clothes will you need for climate changes? How will you clean your clothes?

Safety.   What are the most prevalent crimes and where do they occur? How can you increase your safety? Are abduction and kidnapping of nonlocals common? How about terrorist activity? What are local attitudes toward people from your home country? Do you have emergency numbers for police, ambulance, and fire? Do you know what areas to avoid? (For more on personal safety, see Chapter 4.)

Socializing.   How will you meet people and develop lasting relationships? What are popular social activities in the host country? How can you join a health club or place of worship? Is it OK to socialize with people from work? Is it appropriate to entertain in your home? How do men and women behave toward each other in personal and professional situations?

Sightseeing.   Do you know the tourist hot spots in your host country and how best to explore them? When can you take your vacation and how much time are you allowed? Where are the best places to take the kids? How can you find out about the places few tourists know about but locals enjoy?

PERSONAL AND PROFESSIONAL SUPPORT

Being prepared also means knowing that you're not the first person to take your family abroad on an international assignment. Before you leave, seek out support wherever you can find it. A spouse or other family members are logical choices. Try to find other families who have relocated to your future host country for insights and inside scoops on how to survive there.

Begin developing relationships with other businesspeople already at work in the host country—well in advance of your departure. You may have an opportunity if you're traveling to and from your host country on business before your actual long-term assignment begins. Get to know your host country colleagues in advance, if possible, so they can welcome you when you arrive.

Finally, begin seeking out possible support for your family in the area where you'll be living. Perhaps there is a group of expatriate families who socialize together and are anxious to help newcomers ease into the culture. Experienced expatriates are often happy to introduce you to their "local" friends so that you can quickly make personal connections with people of your host country.

SUGGESTED READING

- *Craighead's International Executive Travel and Relocation Service* (Craighead Publications, Darien, CT, 1993) "International Executive's Passport to Over 70 Countries." This is updated monthly and it explains local business customs, visa and pre-departure requirements, currency exchange, transportation, and travel tips. It is geared more toward business travelers than tourists.
- *Intercultural Press* offers many excellent country-specific guides. Call or write for a free quarterly catalog. Address: P. O. Box 700, Yarmouth, ME 04096. Phone: 207-846-5168. Fax: 207-846-5181. E-mail: interculturalpress@mcimail.com.
- *Local Expert* series (Strategic Mapping, Inc., Santa Clara, CA). This is a software mapping series for 100 cities around the world. It indicates mail and fax services, protocol, messenger services, resources, secretarial services, service centers, and translations. Cost is $99 for the program; each city map is about $20. Call 800-442-8887, extension 1011.
- *Survival Kit for Overseas Living* by L. Robert Kohls (Intercultural Press, Inc., Yarmouth, ME, 1984). "A practical, lively guide filled with do-it-yourself instructions for making sure when you go abroad you remain effective and healthy and, above all, enjoy yourself."
- *Tips for Americans Residing Abroad,* Superintendent of Documents (U.S. Government Printing Office, Washington, D.C.) S/N 044-000-02024-6. $1.00. Information on dual citizenship, tax regulations, voting, and overseas consular services.
- *U.S. Customs Service* brochures. Free. Includes such titles as "Know Before You Go," "Importing a Car," "Travelers' Tips on Bringing Food, Plant and Animal Products to the U.S.," and "Trademark Information for Travelers." These brochures will help you avoid problems when re-entering the United States.

28

FAMILY MATTERS

After a long flight, Anne Greene and her children—Laura, 14, and Alex, 11—arrived at their hotel in Tokyo. Hungry and tired, they began walking around looking for a restaurant in which Anne, who had a working knowledge of Japanese, could order. But Anne couldn't find one. After forty minutes, she recalls, "I started to sweat. I started to get a pit in my stomach. I thought, what have I done? I have brought my children to a place where I can't even feed them."

International assignments pose many challenges. But contending with a spouse or child's unhappiness—while you're making your own adjustments to a new culture, new job, and new life—can be the greatest challenge. According to a survey of international managers conducted by the Society for Human Resource Management and Commerce Clearing House, one of the worst aspects of transferring overseas is family problems. Expatriates agree that it is impossible to have an unhappy family and a happy overseas assignment.

Difficulties don't just happen the first night, week, or month. Greene finally found a restaurant that first evening and all was well. Later, however, Laura's problems with school and culture shock threatened the family's stability—not to mention Greene's success in her assignment. Family problems can also be caused by a spouse or child's separation from their home culture, friends, or extended family.

Multinational corporations are realizing the importance of family stability and happiness during an employee's overseas assignment. To help ensure a family's adaptation, cross-cultural and language training are becoming a standard part of compensation packages. Training can help dispel children's fears of foreign foods, people, and customs; help them affirm and understand their own culture; and make it easier for them to talk about their fears and excitement. (See Chapter 32 for more on the importance of cross-cultural and language training.)

FINDING FULFILLMENT: ALONE AND WITH FAMILY

The nucleus of family is extremely important during an overseas assignment. You must respect each other's situations, and that respect begins with knowing your own feelings, limitations, and skills and how and when to communicate them.

Some Guidelines
- Family stability is critical to your success.
- A healthy balance between work and family in the early stages of the assignment is crucial, and you must stick to it.
- Limited travel during the first three to six months overseas (if at all possible) will ease the cultural adjustments you and your family are making.
- Good business communication skills can work at home. Your spouse needs you to be a good listener. Take his problems seriously and work with him to develop solutions.
- All family members have equal say and power in determining the family's quality of life.

Before leaving, it's a good idea for everyone in the immediate family to clarify their expectations, fears, and doubts. You can do this by taking the time—as a family—to complete the following exercises.

Exercise 1: The Pros and Cons

You and, if relevant, your spouse, and older children can complete a list of pros and cons about moving overseas. Everyone experiences some losses and some gains, and it helps to put those thoughts down on paper.

Losses and Gains When Going Abroad
Losses might include:

- Leaving your home
- Leaving family and friends

- Initial loss of independence
- Language fluency
- Familiar roles and routines

Gains might include:

- A broader perspective about life and work
- New friends
- A new lifestyle
- A new language
- Travel
- A new identity with new roles and responsibilities
- New experiences you never expected to have
- Learning about a foreign country and culture
- Time alone with yourself and with family
- A chance for soul-searching and reflection
- Time to reevaluate your life and priorities
- An opportunity to cultivate new interests

Take a good look at your own list. As you'll probably see, the list of gains is usually much longer than the list of losses.

Exercise 2: Finding Happiness

Next, brainstorm ways of finding happiness or fulfillment in the new country. Actively pursue the ideas that will help you realize the "gains" you listed. Here are some sample strategies.

- Network with others at work.
- Tap into the international transferee or expatriate community.
- Take the time to be accepted by others by building trust and credibility according to cultural values; getting the proper endorsements and introductions; creating and maintaining the right image.
- Get involved with groups that engage your interests and hobbies, as well as organizations, health clubs, or places of worship.

"In creating a meaningful life abroad you have to take the initiative to do things outside of your work," says Vivien Godfrey, a single woman executive who came to the United States from Britain on a two-year assignment. "Do things you really love doing, and you'll meet people who also enjoy doing them."

Exercise 3: Personal Inventory

This personal-qualities inventory helps identify your current strengths and skills. These can help you and your family to cope during tough times abroad.

- What personal qualities, strengths, and skills do I have that will serve me and my family in the host country?
- What personal qualities, strengths, and skills do I need to better serve myself and my family in the host country?
- How will I acquire these qualities, strengths, and skills?

Exercise 4: Making Friends Abroad

Encourage your family to discuss some of the following ways to make friends in a new country.

- Start a discussion group with other international transferees who have similar interests (women's roles, children, hobbies, politics, etc.).
- Take language classes.
- Invite neighbors for walks or coffee.
- Take walks in your neighborhood.
- Sign up for classes at a local vocational school or community college or university.
- Volunteer for a local, national, or international cause.
- Become active in an international student exchange program or cultural exchange organization.
- Teach English.
- Get involved with a religious community of your choice.
- Encourage your children to make friends in the neighborhood so you can get to know their parents.
- Help an elderly neighbor.
- Get to know spouses or your spouse's colleagues.
- Seek out people from your own country who have an international network of friends.
- Be sincere.
- Show humility.
- Follow through with suggestions and ideas.
- Be a giver, not just a taker.

"The first thing to do after moving to another country is to join some sort of group or organization," adds Catherine Tenke Teichert, an assistant vice president of new business development for a U.S. financial institution. "I knew a Canadian ambassador's wife in Kuwait who had lived in Paris for many years. She was determined to make French friends and avoided expatriate women's leagues. Not once was she invited to a French home."

Karen Dorian, a single American woman and sales and marketing development manager, made friends by joining American clubs, chatting with neighbors, and finding a church community in which she was comfortable. "I truly jumped into the culture personally and professionally," she says. "Many North Americans stay close to home while on assignments. Get out and meet those local people! They'll help you."

THE OVERSEAS SPOUSE

Consider the following facts:

- Today, about 60 percent of North American married couples are dual-career couples.
- About half of U.S. transferees have spouses who worked before relocating. (*Source:* Windham International and the U.S. National Foreign Trade Council.)
- Global companies are expanding in areas of the world where spouses of expatriates have a tough time finding jobs, much less staying on their own career track.
- Of fifty-one U.S. multinational corporations surveyed, one-third allow international-commuter marriages to assist working spouses of employees transferred abroad. That number is likely to double in five years. (*Source:* a 1991 survey by Runzheimer International, Ltd., as reported in *the Wall Street Journal*.)

Nearly all prior research on spouse adjustment has focused on the wife's experiences as a "trailing" spouse. However, the situations in which expatriate wives have historically found themselves remain equally as difficult and intense for the growing number of husbands (working and nonworking) who accompany their wives on international assignments.

Some husbands find work in the same country without too much disruption to their careers. Others look for work once they've arrived in the host country; however, many countries will not grant work permits to so-called trailing spouses of either gender. To overcome this obstacle, some couples are choosing international commuter marriages. That way, both partners can continue on their career tracks, albeit in separate countries.

Some accompanying husbands, by choice or because they cannot find work, assume the role of "house-husband," taking charge of children and household duties much as wives have always done.

For the accompanying spouse, regardless of gender, extensive research confirms that:

- Spouse adjustment is the key to an employee's effectiveness during an international assignment.
- A spouse's dissatisfaction is the single most important reason for early return.
- The accompanying spouse needs to find meaning and happiness while being able to provide support to the working spouse.

Fred Valentine, who moved from the United States to London with five-year-old son Heath and wife Mary Upggren on her assignment, sums up the critical role of the spouse: "If you can't be a support to a working partner—providing emotional and job-related support, and help with stress and the kids—it will ruin both of your experiences overseas."

Turmoil When Living and Working Abroad Isn't Limited to North American Families

Marital discord and children's unhappiness are more common than not among European families transferred abroad. One study conducted by Settler International (which is affiliated with Europe Assistance, a European insurance company) shows that among expatriates the divorce rate is 49 percent higher than the rate for couples who don't transfer abroad. The study also shows that highschool students following the technical-education route experience a 50 percent higher failure rate. In total, the study shows, three couples out of five do not survive "in exile," even in "golden exile" (i.e., where there are many executive perquisites).

—Reported in the French magazine *L'Expansion* (September 1995).

Lack of Support

What makes spouse adjustment so difficult? Simply that, most often, a spouse faces adjustment challenges alone. Especially at the beginning of your assignment, you will simply not have much time or energy available for your spouse since your new job will provide a tremendous amount of stress and pressure. And, unlike your spouse, you'll already have some built-in professional support to help you through this critical initial adjustment period. A network of business acquaintances and colleagues will be immediately available to you. Most of your colleagues are likely to be tolerant of you and your mistakes while you learn the ropes. However, if your husband is not employed outside the home, he loses the structure of a daily routine and a built-in support network. In exchange, he faces an overwhelming array of role, relationship, and environmental changes. These changes include:

- *Loss of identity.* At first, he may feel as if there is no depth to his role. There may be little or no professional side to his life, and he may feel as though his new role as househusband is thankless and mundane.
- *Greater contact with the so-called "raw" culture or local people who may have little or no previous contact with people from other countries.* If he is in charge of shopping, settling the household, sightseeing, and child care, he will be more immersed in the culture than you. Because he copes with an unfamiliar culture and language on a daily basis, he may feel more anger and frustration at that culture. Local people are likely to be less tolerant and supportive of his mistakes. Here is where cross-cultural and language training can really help. A facility with the language will make a huge difference when asking questions, shopping, or using public transportation. (See Chapter 32 for more on language training.)
- *Isolation and lack of support systems.* Not only has he lost his professional support network, but he has no family or friends to help him out. That means he lacks close relationships outside your marriage. At the same time, you may be working longer hours and traveling more. It's up to him to make new friends, as he has none of the "instant" friends that you do at work.

Creating a New Life

As a result, trailing husbands often face a bottomless chasm between their needs and your ability and availability to meet those needs. Professor Nancy Adler of McGill University calls this "the availability gap."

In adjusting to a new culture, it's important for the trailing husband to:

- Know himself and what he wants out of the transfer and out of life.
- Take responsibility for creating the life he wants to live.
- Treat the move as permanent, no matter how temporary.
- Persevere and be patient.
- Begin language training immediately.
- Become the cultural specialist for the family. In other words take the role of one who plans most of the family's travels, outings to sporting events, entertainment venues and cultural institutions, and other adventures.

"It was never boring," says one expatriate husband. "We did constant cultural sightseeing, whether it was museums, art galleries, parks, or sports. I wanted our time abroad to be meaningful for my son. I wanted him to be aware of what another culture is all about—different food, languages, ways of dressing and behaving. My whole purpose was that he'd have a great time and realize something about another culture."

YOUR FAMILY'S EMOTIONAL
AND PHYSICAL NEEDS

A businesswoman and mother on an international assignment must not only balance the hours and stresses of a new and demanding job, along with the difficulties inherent to daily life in a new country, but she must also look after the physical and emotional health of her family in the new culture. This task, of course, begins long before leaving home. It starts while you're weighing the pros and cons of moving your family overseas. You can prepare for the emotional difficulties of moving by reviewing past events that may have affected your family's stress level and stability. Ask yourself:

- How many moves have we made?
- Where did we move to and from? Which moves were difficult and why?
- Were the children at a sensitive age or grade in school at the time of a difficult move?
- How did various family members handle the experience?
- Has divorce or separation or a family member's death occurred recently?

Whether you're single or have a partner and/or children, your overseas assignment will affect your extended family members and close friends. For single adults, friends often provide "family" support. Consider how extended family members and close friends will respond to the move as well. Ask yourself:

- Are we close to extended family?
- How often do we visit or communicate with close family and friends?
- What if we couldn't communicate with them so easily for a long period of time?
- How would moving to another country affect our relationship with our family?
- What obligations and responsibilities to extended family members and close friends would we leave behind? How could we resolve such obligations before leaving?
- How will we involve them in important personal issues, problems, or decisions we might face in the host country?
- How can we keep them up to date with the important personal changes and growth that we experience overseas?

Family Safety and Emergencies

Consider safety issues, too. Myriam Botero, a computer-application developer, was comfortable moving her family to Minneapolis because it was a safer city than Bogotá, Colombia. Conversely, Ellen Glatstein, an international marketing consultant who moved to South Africa as a result of her husband's assignment, was concerned about relocating her family to Johannesburg, where crime is on the rise. She had to consider how she might decrease the risks to herself and her family.

Prepare for home-based emergencies before you move. What will you do if a family member dies or has a serious illness or accident? If you'll be leaving behind aging parents, make sure you have a flexible visit-home schedule in case special needs arise. One woman's mother died while she was on assignment in New Zealand. "Fortunately," she explains, "my company's policy made dealing with family emergencies easier. So I never looked back or had regrets with regard to how the situation was handled."

Finally, make sure you also develop contingency plans for emergencies involving your property, banking, or investments.

YOUR KIDS' EXCELLENT ADVENTURE

Breaking the News

Break the news to your kids when you are together as a family. Present it as a decision that you and your spouse have carefully made together. Try to showcase it as exciting news—that you are lucky to be able to participate in this experience as a family. Allow your children to discuss their feelings, which may range from genuine excitement to raging anger. Avoid downplaying negative feelings; instead, try to empathize with them and offer to discuss coping techniques—when they're ready.

"Don't presume your young children understand the move," recommends Brenda Wyley, a well-traveled expatriate of Ireland. "They only understand by doing. The best thing you can do is play games, like 'let's take a trip.' And make the prospect very positive, as in 'look at all the fun things you'll do and learn.' We tried out 'what ifs,' " she explains. "Like, 'What if after a week you decide you don't want to be here?' If they said, 'We want to go home,' then we talked about that." At the same time, Brenda notes, "You can't stress enough that they'll still have their same bed, same toys, same clothes. They don't believe you until you arrive, and then they say, 'Mom, look, my same bed, my same toys.' "

Getting children excited about the adventure ahead is a good way to prepare them for life abroad, ease departure, and settle them into a new culture. To this end, take pictures of local sights during your look-see trip. That way, your children will have something visual to help them understand where they are going.

Talk to your children's teachers about including a unit on your future host country in their classwork. Perhaps your children could share with their class an album of photos from your look-see trip. Also, help your children assemble a list of friends' addresses so they can have pen pals after the move.

Tips to Help Children Prepare for Moving Overseas

- Help them pack favorite things to take along.
- Visit favorite places with them before leaving.
- Throw a farewell party.
- Assemble a scrapbook about home, school, family, and friends.
- Make flight arrangements together.
- Develop plans with friends and family who can visit.

Packing Your Child's Overnight Case

Air travel, even with small children, can be enjoyable—if you're prepared. Plan carefully what you'll carry on the airplane to help the children feel comfortable and keep them entertained. Items might include:

- Their favorite toys
- Disposable training pants if your child is only recently toilet trained; time changes can upset training
- Comfort items such as a special blanket or teddy bear
- Pajamas, toothbrush and toothpaste, and washcloth (on extra-long flights) and extra changes of clothes in case of spills or sickness
- Something to suck or chew on to relieve discomfort from cabin pressure (pacifier or bottle for babies and toddlers; gum for school-age children)
- A few favorite books, magazines, or coloring books
- A few fun surprises or games, and, of course, snack food
- A reusable water bottle for thirst and quick cleanups

As one experienced mother says, "I try to have a new game, toy, book, or other diversion along for each hour of the plane trip. That makes a long ride a lot less bumpy!" Also, don't forget motion-sickness medicine for your child. You may need to administer more than one dose during long flights. Before takeoff, gather a few motion-sickness bags and put them within easy reach so you can react quickly.

Settling In

Once you arrive, you'll be consumed with getting to work, setting up your household, and adapting to your new country and community. Some women opt to take it slowly, giving themselves the first month or two to settle the household; others like to have theirs ready within days.

"During the first few days it's crucial that things go smoothly," says one savvy expatriate. "Planning is so important. It's so important to start properly to set a positive tone. Usually we're unpacked and living in the house two days after we arrive. This helps us get into the groove because we're up and running." But this also means allocating some time at the beginning of your assignment just to get organized.

One priority many agree on is quickly settling their children. Children need lots of time and attention and a feeling of security to help them adjust. And families have many creative ways of helping children settle in quickly and comfortably. It's a good idea to set up their bedrooms first, followed by family areas you will share in common, such as the kitchen and den. This will help give your children that sense of security and continuity.

After numerous international transfers, Brenda and Shay Wyley have developed a process that works well for them. Brenda and her two children do not make the move until all their things are shipped and placed in the new house. Shay goes ahead to start his new job and arrange the house. Brenda comes a month later with the children on a flight that lands in daylight hours, "so it's not so dark and scary for the kids, arriving and moving into a dark, new house." Shay picks them up, makes the kids lunch, and puts them down for their afternoon nap—leaving quiet time for the couple to catch up.

If possible, obtain a car and a map early on, so you can learn the area a little bit before having the pressure of getting things done. It's easier to discover how to get around while you expect it to be frustrating, rather than waiting until later when you think you should be over this hurdle or when you are in a hurry.

A Family Opportunity of a Lifetime

Set priorities before you become caught up in a whirlwind of work, social and school events, and other obligations. First, settle the children in play activities and school as quickly as possible. Then make sure you have time to relax and explore your new setting with your family.

One American family found that they spent more time together on assignment than they probably would have at home. They didn't have the obligations they formerly faced—to friends, school, and community—so they explored the city, hiked, and traveled. A family can really pull together when it's in an environment with lots of unknowns. As one internationally employed mother explains, "At a time when families are usually flying apart—the teenage years—I felt really lucky that I had this opportunity to spend time with my kids."

The Glass Is Half Full

As a family, try to prepare for each international move by considering worst-case scenarios, from homesickness to health problems, to education, to loneliness. Once you identify these situations and emotions, they are easier to cope with. You can't assume you'll be fine because many times you won't.

But most families prevail and thrive as a result of openness and a positive attitude toward the experience.

Looking at situations negatively can be habit forming. Once that happens, it's harder to get yourself out of such a rut. You don't want to regret this exciting time in your life. Always try to be realistic. But do maintain a positive, upbeat attitude. "Attitude is everything," says Brenda Wyley. "For us, the glass is always half full."

29

ON-THE-JOB CHALLENGES

Congratulations. During your international assignment you get to live in two worlds—that of the home office (where you came from) and the international office (where your assignment is). When you favor the home office's take on things, your international colleagues may think you're a spy, "one of them." Animosity, isolation, even sabotage of your projects can result. Conversely, when you try to explain to the home bosses how things really work in Tanzania or Paris, they may raise their eyebrows, saying, "She's going native. We can't trust her." You could be excluded from important meetings or dropped from key communications.

Here's how to walk the tightrope between the home office and the international office as you face the five unique challenges of an international assignment.

CHALLENGE 1: LIVING WITH TWO REALITIES

- *Keep in touch with both realities.* Don't favor one or the other. You need both perspectives to meet your objectives.
- *Bridge the gap.* You're the liaison—often a thankless task. The most important contribution you may make during this assignment is taking the time to help both sides understand each other.
- *Invite your superiors to your new location.* Explain how things work. Show them the good, the bad, and the ugly. Paint a realistic portrait of the challenges and limitations you face daily and demonstrate how you achieved success.
- *Make sure the locals know you have headquarters' support.* This will add to your credibility and help you secure local cooperation when the going gets tough.

- *Don't forget whose side you're on.*   Remember who sends your paycheck—don't lose sight of your employer's objectives. Balance your responsibility to the home office against the demands of your local situation.
- *Find a "cultural interpreter."*   This can mean one or two trustworthy people outside the job, and one in the workplace, who can help you understand how business works in the new culture and why people do the things they do.
- *Set realistic expectations on both sides.*   Get consensus before you start, and keep checking in.
- *Understand all policies and procedures before you go overseas.* Know the local protocol for hiring and firing as well as any legal complications.
- *Keep communicating and educating.*   The more both sides communicate, the more likely you are to succeed.

CHALLENGE 2: STAYING IN THE LOOP WITH THE HOME OFFICE

- *Stay plugged in.*   Communicate regularly with colleagues and bosses back home. Out of sight is usually out of mind on the international assignment.
- *Set up a support network at headquarters before leaving.*   Who can help you at home when the going gets tough? Who in personnel can assist you in case of emergency? Find a corporate mentor or advocate who will keep you up to speed on corporate changes and bring your name up frequently to management.
- *Take regular business trips back to the home office.*   Nothing takes the place of in-person appearances for demonstrating your commitment to the organization and advertising your overseas accomplishments.
- *Invite your home-office colleagues to your international site.*   They can then see how you successfully balance the resources and constraints that affect your ability to meet objectives.
- *Share your success or new information with the home office frequently.* Promoting your achievements and know-how will keep your name "top of mind." This is critical for assuring a meaningful post when you return from your assignment.
- *Get regular performance reviews.*   Make sure your job description and objectives don't change without your knowledge or involvement.

CHALLENGE 3: GETTING MORE
LANGUAGE TRAINING

Why? Because without language training:

You are at the mercy of others.   Information can be screened, altered, even censored from you. You're not an equal in the communication process, so you can't be an equal business partner.

You lose credibility.   It's a fact that when someone doesn't speak our language we somehow think she's not quite as smart as we are.

You waste time.   You need translators, interpreters, or other helpful intermediaries just to greet someone.

CHALLENGE 4: DEALING WITH CHANGES IN
YOUR PRIORITIES AND GOALS

Initially, you may be determined to accomplish your objectives as fast as possible. Remember, though, that while change may be a vital aspect of the North American business culture, many overseas cultures resist it. Proceed with caution.

The longer you stay, the more you may start questioning some of the home office's goals and objectives. Or you begin to think that there are faster, cheaper, or easier ways of attaining those goals—things the home office just doesn't know about. This is normal, but, again, proceed with caution.

Work through the chain of command—don't bypass it. Do this even if you think you understand better than the home office what your site needs to be successful. If you bypass the proper channels, your international assignment could come to an abrupt and unhappy conclusion.

CHALLENGE 5: BUILDING MULTICULTURAL
TEAMS THAT WORK

- Concentrate on this task from the beginning to ensure success.
- Allow for the time and training needed to build effective global teams.
- Remember that much of the time you'll spend overcoming people's differences—whether they relate to culture, gender, or race. It's your job to

convince people they have enough in common to meet the company's business objectives.

• Have your team—together—identify common goals and objectives from the outset. Agree on the steps and fallback positions for achieving them.

• Encourage the team to develop and adhere to norms for communication and conflict resolution.

SUGGESTED READING

- *Cultural Environment of International Business* by V. Terpstra (South-Western Publishing, Cincinnati, 1978).
- *International Business Communication* by David Victor (HarperCollins Publishers, New York, 1991).
- *International Dimension of Organizational Behavior* by Nancy J. Adler (Kent Publishing Company, Boston, 1986).
- *A Manager's Guide to Globalization* by Stephen H. Rhinesmith (Irwin Professional Publishing, Chicago, 1996).
- *Managing Across Borders* by Christopher A. Bartlett and Sumantra Ghoshal (Harvard Business School Press, Cambridge, MA, 1989). The guide offers practical approaches for addressing the challenges of today's global environment and focuses on how to organize worldwide and implement global strategies.
- *Managing Cultural Differences* by Philip R. Harris and Robert T. Moran (Intercultural Press, Inc., Yarmouth, ME, 1987).
- *Mindsets: The Role of Culture and Perception in International Relations* by Glen Fisher (Intercultural Press, Inc., Yarmouth, ME, 1988).
- *The New Expatriates* by Rosalie L. Tung (Ballinger Publishing Co., Cambridge, MA, 1988).
- *Dynamics of Successful International Business Negotiations* by Robert T. Moran and William J. Stripp (Gulf Publishing Co., Houston, TX, 1991).
- *How to Negotiate Anything with Anyone Anywhere Around the World* by Frank L. Acuff (Amacom—American Management Association, New York, 1993).
- *International Negotiation: A Cross-Cultural Perspective* by Glen Fisher (Intercultural Press, Inc., Yarmouth, ME, 1980).
- *Managing Intercultural Negotiations: Guidelines for Trainers and Negotiators* by Pierre Casse and Surinder Deol (Intercultural Press, Inc., Yarmouth, ME, 1985).
- *Riding the Waves of Culture* by Fons Trompenaars (Irwin Professional Publishing, Chicago, 1994).

30

CULTURE SHOCK

Culture shock is very much a reality for women in international business. Detect it early and you can isolate the events that make you feel disoriented or depressed, or find ways to alleviate or avoid those situations.

WHAT IS CULTURE SHOCK?

Cross-cultural expert Robert Kohls defines culture shock in his book *Survival Kit for Overseas Living:*

> The psychological disorientation most people experience when they move into a culture markedly different from their own. It comes from the experience of encountering ways of doing, organizing, perceiving or valuing things which are different from yours, and which threaten your basic, unconscious belief that your culture's customs, assumptions, values and behaviors are "right."

In other words, everything familiar to you—from routines, traffic patterns, food, and language, to value and belief systems—is gone. You feel as if the rug's been pulled out from under you. All your cultural cues are cut off and invalid. You may be functioning as an adult, but you feel like a helpless child. You're living with ambiguity and unknowns, questioning your own values and beliefs. As a result, you experience fatigue, frustration, discomfort, irritability, maybe even bitterness and resentment, and probably homesickness and depression.

For a time after her family moved from California to Mexico, one transferee became tired of hearing people speak a different language, of seeing nothing familiar, of studying every food label at the grocery store, of standing in line for milk. She was beginning to experience culture shock.

The combination and intensity of culture shock symptoms vary, depending on such issues as:

- The length of stay
- The purpose of the trip (tourist/business travel versus living in the country)
- Contact with the local or "raw" culture
- The number and type of cultural differences
- Finances and housing decisions (staying among other expatriates or living within the "raw" culture)

THE CULTURE SHOCK PROCESS

The Honeymoon

You may first sense culture shock as you are making preparations for your move. Once you arrive in your new country, this sense will probably be replaced by a honeymoon period. Culture shock effects are still limited at this point. All the country's sights, sounds, smells, and tastes may seem exciting, even romantic. Or hilarious.

Even though Anne Greene, a marketing executive for an international food company, knew some Japanese and had traveled in Japan prior to her assignment, she became frustrated with not being able to jump into her car and run errands. "I was walking everywhere because we didn't have a car, it was 100 degrees, and I didn't even know where to buy a wastebasket," she recalls. Plus, she couldn't read anything written in Japanese. This meant, among other things, that Greene couldn't run any of the appliances in her home. "Think of it," she recalls, laughing. "Every appliance in Japan—even the telephone—has a million buttons and you can't read them. Even the toilet had five different modes."

The Real Thing

Several weeks or months into the assignment, real culture shock sets in. Life in the new culture often seems more frustrating than it's worth. You will probably complain about everything. You can't find street addresses, you get lost, you don't speak the language, you panic, and you're self-critical when you realize how inadequate you feel. Sometimes it's one brief moment, sometimes it's a few minutes, sometimes it's an ongoing condition that leads to depression.

As one woman explains, "You're absolutely buried by the daily complications of life and the constant need to dig yourself out. It's mentally exhausting because there's no routine."

Symptoms of Culture Shock

Look for these warning signs:

- You become disoriented, listless, tired, moody, overwhelmed, unproductive. You feel isolated.
- Your problems seem bigger than life. For example, if you can't complete a seemingly simple task, you blow up.
- You find yourself living in extremes: you stay away from people and new places, you cry or get angry a lot, you can't sleep except during the day, and so on.

Culture shock also affects your professional life:

- Communication breaks down between you and your colleagues at the home and host offices.
- You start making ill-considered decisions, or use poor judgment.
- You can't fulfill your job responsibilities in a timely, efficient manner.

If you don't deal with culture shock positively, it can cause friction that may damage your most important business relationships. In extreme cases, culture shock can result in severe depression and personal problems.

COPING WITH CULTURE SHOCK

Eventually, as a means of self-preservation or survival, you'll begin a sometimes long, slow climb toward dealing with the culture. You'll realize that you can't change the local culture, even if it appears nonsensical, illogical, perhaps even dangerous. You'll start to identify aspects of the culture that you can appreciate or at least relate to. This is the beginning of acceptance.

To help you in that climb toward acceptance, look for support from both personal and professional acquaintances and from your company.

Find People Who Can Help You

It's important to find and talk to people who can provide moral support and assistance with routine tasks. Greene met a woman through her daughter's school who took her to a store where she could purchase household goods. One of her son's teachers, who lived nearby, escorted her around the neighborhood to various stores. And her boss's secretary stopped by on a Saturday and showed Greene how to work her appliances. Greene also joined a professional group called Foreign Executive Women, with the appropriate acronym FEW, of 200 women just like herself.

Overcome Communication Barriers

Surmounting language barriers or communication difficulties can also help ease you out of isolation. Continued language instruction is essential for both your family and you to further self-sufficiency at home and on the job. Even North American women who are transferred to English-speaking countries will encounter difficulties because of different vocabularies and communication patterns. For example, British formality often compels the British to tone down their enthusiasm to the point where you are unclear whether they are pleased or displeased with a given situation. Australians and Irish use communication to constantly reinforce their professional relationships. While you may think they are wasting precious time on chitchat, in reality they are reinforcing their loyalties and sharing useful information. North American women should carefully study and adapt to communication flow and protocol in their host countries to "stay in the loop" and thereby lessen these feelings of alienation and isolation.

In many countries, women need to take the initiative in communicating with others in business and establishing a social life. Don't wait for things to come to you. From a business standpoint, getting used to and being a good communicator with the telephone, fax machine, and e-mail are very important. "When you're off somewhere in the world and trying to get the job done and fit in, you've got to be very comfortable with really wanting to communicate. Overcommunicating is good," insists one international executive.

Enlist Your Company's Support

Your company should also help you through culture shock by:

- Giving you easy access to home via e-mail, fax, and interoffice mail.
- Educating you further about culture shock and providing support.
- Providing ongoing language instruction for you and your family.
- Giving you ample time to adjust to the new culture.
- Not expecting you to rush off on "global" trips while in the midst of culture shock.
- Problem-solving with you on a proactive basis.
- Directing you to a good host or mentor in your new country.
- Identifying social organizations and expatriate groups you might join to begin making friends and integrating into the local community.

Take Care of Yourself

Make time for relaxation and exercise. Eat healthy meals. Writing about your feelings and experiences in a journal can help, too. Balance social activities and restful time. And realize that you will make mistakes and look silly. At that point, you usually have two choices: get angry or laugh at yourself. Which feels better? Try to keep your sense of humor.

Culture Shock Is a Growth Process

After working through the phases of culture shock, you'll have a variety of new skills. Perceptions about yourself will also change. These changes might include:

- Becoming more independent, flexible, adaptive.
- Enjoying new experiences.
- Taking more responsibility for your adjustment.
- Identifying your own stereotypes and those others hold of you.
- Acquiring new cultural knowledge.
- Letting go of judgmental, intolerant behavior.
- Achieving maturity.
- Refining your decision-making skills.
- Gaining objectivity.

- Improving organizational and communication skills.
- Acquiring new language skills.

After working through culture shock, you'll find your horizons tremendously broadened—from politics to food, culture to body language, work habits to communications. You'll feel confident once again. You'll be full of new knowledge and experience. And you'll be anxious to return home and share everything you've learned with friends, family, and colleagues.

There's only one glitch—reverse culture shock. Chapter 31 covers repatriation and reverse culture shock in detail.

SUGGESTED READING AND RESOURCES

- *Culture Shock* by Adrian Furnham and Stephen Bochner (Methuen, New York, 1986).
- *Culture Shock! A Wife's Guide* by Robin Pasco (Graphic Arts Center Publishing Co., Portland, OR, 1993). (Part of the *Culture Shock!* series, which provides cross-cultural guidebooks for twenty-three countries.) This book helps wives of corporate transferees develop strategies for dealing with culture shock, general adjustment, socializing, making friends, working, and returning to the United States after the assignment. Husbands will find this interesting reading, too.
- *On Being Foreign: Culture Shock in Short Fiction* by Tom Lewis and Robert Jungman, eds. (Intercultural Press, Inc., Yarmouth, ME, 1986).
- *Culture Shock and the Problem of Adjustment in New Cultural Environments* by Kalvero Overg. From *Culture, Communications and Conflict: Readings in Intercultural Relations*, edited by Gary R. Weaver (Ginn Press, Needham Heights, MA, 1994).
- *Understanding and Coping with Cross-Cultural Adjustment Stress* by Gary R. Weaver. From *Culture, Communications and Conflict: Readings in Intercultural Relations*, edited by Gary R. Weaver (Ginn Press, Needham Heights, MA, 1994).
- *Host country orientation services* are located in many major cities around the world. One example is Focus Information Services, a nonprofit resource center for international residents in London. If you're relocating to London or nearby, contact Focus Information Services for all the answers to your questions about the "ins-and-outs" of living in London, including how to find goods and services, schools, medical care, courses, recreational activities, child care, and employment assistance. Focus of-

fers an information phone line, career networking, seminars, a lending library, newsletter, and a calendar of London events. Write to Focus at 13 Prince of Wales Terrace, London W8 5PG. Phone: 011-0171-937-0050; fax: 011-0171-937-9482.

- *The Art of Crossing Cultures* by Craig Storti (Intercultural Press, Yarmouth, ME, 1990).

31

REPATRIATION AND REVERSE CULTURE SHOCK

REPATRIATION PLANNING

Ideally, you should start to prepare for your repatriation before you transfer overseas. Realistically, you have all you can manage just seeing to the details of your move and starting a new job. Once you've got your culture shock under control and are functioning well in your job, you can start to plan for repatriation.

Some of the most immediate things you need to consider concern your household and family. These include:

Housing.   Where will you live? (If you've sold your house, will your company help you buy a new one?) Will you live in the same location and neighborhood? How far are you willing to commute? How much will housing cost on your return? What do you need to do to get a loan?

Schools.   Will your children return to their previous school? How will the level of difficulty and pace differ from the school they're attending in the host country? Would you considering enrolling them in an international school? What is the school's reputation and the likelihood of your children being accepted? What are the pros and cons? When does school begin and end? Is bus service available? What activities will your children participate in after school?

Transportation.   Will you by a car or lease one? Will you need to update your driver's license and car insurance? Do you need easy access to public transportation?

Money and Banking.   Where will you bank and what kinds of accounts do you need to set up? How will you transfer funds from your host country? What, if anything, do you need to do concerning your investments?

Health Care.   Will you have the same doctors when you come back? The same health insurance? For emergencies, which hospital will you go to? Where is the closest twenty-four-hour pharmacy?

Safety.   How have crime and types of crime changed since you left? What new safety precautions will you need to know? What neighborhoods will have become less or more safe?

Planning for the Job You'll Return To.   You should place this near the top of your repatriation "to-do" list. At least one year before your return date, initiate a discussion with your human resources representative and the director of the business group who sent you on assignment. Make a point to meet with them every time you visit home. Keep them informed of your developing interests and skills and learn about organizational changes. Strategize with them about where you might fit in the organization when you return.

TAKE CHARGE OF YOUR CAREER

There are serious risks to ignoring career planning while you're abroad. Leaving your career in the hands of others can lead to bitter disappointments and a stalled career.

Most companies assure the international transferee that an overseas assignment will advance her career. They tell her it will help her do her new job at home better because of the skills and expertise she will gain overseas, and will be a steppingstone to a higher position. It will increase her credibility among peers and superiors and probably lead to a promotion. In reality, only 46 percent of former expatriates are promoted when they return home. (*Source:* "The Trip Home" Kathryn Welds, *HRMagazine,* June 1991, p. 113.)

Returnees who find themselves in an undesirable job feel invisible. They sense that the company doesn't know quite what to do with them or doesn't appreciate the sacrifices they made for the organization. It seems as if the old saying "out of sight, out of mind" really is true. Relationships with supervisors, peers, and colleagues feel strained because they've returned with loads of ideas, suggestions, country knowledge, and improved management skills and no one appears interested.

Many repatriates also find their reentry job boring. It lacks the excitement, challenge, responsibility, authority, status, and autonomy they enjoyed overseas. In fact, their reentry job may have diminished responsibilities and decision-making power, with little incorporation of the international skills acquired abroad.

You can beat the repatriate blues if you are proactive and successful in securing a job that moves you up the career ladder and allows you to use the skills you've developed overseas.

EASING PROFESSIONAL REENTRY

Even if you return to a stimulating job, you may feel hopelessly behind with such new technology as e-mail, computer networks, voice mail, and Internet access. The key is to prepare for your return while you're abroad, by staying up to speed with changes and securing the professional support you need to make a smooth transition.

Tips for Professional Reintegration

•   Undergo repatriation training through a reputable cross-cultural training organization. (See Chapter 32 for information on cross-cultural training.)

•   Obtain accurate new information about corporate operations from your manager and human resources representative.

•   Use the same skills to adjust to the home office as you did when adjusting to the international office—anticipating and tolerating ambiguity, remaining open-minded, seeing the value of difference, and asking questions. Give yourself several months to adjust.

•   Incorporate special competencies developed abroad into your current position.

•   Try not to judge the home office against the international organization.

•   Establish your credentials and credibility with people in your new work group.

•   Share your frustrations with a trusted colleague who has successfully repatriated after an international assignment.

•   Be realistic when setting your goals and objectives. Build extra time into schedules so deadline stress isn't overwhelming.

•   Take time to evaluate and select the right opportunities. Forecast likely results and develop backup plans.

•   Break problems into manageable, sequential steps.

•   Participate in technical training to get "up to speed" on advancements in office technology.

•   Reestablish ties with former colleagues—but listen to them first before telling them about all your adventures! They have gone through important changes in their lives, too.

- Present work-oriented country and culture information to interested groups of co-workers.

REVERSE CULTURE SHOCK

Regardless of how long you've been away, you'll feel a jolt of reverse culture shock when you return home. Sometimes, reverse culture shock is more intense than culture shock because people don't anticipate it or believe it will occur.

Here's what you can expect. At your company's international office in the host country, you were at first part of the "minority," the "odd woman out." But you soon became a big fish in a small pond. You had a new identity from living in a foreign country, developing a variety of new job skills and responsibilities, and experiencing the growth process inherent in culture shock. After reentry or repatriation, however, you're once again the "odd woman out." You're now part of a huge organization with colleagues who haven't shared your experiences. You are confronted with changes in both the office as well as in your personal and home life. There may even be new business buzzwords you have to learn. Plus, colleagues and friends might look at you differently, as maybe a little dangerous, unnerving, or simply unknowledgeable. Your confusion, anxiety, or difficulties with reverse culture shock may reinforce this negative perception.

While dealing with reverse culture shock on the job, don't be surprised if you employ one of these common coping strategies:

- You struggle to regain your former status.
- You try to redefine your relationships based on new values you've acquired.
- You seek out new relationships because your values have shifted.
- You try to change others to fit "the new you."

For most women, an overseas assignment is a powerful, life-altering experience. It is therefore unrealistic to expect things to go "back to the way they were" before the transfer. "My personal and professional development experience during my two years in Japan was absolutely the pinnacle," says Anne Greene. "Japan was really hard at the beginning. But after I climbed out of the hole of culture shock, living and working there was just one incredible experience after another. It's been tremendously hard being back."

EASING PERSONAL REENTRY

Smoothing the personal process of readjusting to your home country will require effort, but the payoff is peace of mind, stronger personal relationships, and continued growth and learning.

While abroad, you should correspond regularly with colleagues, friends, and family at home. You're not the only one whose life has changed and you will receive more support from friends and family on your return if you acknowledge this. You should also stay on top of current events at home. If your goal is to slide back into the mainstream, you'll want to be *au courant* about news events, social trends, and popular culture. Newspapers, magazines, and occasional videotapes of TV shows and movies from home will keep you plugged into your culture.

After returning home:

• Take it easy. Readjustment takes time and energy; some experts compare it to a major life trauma (such as death or divorce) in its emotional intensity and duration.

• Communicate with family members about your feelings. Children especially need more attention. They may feel as punished, insecure, and inadequate on return as they did while adjusting to the host country.

• Find support for sharing feelings and experiences about living and working abroad. One way is to seek out other international "returnees" or expatriates. You may discover you have a lot in common.

• Incorporate skills you learned overseas into daily life.

• Participate in international activities in your community.

• Continue studying a foreign language and join a discussion group.

• Host international guests in your home.

• Maintain and continue friendships made abroad.

• Explore your neighborhood or city. Visit new museums and parks, try new restaurants, take up new activities.

• Write about your overseas experience.

• Enjoy travel, but recognize that constant travel may be a form of escape.

SUGGESTED READING

• *Cross-Cultural Reentry: A Book of Readings,* edited by Clyde Ausin (Abilene Christian University Press, Abilene, TX, 1986).

- *Going Home: A Workbook for Reentry and Professional Integration,* by Martha Denney (NAFSA, Washington, D.C., 1987).

32

CROSS-CULTURAL AND LANGUAGE TRAINING: DON'T LEAVE HOME WITHOUT THEM

WHY DO YOU NEED CROSS-CULTURAL AND LANGUAGE TRAINING?

Fact: Studies show that, in the last decade, as many as one-third of expatriates sent on international assignments have returned home early. Another one-third are "brown-outs"—they stay for the duration, but don't achieve the corporation's objectives.

Reason: The transferee, and/or her family, were unprepared and unable to live in the host country. In other words, they simply could not adapt.

Result: The cost to corporations falls between $2 and $2.5 billion a year, according to J. Stewart Black, a professor at the American Graduate School of International Management. The figures per employee? Your company will probably spend three to five times your base salary to place, sustain, and retrieve you and your family. A typical, successful three-year assignment can cost a company as much as $1 million.

Result: Assignment failure can affect you and your family personally, from coping with the lack of a home or a job on return, to depression, marital discord—even divorce or alcoholism.

Remedy: Cross-cultural training and language instruction. Get cross-cultural training before you go. Language instruction should begin well in advance of your transfer and continue during your assignment. Cross-cultural and language training will equip you with the awareness, skills, tools, and resources you need to perform effectively across national and cultural boundaries.

Research shows that cross-cultural and language training dramatically increase your chances of success on an international assignment—at home as well as at work.

Why? Because they:

- Increase your self-sufficiency and confidence.
- Save corporate time and money by increasing your productivity.
- Make you aware of how and where to ask for help.
- Ready you and your family for a once-in-a-lifetime opportunity.

The challenges of an international assignment are myriad and intense. Anything you can do to prepare yourself for situations you will inevitably confront will help you. Cross-cultural and language training are invaluable preventatives to frustration and anxiety as you navigate cultural differences on assignment.

There are many kinds of cross-cultural training. Pre-departure or relocation training gives international transferees and their families information and tools to ease their adjustment to living and working in a new country. If pre-departure training isn't included in your assignment letter or compensation package, lobby for it. It's an essential part of your preparation.

During the last decade, corporations have been recognizing the benefits of cross-cultural training. Recent human-resources studies by the Society for Human Resource Management show that 65 to 70 percent of the U.S. companies surveyed offer some kind of cross-cultural training. However, the same study notes that up to three-fourths of international transferees say they could have been more successful if they'd had additional pre-departure training and that their families needed more cultural training to make the transition abroad.

Domestically based international businesswomen should note the following: Many businesses are increasing the success of individuals working in the international arena of a U.S. firm by providing them with other kinds of cross-cultural training.

"For various assignments, my company has recommended I enroll in cross-cultural training, and it is certainly valuable," observes Vivien Godfrey, an international marketing executive. Cross-cultural training before working in Germany gave Godfrey "ideas about how to prepare differently for meetings and business interactions there." She also learned about subtle, yet critical, differences between the United States and her home country, England. Then, before being sent to Japan, cross-cultural training helped her learn about building effective relationships and the value of business protocol. Even little things like knowing about correct seating plans in conference rooms enhanced her credibility with Japanese business partners and added to her success overseas.

WHAT CROSS-CULTURAL TRAINING SHOULD INCLUDE

Leading cross-cultural training expert Robert Kohls believes that quality pre-departure or relocation training for international transferees should include:

Basic Training.   Every good cross-cultural training program begins by taking a good look at how you function within your own culture. Topics might include:
- Understanding your own culture and how it affects your behavior.
- Comparing home and host cultures.
- Defining culture shock and how to live through it.

Logistics
- What to take
- Setting up your household
- The local economy
- Visa and passport requirements
- Residence and work documents
- Legal requirements
- Housing (see page 176 for more on housing)
- Utilities/appliances
- Electric current
- Weights and measurements
- Mail
- Telephone, cables, faxes, etc.
- Transportation
- Banking
- Insurance
- Schools
- Currency
- Climate/weather
- Legal holidays
- Servants and services
- Survival needs
- Support systems
- Making friends (for children, too)
- Establishing a routine
- Finding where to buy what you need
- Entertaining guests
- Leisure activities
- How family members can support each other
- Maintaining old ties and friendships
- Security and safety

Deep-Culture Studies. This is critical to cross-cultural training. Topics include:
- Demographics
- Ethnic composition
- History, geography, politics, economics
- Education system
- Religious/philosophical beliefs
- Inventions and scientific achievements
- Sports and games
- Places of scenic and historical interest

Language Training. You should start this well before leaving and continue on your arrival in the host country. (For more on language training, see page 218.)

Nonverbal Communication. This includes gestures and body language.

Family Health Considerations
- Assessing special health needs
- Learning where to find doctors, dentists, etc.
- Know which prescription and nonprescription medications to take along

Social Do's and Taboos. This includes etiquette for business and nonbusiness situations.

Business Practices and Procedures*

Cultural Mindset

- National character traits in host country
- Values
- Implicit cultural assumptions
- Thought processes

Current Events and Issues

Problems Expatriates Face

---

*A note of caution: this subject is often brushed over. Demand cross-cultural training that can help you understand specific business norms and practices in your new country, such as negotiation style, meeting and presentation style, common management practices, and preferred conflict-resolution methods. If your facilitator can't do this, look elsewhere.

(*Source: Training Know-How for Cross-Cultural and Diversity Trainers*, L. Robert Kohls with Herbert L. Brussow.)

CHOOSING THE BEST PRE-DEPARTURE OR RELOCATION TRAINING PROGRAM

When selecting a cross-cultural training company, be suspicious of off-the-shelf, quick-and-dirty solutions. Your cross-cultural training program should be customized to fit your specific needs.

Quality pre-departure training for you and your family can be narrowed down to five basic steps:

1. *Needs Assessment.* Your trainer should take the time to learn about you and, where appropriate, your family. A thorough needs assessment examines your work and family background, job objectives, length of assignment, challenges and strengths, languages spoken, and critical business and personal issues that could have an impact on your success.

2. *Customized Design.* Based on the information gathered during the needs assessment, the trainer creates a personal profile of you and, where relevant, your family. A customized design ensures that the training will help you professionally—as well as personally. The training should address specific business challenges you will face. That means customizing it to your position and function within your company, and the country and region of your relocation.

3. *Training/Consultation.* Before you leave, corporations typically provide two to five days of cross-cultural training for you and, if you're married, your spouse and family. Many companies also offer destination services. Destination service companies help you locate schools, homes, and other services you need to live in a new country.

4. *Summary Report.* This report is addressed to you and your employer and identifies the hurdles and challenges you'll most likely confront in the host country. It includes business and personal issues you may still need to clarify with your company. It can also include a variety of personal and professional action plans to help you transfer training skills directly to your job and private life.

5. *Follow-Up.* Adjusting to a new country takes months, even years. Quality cross-cultural training providers will contact you once you've arrived

in the host country and check up on you regularly. They'll ask if you need additional support services and then work with your company to get you that help.

A Caution

Make sure the facilitators and trainers you work with are professionals who have lived and worked abroad and studied other languages. Your training program should also include a co-facilitator or guest speakers who have lived and worked in the country where you are going. Before signing on the dotted line with a cross-cultural training firm:

- Check biographies of the company's principals and trainers/facilitators.
- Research the company's reputation.
- Ask for recommendations from past participants.

Finally, remember that cultures change fast. Make sure the cultural information being shared with you is up to date. Ask your trainers/facilitators where and when they did their research.

LANGUAGE INSTRUCTION

Cross-cultural training and language training go hand in hand. Each enhances your learning of the other. And both are indispensable preparation for an international assignment. As with cross-cultural training, learning a new language doesn't happen in a week or a month. It takes several years. And language learning is an invaluable tool in understanding a new culture, communicating, and experiencing success abroad. Finally, as with cross-cultural training, the cost of language training should be included in your compensation package.

If you find language instruction on your own, you can use many of the same criteria you used to choose cross-cultural training.

Steve Iverson, President, Iverson Language Associates, Inc., Milwaukee, recommends that businesswomen take the immersion route—eight hours a day for a week or spread out over six months, where all coursework is conducted in the language being learned. "Most people are interested in learning conversational language, which teaches survival skills like numbers, introductions, how to respond in situational language at the hotel and airport," he says. "This way you start with speaking, repeating the instructor's words, then later you can look at grammar." After the course is completed, reinforce your learning with language tapes, videos, or CD ROMs.

In choosing a language instructor, first meet and talk with the potential instructor about your needs and goals. If you don't "click" with the instructor, keep looking. Of course, you must find someone experienced in language instruction who's familiar with the nuances of conversation in the region of the country in which you'll be living and working. But you also need someone who will motivate and interest you, someone who is encouraging, someone with whom you are comfortable making mistakes. If you don't make mistakes, you can never improve.

Before your transfer, it's critical to get regular language training at home or at the office for as long as you can. You don't have time *not* to learn a language. You will always be disabled without it.

Women returning from assignments sing the same sad song: "I wish I'd taken more language training before I left—and definitely while I was there. But I just got too busy." One of your primary keys to success is knowing the language, being as fluent as possible. Language is the key that unlocks the secrets of a new culture. Once abroad, continue your language training. Try to find a trainer who can meet you while you're at work. And make sure your family members continue their language training as well.

At Home in a Global Environment: Cross-Cultural Training for the Businesswoman Not Living Abroad

In our rapidly changing global business environment, businesswomen need every advantage they can get. Knowing how to extract the best out of the business environment in which you'll be operating gives you that advantage. This is the objective of cross-cultural training.

There are many kinds of cross-cultural training:

- Intercultural awareness training. This is essential if you're about to enter the international arena or are expanding your international scope.
- Multinational team building. Make sure training includes a skilled facilitator.
- Intercultural communication skills. This is especially im-

portant for those working globally through such media as telephone and e-mail correspondence as well as for businesswomen conducting business face to face.

- Joint venture preparation. The trainer should work well with teams from both your company and the international company you're poised to work with.
- International human resources management. This enables personnel to help transferees with such financial issues as compensation and tax equalization, as well as culture shock and repatriation.
- Americanization training for non–U.S. transferees.
- International negotiation facilitation.
- Protocol training for receiving international representatives into your company. This teaches you to treat your visitors with respect and cultural sensitivity.

(*Source:* Excerpted in part from *Training Know-How for Cross-Cultural and Diversity Trainers,* L. Robert Kohls with Herbert L. Brussow.)

The following organizations can provide tips on finding quality cross-cultural training in your area:

SIETAR International (Society for Intercultural Education, Training and Research), 808 17th Street NW, Suite 200, Washington, D.C. 20006; telephone 202-446-7883. There are chapters in every U.S. major city. To contact the national headquarters, write to 733 15th St. NW, Suite 900, Washington, D.C. 20005; telephone 202-316-4278. SIETAR publishes intercultural training books, a newsletter, and a journal. The latter two are included in membership, along with discounts on publications and programs. SIETAR publishes a bi-monthly international newsletter called "Communique," and also sponsors a number of conferences annually for members and nonmembers. Conference speakers are leaders in the field of cross-cultural communication and training.

American Society for Training and Development (ASTD). Some chapters within ASTD have an international special interest group that sponsors monthly informational meetings with speakers on international business topics. ASTD's national headquarters is 1640 King St., Alexandria, VA 22313; telephone 703-683-8100.

SOURCES FOR HELP

- *Intercultural Press.* This publisher offers the best selection of cross-cultural communications titles available. Its collection of works has something for everyone, from seasoned international business professionals to teachers and psychologists. To receive a quarterly catalog of new and recent titles and bestsellers, write to P. O. Box 700, Yarmouth, ME 04096; telephone 207-846-5168.
- *Sage Publications, Inc.,* 211 West Hillcrest Drive, Newbury Park, CA 91320. Specializes in texts on cross-cultural communication. Request a catalog of publications.
- *Kennedy Center Publications,* Brigham Young University, 280 Herald R. Clark Building, P. O. Box 24538, Provo, UT 84602-4538; telephone 800-528-6279. Request a catalog of publications.
- *American Ways,* by Gary Althen (Intercultural Press, Yarmouth, ME, 1988).
- *The Art of Crossing Cultures,* by Craig Storti (Intercultural Press, Yarmouth, ME, 1990).
- *The International Business Book: All the Tools, Tactics, and Tips You Need for Doing Business Across Cultures,* by Vincent Guy and John Mattock (Intercultural Press, Yarmouth, ME). Includes case studies, checklists, games, and quizzes to challenge your assumptions about other cultures and offers practical advice on crossing cultures in business.
- *Understanding Cultural Differences: Germans, French and Americans,* by Edward T. and Mildred Reed Hall (Intercultural Press, Yarmouth, ME, 1989).

SOURCES FOR LANGUAGE TRAINING

- Investigate your local universities, community colleges, and technical schools for language instruction. Many offer night courses for scheduling flexibility. Many American cities also have private language schools. Check the Yellow Pages of your telephone directory under "Language Schools" to find the schools in your area.
- *Berlitz International.* This worldwide language school has its headquarters in Princeton, NJ; telephone 609-924-8500. Call 800-257-9449 for information on the school nearest you. Berlitz teaches all languages, including English. Choose between private and group lessons with native-fluent instructors. You'll find the teaching approach less academic than

high school or college courses. Berlitz emphasizes practical and conversational speaking skills.

- *Berlitz Publications.*   Berlitz offers publications for self-study and travel. Its home study courses, "Think and Talk," are available on cassettes, audio CDs, or CD ROM. Berlitz claims these courses are equivalent to two years of high school instruction. Advanced instruction is available for Spanish, French, and German. "Berlitz and You" is a self-study English course available in individual packages targeted to speakers of specific languages, for example, "Berlitz and You for French Speakers."
- *Alliance Française.*   This is a nonprofit organization sponsored by the French government offering French language instruction and cultural programs to its members. There are over 1300 independently run associations in 130 countries around the world. Many chapters also offer an extensive lending library, translation and interpretation services, and a business French diploma. Check the phonebook to see if there's a chapter in your area. Or call the national office at 202-966-9740. The address is 2819 Ordway St. NW, Washington, D.C. 20008. The international headquarters are located in Paris at 101 Boulevard Raspail, 75270 Paris. Telephone 011-45-44-38-28; fax 011-45-44-89-42.

PART FIVE

HELP FOR THE INDEPENDENT BUSINESSWOMAN WHO WISHES TO WORK ABROAD

If you decide you'd like to live and work abroad, but you don't have a company to send you, dozens of magazines and books can help you get overseas on your own steam. The tips and resources in Part Five will show you how to plan and execute your job search, arrange visas and work permits, locate housing, and get settled in your new country.

33

TIPS FOR THE INDEPENDENT CAREER SEARCH

A world of options awaits the independent woman who wants to pursue an international career in a foreign country. Positions can be found in government agencies, businesses, nonprofits, educational institutions, trade and professional organizations, consulting firms, import-export companies, and contractors.

Here are some factors to consider in your research for the perfect global job:

1. Tailor your search so your goals and interests fit with the type of organization you choose. For example:
   - Make money—join a multinational corporation
   - Have an adventure—lead treks in the rainforest
   - Pursue a cause—work for Amnesty International

2. Consider where you want to live and work. This can be as broad as anywhere overseas or as specific as one country.

3. Make an inventory of the travel documents you will need: visa, work permit, residence permit, and so on. Is a work permit necessary? Who sponsors the work permit? Can you get the work permit in the country? How will you obtain a visa?

4. Make a study of the workplace. What are the labor laws affecting foreign workers in the country or countries of interest to you? Are there unions; are they powerful?

5. Take time to learn about the job or career you have chosen. What does the job entail, and how does it differ from the same position here in North America?

6. Review your finances. What is the cost of living in your chosen country? Find out the average salary/wages for your profession. This is especially

helpful in wage negotiation. Will your salary allow you to support yourself and live within your comfort range? Will you be able to find affordable housing?

7. Determine the typical benefit package for your chosen job or profession. Does it include medical insurance, retirement planning, life insurance, company car, or paid vacation? What benefits are you willing to live without?

8. Learn all you can about national security and personal safety. What is the political situation? Is there fighting or unrest? What is the crime rate? Learn about the advantages and disadvantages of daily life. Are you sure you will feel safe in this country?

9. Consider the needs of individual family members. What are the professional opportunities for your spouse? What educational options are there for your children?

10. Examine your long-range goals. How would a global job fit? Does it need to?

RESOURCES

Directory of Work and Study in Developing Countries is a guide to paid and voluntary work and academic opportunities with over 400 organizations in over 100 developing countries. (Vacation-Work, 9 Park End Street, Oxford, OX1 1HJ England).

International Jobs: Where They Are (and) How to Get Them by Eric Kocher (Addison-Wesley Longman Publishing Company, Reading, MA, 1993). This book is required reading for anyone seeking employment overseas. It offers advice on career selection, education, and job hunting strategies; it also contains region-by-region job market assessment and information on a wide variety of international employment spheres from government and business to nonprofits, communications, and teaching. The outstanding bibliography is worth the price of the book.

Overseas 1995 Summer Jobs: Your Complete Guide to Thousands of Summer Employment Opportunities Abroad, edited by David Woodworth (Vacation-Work, 9 Park End Street, Oxford, OX1 1HJ England, 1995). A lively book covering more than 30,000 summer jobs in over fifty countries around the world. Includes job descriptions, application procedures, getting visas and work permits, and a country-by-country overview of job situations for nonnationals.

International Career Employment Opportunities.   This bi-weekly report identifies and describes more than 500 current international career positions with U.S. employers in all sectors of the job market, including government, corporations, and nonprofits, as well as with the United Nations and other international government organizations. Includes positions requiring little or no experience. The job postings are categorized in eight sections: (1) International Understanding; Education; Communication; Exchange, (2) Foreign Policy; Research; Intelligence, (3) International Trade and Finance, (4) International Environmental Programs, (5) International Development Assistance, (6) International Program Administration and Technical Support, (7) International Internships, and (8) International Health Care Professionals.

Try looking for this highly useful publication in your local reference library, your state trade office library, or local university libraries. It is published by the Carlyle Company, a Brubach Corporation Company, Rt. 2, Box 305, Standardsville, VA 22973. Phone: 804-985-6444; fax: 804-985-6828.

International Employment Gazette. This periodical calls itself "The #1 Source for Overseas Jobs." It comes out every two weeks and is sold by subscription (6 issues for $35; 13 for $55; and 26 for $95) and at newsstands. Each issue contains details on over 400 current international job openings. You may be able to locate this publication in your city or university library. The *Gazette* also offers a subscription service called the International Placement Network that provides comprehensive personalized reports about current job openings geared to the subscriber's occupational and geographic interests. You can access job openings already published in the *Gazette* as well as those with employers who accept applications. The *International Employment Gazette* has a three-page section of international jobs in every other issue of the periodical "National Business Employment Weekly" of the *Wall Street Journal*. Contact the publisher of the *International Employment Gazette,* Global Resources Organization, Inc., at 220 N. Main Street, Suite 100, Greenville, SC 29601. Phone: 800-882-9188; fax: 803-235-3369; e-mail: intljobs@aol.com.

Impact Publications, located in Manassas Park, Virginia, has some excellent international job-hunting titles available through the *International Employment Gazette* (see above). Four titles from Impact Publications are as follows:

Almanac of International Jobs & Careers: A Guide to Over 1001 Employers!, 2nd edition, by Drs. Ron and Caryl Krannich, 1994. In this tome, you will find complete contact information for governments, businesses, consulting firms, nonprofits, and universities. Includes special chapters on internships and teaching.

The Complete Guide to International Jobs and Careers, 2nd edition, by Drs. Ron and Caryl Krannich, 1992. This book evaluates the outlook for international jobs, outlines job opportunities, and identifies productive job-hunting strategies—including resume writing, networking, and interviewing. You'll also learn about major employers hiring international specialists and find specific chapters on the travel industry and starting an international business.

Jobs for People Who Love Travel by Drs. Ron and Caryl Krannich, 1995. Globe-trotters will be intrigued by this book about jobs involving travel both at home and overseas, including government and travel industry positions. It also provides job-hunting tips and employer contact information.

Guide to Careers in World Affairs, 3rd edition, edited by the Foreign Policy Association, 1993. Updated for the 1990s, this guide describes hundreds of major employers in international business, consulting, finance, banking, journalism, law, translation/interpretation, nonprofits, government, and the United Nations. Includes internships, graduate programs, job strategies, and contact information.

Overseas Employment Newsletter. This is a news service for job seekers in all sectors of the economy, including government, corporate, and nonprofit. Write to them at 1255 Laird, Suite 208, Mount Royal, Quebec, Canada H3P2T1. Phone: 514-739-1108; fax: 514-739-0795.

American Jobs Abroad (Gale Research, Detroit, 1994, $55). This volume offers job seekers a listing of over 800 companies and organizations with operations overseas. It profiles individual countries with statistics, government contacts, and social services.

Looking for Employment in Foreign Countries, 9th edition (World Trade Academy Press, New York, 1992). Consult this book to learn how to find jobs abroad with for-profit corporations and nonprofit and voluntary organizations and government agencies. It includes sample resumes and cover letters and work permit requirements, and details thirty-seven countries. The book also lists opportunities for teachers.

Vacation-Work Publishers at 9 Park End Street, Oxford OX1 1HJ England, publishes or distributes an excellent series of books for finding temporary work around the world. Many titles are available in the United States from *Peterson's Guides,* 202 Carnegie Center, P. O. Box 2123, Princeton, NJ 08543-2123. Here are some examples:

Work Your Way Around the World
The Directory of Jobs and Careers Abroad
The International Directory of Voluntary Work
Kibbutz Volunteer
Live & Work series, a selection of books giving full information for people wanting to live and work in individual countries temporarily or permanently.
Teaching English Abroad
The Teenager's Vacation Guide to Work, Study and Adventure
The Directory of Work and Study in Developing Countries
Jobs in Japan

Transitions Abroad. Journal for international education, living, working, and traveling abroad. Published five times per year along with an annual "Educational Travel Resource Guide." $19.95. Write to *Transitions Abroad* Subscriber Service, Box 344, Amherst, MA 01004.

How to Get the Job You Want Overseas, revised, by Arthur Liebers (Pilot Books, New York, 1990).

How to Get a Job in Europe: The Insider's Guide by Bob Sanborn (Wiley, New York, 1988).

Making It Abroad: The International Job Hunting Guide by Howard Schuman (Wiley, New York, 1988).

Another way to research international job opportunities is to consult directories of international organizations, corporations, nonprofits, and so on. Many of these directories are cost-prohibitive for the average person, but they can be found at your local business library. To start, look for international directories by Standard & Poor or Dun & Bradstreet. Other publications that may be helpful to you include:

Encyclopedia of Associations: International (nonprofit) Organizations 29th edition (Gale Research, Detroit). Annual directory of 14,500 nonprofit international organizations.

For international banking, check *Polk Bank Directory: International Edition* (Polk, Nashville, TN, 1993), or *Thomson Bank Directory* (Thomson Financial Publishing, Skokie, IL, 1996).

International Corporate Yellow Book (Leadership Directories, Inc., New York). This is a semiannually updated directory of over 1000 leading international companies and their top executives. It includes addresses, phone/fax/telex, and information about their business. The *Yellow Book* is organized by major geographic areas of the world.

Directory of Multinationals, 4th edition (Stockton Press, New York, 1992). This resource offers profiles of 450 of the world's biggest multinationals. It lists each company's sales and financial performance and values of exports.

Directory of the World's Largest Service Companies—Series I. Moody's and the United Nations Centre on Transnational Corporations produce this publication. It lists approximately 200 companies and covers fourteen service industries.

Directory of American Firms Operating in Foreign Countries (World Trade Academy Press, New York, 1996).

Directory of Foreign Firms Operating in the United States (World Trade Academy Press, New York, 1992).

If you desire help in organizing a research strategy for your international job hunt, consult these publications:

How to Find Information about Companies (Washington Researchers, Washington, D.C., 1994).

How to Find Information about Foreign Firms, 5th edition (Washington Researchers, Washington, D.C., 1993). This resource gives you ten steps for evaluating foreign companies. It details U.S. and non–U.S. organizations, associations, government agencies, country experts, and databases.

International Business Information: How to Find It, How to Use It by Ruth A. Pagell and Michael Halperin (Oryx, Phoenix, AZ, 1994). The authors provide electronic and print business information services and discuss basic elements of trade and finance, politics and organizations.

Where to Find Business Information: A Worldwide Guide for Everyone Who Needs the Answers to Business Questions, 2nd edition, by David Browstone & Gorton Carruth (Wiley, New York, 1982).

The U.S. Peace Corps is looking for volunteers with business skills to serve in forty-eight countries abroad. "Peace Corps invites you to apply no matter where you are in your career," states the organization's recruitment brochure. For more information, call 800-424-8580. Or write Peace Corps, Room 8500, 1900 K Street, NW, Washington, D.C. 20526.

Christian Placement Network (Interchristo). This operation puts you in touch with Christian nonprofit organizations needing your skills and abilities in the

United States and overseas. 19303 Fremont Avenue North, Seattle, WA 98133-3800. Phone: 800-426-1342.

Co-Ordinating Committee for International Voluntary Service. UNESCO 1 rue Miollis, 75015 Paris, France. Phone: 45-68-27-31; fax: 42-73-05-21. UNESCO publishes *Volunteering in the 90's* in two volumes: Europe and North America and Africa and Asia. Each volume contains over 120 organizations. They also publish *Africa Directory.* Write to the address above for a complete list of publications.

PART SIX

ADDITIONAL
RESOURCES

To help you locate resources quickly, the items in this part are organized into categories. Many of those categories correspond to topics we have addressed in this book.

If you know of a resource for women in international business that you think should be added to future editions of this book, kindly contact the publisher. The authors are grateful for your input.

ESSENTIAL RESOURCES

Obtain these immediately!

Bibliography of International Resources, 8th edition, September 1994. This complete and dizzying 240-page compilation of printed, computer, video, audio, and even human resources will show you the world of international information and contacts that await you. It was compiled for the Minnesota Trade Office (MTO) International Library by Marilyn C. Gahm, whom the MTO designates the best librarian in the state. It includes title index and publisher contacts. Prices of materials are included. This is a "must-have" and can be yours for $15. Call the Minnesota Trade Office International Library at 800-657-3858. They are located at 1000 Minnesota World Trade Center, 30 E. 7th Street, St. Paul, MN 55101-4902.

Intercultural Press Catalog. This publisher offers the best selection of cross-cultural communications titles. There is something for everyone, from seasoned international business professionals to teachers and psychologists. Get yourself on their mailing list immediately to receive a free quarterly catalog of new and recent titles and bestsellers. Write to them at P.O. Box 700, Yarmouth, ME 04096. Phone: 207-846-5168; fax: 207-846-5181; e-mail: interculturalpress@mcimail.com.

Going International: How to Make Friends and Deal Effectively in the Global Marketplace by Lennie Copeland and Lewis Griggs (Plume—Random House, New York, 1985). This excellent handbook belongs in every woman's international library. It gives you solid advice for international business effectiveness, protocol guidelines, and a special chapter for women in international business. In the appendix you will find a country-by-country protocol rundown. Also available from Griggs Productions is a set of videos that illustrate the themes in the book through dramatizations and discussions led by cross-cultural business experts. The titles include (1) *Bridging the Culture Gap,* (2) *Managing the Overseas Assignment,* (3) *Beyond Culture Shock,* (4) *Welcome Home Stranger,* (5) *Working in the USA,* (6) *Living in the USA,* and (7) *Going International—Safely.* Videos are available for preview, rental, and purchase. Nonprofits receive a discount. Phone: 800-210-4200; fax: 415-668-6004. Griggs Productions is located at 2046 Clement Street, San Francisco, CA 94121-2118.

RESOURCES FOR WOMEN

Competitive Frontiers: Women Managers in a Global Economy by Nancy Adler and Dafna N. Izraeli, eds. (Blackwell Publishers, Cambridge, MA, 1994). Ms. Adler, of McGill University in Montreal, is a worldwide expert on women in international management. This collection of writings covers the globe, exploring the link between global competitive advantage and greater numbers of women in management roles. The book exposes "the myths which have prevented many companies from fully utilizing talented women in their global workforce."

International Businesswoman of the 1990's: A Guide to Success in the Global Marketplace by Marlene L. Rossman (Greenwood Press, Westport, CT, 1990). Offers advice on preparing for a career in international business, international negotiating, global marketing, life on the road, career and family, and how women can conduct business in specific world regions.

International Dimensions of Organizational Behavior by Nancy Adler, 2nd edition (Wadsworth, Belmont, CA, 1991).

Megatrends for Women by Patricia and John Naisbitt (Villard, New York, 1992).

Reach for the Top: Women and Changing Facts of Work Life, edited by Nancy A. Nichols (Harvard Business School Press, Boston, 1994).

Women in Management Worldwide, edited by Nancy J. Adler and Dafna N. Izraeli (M. E. Sharpe, Inc., New York, 1988).

Women's Employment and Multinationals in Europe, edited by Diane Elson and Ruth Pearson (Macmillan, London, 1989).

Working with Japan Series: Women in Business. This is one video in a seven-part series on Japan. It is produced by ITRI, 1750 Buchanan Street, San Francisco, CA 94115. Phone: 800-626-2047. They offer a discount for non-profit/educational organizations.

Organization of Women in International Trade (OWIT). OWIT is a not-for-profit association dedicated to professionals engaged in international trade and related business areas and services. It provides a valuable forum for members to exchange views, ideas, and information on current trends and developments in their field. The organization also offers opportunities to its members to enhance their knowledge and skills through educational programs, panel discussions, monthly newsletters, and special events. Membership is open to professionals in the international trade community. Meetings are held monthly and there is an annual national convention. Individual and corporate memberships are available.

There are chapters throughout the United States and in Bermuda and Mexico. For information on joining or starting a chapter in your area, contact OWIT Vice President Donna Murray, CaroTrans International, c/o 8423 104th Avenue, P.O. Box 331, Pleasant Prairie, WI 53158. Phone: 630-860-7588; fax: 630-860-7698; e-mail: DURKE1901@aol.com.

NAWBO—National Association of Women Business Owners. According to NAWBO, women-owned businesses employ 30 percent more people than the Fortune 500s. By the year 2000, 50 percent of all businesses will be owned by women. NAWBO is an organization for women business owners that offers "exceptional peer networking, mentoring, visibility in media and community, leadership training, and education." Many members are active in international business. NAWBO chapters are located in fifty-two cities and represent more than 30,000 businesses worldwide. Membership is open to sole proprietors, partners, and corporate owners. The mailing address is 1413 K Street, NW, Suite 637, Washington, D.C. 20005. For information, call 301-608-2590. NAWBO is affiliated with Les Femmes Chefs d'Entreprises Mondiales (World Association of Women Entrepreneurs) in 33 countries.

Women's Colleges: The Inside Guide to More Than 70 of These Popular Schools—Proven Training Grounds for Successful Women Leaders by Jo Anne Adler, with Jenifer Adler Friedman (Prentice-Hall, New York, 1994). This guide details each college's educational mission, campus and student life, enrollment, and majors. Many of the institutions profiled offer international relations and economics, international business, and area studies.

INTERNATIONAL EDUCATION AND INTERNSHIPS

High School

American Field Service (AFS).   AFS is the world's oldest and largest nonprofit high school student and teacher exchange program. It was founded by ambulance drivers during World War I and II. Its mission is world peace and intercultural understanding. There are opportunities both for people seeking educational exchange and for volunteers. With AFS, you can select from over fifty countries in Europe, Africa, the Americas, Asia, and the Pacific. Programs include academic year for high school students, interim programs for high school graduates, and summer programs. Financial aid and scholarships are available. AFS operates five regional offices around the United States— in Portland, OR; Los Angeles; Minneapolis/St. Paul, MN; Springfield, MA; and Annapolis, MD. To learn more about becoming an exchange student or host, call 800-876-2377 and you will be connected automatically to the office in your region. To receive a free AFS catalog, write to Program Information Office, AFS Intercultural Programs/USA, 220 East 42nd Street, New York, NY 10017.

Youth for Understanding (YFU).   Established in 1951, YFU is a nonprofit educational organization dedicated to creating a more peaceful, cooperative world through greater understanding and friendship. It offers exchange programs for high school students in about forty countries. YFU's international center is located in Washington, D.C., and it has ten regional offices across the United States. Programs include summer, semester, and academic year. Contact YFU if you're interested in becoming an exchange student or a host. Scholarships are available. Address: 3501 Newark St. NW, Washington, D.C. 20016-3199.

Sports for Understanding (SFU).   This summer program accepts teenagers between fourteen and nineteen with a minimum 2.0 GPA who are active in their chosen sport. Program participants train and compete with teams in countries around the world. Call 800-TEENAGE (800-833-6243) or 202-895-1122 for information and application forms. YFU's address is 3501 Newark Street, NW, Washington, D.C. 20016-3199.

Directory of Resources for Cultural and Educational Exchanges and International Communication (Washington, D.C., U.S. International Communication Directory).

Orientation Handbook for Youth Exchange Programs by Cornelius Grove (Intercultural Press, Yarmouth, ME, 1989).

The Au Pair and Nanny's Guide to Working Abroad (Vacation-Work: 9 Park End Street, Oxford OX1 1HJ England). This book explains how to get domestic work abroad, including a guide to agencies and country-specific guides.

The Teenager's Vacation Guide to Work, Study & Adventure (Vacation-Work; 9 Park End Street; Oxford OX1 1HJ England).

Undergraduate Study

The Whole World Handbook: A Student Guide to Work, Study, and Travel Abroad (Council on International Educational Exchange, 205 East 42nd Street, New York, NY 10017).

Academic Year Abroad, edited by Sara J. Steen (Institute for International Education, 809 United Nations Plaza, New York, NY 10017-3580). This handbook describes study-abroad programs and internships for college students. It also gives travel tips and financial-aid information.

Peterson's Study Abroad 1995: A Guide to Semester and Year Abroad Academic Programs (Peterson's Guides, Inc., 202 Carnegie Center, P.O. Box 2123, Princeton, NJ 08543-2123). This publication also covers international internships.

U.S. News and World Report publishes an annual ranking of colleges around the country. In the category of undergraduate business schools for 1996, the top five international business programs in rank order are: University of South Carolina at Columbia, University of Pennsylvania (Wharton), New York University (Stern), University of Michigan at Ann Arbor, Georgetown University.

Where in the World Should I Study? A Guide to International Schools by Andrea Bensaia (Imperial Publications, New York, 1993). An international education guide for English-speaking students that features opportunities from high school to post-graduate level worldwide. It also references independent universities and colleges and those that have affiliations with U.S. universities and colleges.

The following are some institutions in Western Europe open to English-speakers. Of course, if you're competent in one or more languages, there is a wider selection of overseas universities to which you can apply.

- American University in Paris
- Franklin College, Switzerland. Offers a B.A. in International Affairs.
- Helsinki School of Economics and Business Administration in Finland
- London School of Economics
- Schiller International University, Berlin, Germany. Offers a B.A. and an M.A. in International Relations, an M.B.A., and an M.I.M. (Master's in International Management).
- University of Wisconsin-Madison's five-year undergraduate major in international business requires fluency in a second language, one year's work abroad, and an internship. Write to Professor Jeff Gehrke, UW-Madison, School of Business, 5151 Grainger Hall, 975 University Ave., Madison, WI 53706-4194 for more information. Phone: 608-265-3579.
- The International 50 is an association of just over 50 American international liberal arts colleges. These are small, selective, independent colleges dedicated to liberal education that have made outstanding contributions in advancing important interests in world affairs. The association has its headquarters at Kalamazoo College in Michigan. To learn more about the colleges in the International 50, call 800-253-3602 or contact the association by e-mail at Admissions@Kzoo.edu.
- The University of Florida in Miami has an excellent undergraduate program for people wishing to specialize in Latin American business.
- The University of Hawaii offers a program for undergraduate students wanting to focus on business in the Pacific Rim countries.
- Other excellent undergraduate programs are available at Memphis State University, the University of Pennsylvania, New York University, and Harvard University.
- Middlebury College in Vermont has undergraduate and graduate degree programs in a large number of languages. Middlebury also offers intensive academic year-abroad programs.

Graduate Study

The top international business graduate programs in the country for 1995, according to *U.S. News and World Report,* are the American Graduate School of International Business (Thunderbird), the University of South Carolina, University of Pennsylvania (Wharton), Columbia University (NY), and Harvard University.

• Thunderbird—American Graduate School of International Management. Thunderbird offers one degree—the Master of International Management, the M.I.M. The school has a reputation as America's premier graduate school for business, turning out graduates who want to be international business leaders. Two features that distinguish Thunderbird are: (1) its placement program, where dozens of employers regularly come to the school to recruit graduates, and (2) its alumni association. You can travel to any major overseas city and find a helpful Thunderbird alumnus. Address inquiries to the Dean of Admissions, 15249 N. 59th Avenue, Glendale, AZ 85306-3399. Phone: 800-848-9084; fax: 602-439-5432; telex: 187123.

• The University of South Carolina's Masters of International Business (MIBS) Program was founded in 1974, and it was the first business school in the nation to require all students to be fluent in a second language, receive cross-cultural training, and complete a six-month internship abroad with multinational companies.

• The Gourman Report rates graduate and professional programs in American and international universities. Its last ranking in 1993 for international relations chose Harvard as the top school, followed by Princeton, Tufts, Johns Hopkins, Georgetown, Columbia, and Yale.

• University of Florida. Miami's School of Business Administration offers a Master of International Business Studies Program combining an M.B.A. with a Master of Science degree in Business. The two-year total immersion program includes a four-month foreign corporate internship, fluency in a second language, and various seminars on doing business abroad.

• Pepperdine University in Malibu, CA, offers a twenty-month Master in International Business program that includes an eight-month internship overseas.

• UCLA's John E. Anderson Graduate School of Management has a twenty-four-month certificate program combining language and area studies with an M.B.A.

• Monterey Institute of International Studies. Monterey's Graduate School of International Management's M.B.A. program requires students to develop a working proficiency in a second language. (You can even take an accounting course in Spanish!) Students work on international business plans on teams with students from around the world. Contact the Admissions Office at 425 Van Buren Street, Monterey, CA 93940. Phone: 408-647-4123.

U.S. News and World Report ranks the top five Ph.D. programs for international economics in this order: Princeton University, Massachusetts Institute of Technology, Stanford University, Columbia University, and Harvard University.

Internships, Scholarships, and Fellowships

•   AIESEC (pronounced eye-sec)–United States: *Association Internationale des Etudiants en Sciences Economiques et Commerciales* or International Association of Students in Economics and Business Management. AIESEC is an organization dedicated to the development of international understanding and cooperation. The association is designed to train and enlighten future business leaders through the exchange of students and ideas around the world. AIESEC offers business internship exchanges, conferences, study tours, training seminars, and cultural exchanges. It has sixty-four member countries and 40,000 members at 532 college campuses around the world and at more than sixty U.S. universities and colleges. Contact AIESEC–United States' National Office at 14 West 23rd Street, New York, NY 10010. Phone: 212-206-1888, or its Central Regional Office at 208 South La Salle Street, Suite 1331, Chicago, IL 60604. Phone: 312-346-8155.

     •   *Rotary Club Scholarships.*   The Rotary Club is a professional organization for businesspeople with chapters in small and large towns around the country. For the purpose of promoting international relations, Rotary offers scholarships to overseas universities. The scholarship program is open to people who have had at least two years of college and there is no age limit. On the form, which you can obtain from your local Rotary chapter, you must list the top five institutes at which you wish to study. Rotary decides which institute its scholarship recipients will attend. Submit your applications two to three years in advance of the time you would like to study abroad. If you are chosen to be a Rotary scholar, you may be asked to represent the Rotary Club both in your host country and in the United States on your return.

     •   To explore the types of financial support awarded annually to graduate and Ph.D. students researching international topics, consult *The Annual Register of Grant Support*, Chicago National Register (Macmillan Publishing, Directory Division, New York). This publication lists national fellow-ships, grants, and awards, indexed by area of study and geographic area.

• *Graduate Fellowships.* Universities use fellowships to recruit out-standing new students to their graduate and Ph.D. programs. They provide monetary support and tuition for at least one academic year. You may be eligible to apply for a fellowship to pursue international study. Prospective students are usually nominated by their chosen major field or graduate school, and you can apply to the director of your major field or of your graduate school. Your university may participate in several international competitions. Appli-cants are usually required to have completed a bachelor's degree as well as have an outstanding academic record, leadership potential, a carefully formu-lated study proposal, cross-cultural adaptability, and a wide range of inter-ests.

The international programs below are offered annually to U.S. graduate students. Many require U.S. citizenship. Information on the location, number and types of awards, and application deadlines is available from your univer-sity fellowship office.

Churchill Scholarships support one year of graduate study at Churchill College, Cambridge University, England. Most are in engineering, math-ematics, and the sciences; some are in the social sciences and humanities. Applicants must be nineteen to twenty-six when the award begins, and must have earned a baccalaureate degree, but not a doctorate. GRE scores are required. Ten awards are offered nationally.

Fullbright Program offers a variety of full and partial grants for one year of study or research abroad.

German Academic Exchange Service (DAAD) provides ten months of study or research in Germany. Applicants must be eighteen to thirty-two.

Luce Scholars Program funds one-year internships in Asia to eighteen people nationally. Individuals from all fields except Asian affairs may apply. Applicants must be under thirty when program begins.

Marshall Scholarships support two years of graduate study at any of ninety-seven British universities. Applicants should have a GPA of 3.7 be-yond the freshman year and be no more than twenty-six when the award begins. Up to forty awards are offered nationally.

Rhodes Scholarships support two or three years of study at Oxford University in England. Applicants must be eighteen to twenty-four at the time of application. Thirty-two awards are offered nationally.

• *International Opportunities: A Career Guide for Students,* published by the David M. Kennedy Center for International Studies, Brigham Young University. Rather than provide a list of employers for students to contact, this book gives you general steps in preparing for an international career. Exercises in the beginning of the book help you identify your interests and goals and focus on a field and type of career that's best for you. There are suggested summer extracurricular activities and internships to orient you toward your international goal, as well as ideas for learning languages. The book suggests ideas for work experience for young people, from internships and volunteer work to government employment. Contact Kennedy Center Publications, Brigham Young University, P.O. Box 24538, Provo, UT 84602-4538. Phone: 800-528-6279 or 801-378-6528; fax: 801-378-7075.

• *International Career Employment Opportunities.* A portion of this bi-weekly report is devoted to international internships, located both in the United States and overseas. See pages 226–227 for further information.

• *International Directory for Youth Internships.* Council for Intercultural Studies and Programs, 777 UN Plaza, New York, NY 10017.

• *International Internships and Volunteer Programs* by Will Cantrell and Francine Modderno (Worldwise Books, Oakton, VA, 1992). Internships and volunteer positions are broken down into five areas: national and international government, academic programs, independent programs, volunteer programs, and miscellaneous international opportunities. The internships address a wide variety of educational backgrounds and experiences.

• The American Bar Association's International Legal Exchange Program helps place law students in internships in overseas law firms. Contact Edison W. Dick, Executive Director, 1700 Pennsylvania Avenue NW, Suite 620, Washington, D.C. 20006. Phone: 202-393-7122; fax: 202-347-9015.

• *Peterson's Internship 1995,* 15th edition (Peterson's Guides, Princeton, NJ, 1995). Lists internships by areas of study and gives details on the organization, the intern's responsibilities, benefits, and a contact. Describes mainly U.S.–based internships. International relations internships are also included.

PROFESSIONAL DEVELOPMENT

The Thunderbird Management Center, a department of the American Graduate School of International Management in Glendale, Arizona (see earlier listing in the graduate school section), conducts customized executive training programs in language and/or business procedure.

Summer Institute for Intercultural Communication (SIIC). This mecca for interculturalists is held every summer in the Portland, Oregon, area. It offers about two dozen seminars on a wide range of cross-cultural communications topics, many of them business focused. Seminars are taught by world-renowned experts in cross-cultural communication. For more information, write to the Institute at 8835 SW Canyon Lane, Suite 238, Portland, OR 97225, or phone 503-297-4622.

National Association of Small Business International Trade Educators (NASBITE). One World Trade Center, 121 SW Salmon Street, Suite 210, Portland, OR 97204. Phone: 503-274-7482; fax: 503-228-6350.

INTERNATIONAL PROTOCOL

Coping with . . . series; various authors on 12 countries (Basil Blackwell, Cambridge, MA).

Culture Shock! series; various authors (Graphic Arts Center Publishing Co., Portland, OR). Includes complete orientation guides to a long list of countries. You can find *Culture Shock!* titles in the travel section of larger bookstores.

Culturgrams. These are condensed reports on country-specific protocol, cultural background and issues, and nuts-and-bolts advice for getting around and getting things done. They cover more than 125 areas of the world and are also available on CD ROM. For a free catalog, call 800-528-6279. They are published by David M. Kennedy Center for International Studies, Brigham Young University, P.O. Box 24538, Provo, UT 84602-4538.

Do's and Taboos Around the World: A Guide to International Behavior, 3rd edition, edited by Roger E. Axtell (Wiley, New York, 1993). A country-specific handbook full of facts, tips, and cautionary tales offered by over 500 international business travelers. Covers etiquette, business protocol, and verbal and nonverbal communication.

Do's and Taboos of International Trade: A Small Business Primer, revised edition, by Roger E. Axtell (Wiley, New York, 1994). Covers how to get started, trips abroad, contacts for assistance, legal aspects, pricing, financing, shipping, distribution, countertrade, communication, and dealing with the Japanese.

Do's and Taboos of Hosting International Visitors by Roger E. Axtell (Wiley, New York, 1990). Helps you anticipate the needs of your guests; how to meet, greet, host, entertain, negotiate, and do business with visitors from other countries.

Do's and Taboos of Using English Around the World by Roger E. Axtell (Wiley, New York, 1995). Offers valuable rules for making yourself understood when communicating with people from other cultures.

Gestures: Do's and Taboos of Body Language Around the World by Roger E. Axtell (Wiley, New York, 1991). Explores the challenges of nonverbal communication across cultures.

Kiss, Bow or Shake Hands: How to Do Business in 60 Countries by Terri Morrison, Wayne A. Conaway, and George A. Borden, Ph.D. (B. Adams, Holbrook, MA, 1994). Discusses cultural overview, behavior styles, negotiation techniques, general protocol, and business policies.

Put Your Best Foot Forward series by Mary Murray Bosrock (International Education Systems, St. Paul, MN, 1994). Four volumes: Mexico/Canada, Russia, Europe, Asia.

A World of Gestures: Culture and Nonverbal Communication [video] University of California Extension Media Center. Available for purchase or rental; preview is also available. This twenty-eight-minute video features demonstrations of nonverbal gestures from dozens of countries.

MISCELLANEOUS

Do's and Taboos of Preparing for Your Trip Abroad by Roger E. Axtell and John P. Healy (Wiley, New York, 1994).   A step-by-step guide on everything you need to consider before stepping off American soil.

How to Negotiate with Anyone, Anywhere Around the World, by Frank L. Acuff (Amacom, New York, 1993). A practical guide to business practices and cultural traditions all over the world. This book covers negotiation style, decision-making practices, relationships, and interesting case studies for more than forty countries.

The Literate Traveller.   An annual catalog filled with current books on all aspects of travel: country-specific, biking, rail, walking, water travel, and so on. This excellent catalog can be obtained by writing 8306 Wilshire Blvd., Suite 591, Beverly Hills, CA 90211, or phoning 800-850-2665.

Multinational Executive Travel Companion: Business Travel Tips Worldwide by Dale Strand and Janet Tracy (Suburban Publishing of Connecticut, Inc., Stamford, CT, 1995).

The Traveler's Handbook, edited by Melissa Shales (Globe Pequot Press, Old Saybrook, CT, 1988). Has over 800 pages filled with separate essays by dozens of experienced travelers—both men and women. Over one-third of the book consists of lists and directories for almost every conceivable need.

Your Trip Abroad (U.S. Government Printing Office, Superintendent of Documents, Washington, D.C., 1992). S/N 044-000-02335-1. $1.25. Information for preparing your trip. Covers passports, customs, visas, vaccinations, insurance.

Stores Specializing in Travel Books

- Rand-McNally has twenty-four stores in major U.S. cities.
- Book Passage, Corte Madera, California, offers free of charge a mail-order catalog specializing in travel books of all kinds. Phone 800-321-9785 for a copy of this forty-eight-page catalog.
- Books for Travel in St. Paul, Minnesota, publishes a bi-monthly newsletter. Address: 857 Grand Ave., St. Paul, MN 55105. Phone: 612-225-8006.

Passports, Visas, and Work Permits

Apply for passports and visas at the main branch of your city post office.

The Council on International Educational Exchange (CIEE) in New York is the largest provider of work permits. The Council has a reciprocal agreement with several countries through which it obtains more than 5000 work permits each year for U.S. students in exchange for helping international students find work in the United States. For a $160 fee, students receive a work permit, good for three to six months.

Travel Safety

Americans Abroad.   U.S. Department of State. It's free (Order No. 557X) from R. Woods, Consumer Information Center, P.O. Box 100, Pueblo, CO 81002. Tells you how to obtain a passport, avoid terrorist incidents and crimes, and find legal assistance.

Consular Affairs Bulletin Board.   Operated by the U.S. State Department's

Bureau of Consular Affairs. Offers travel warnings and helpful tips to travelers. Free computer access via modem. Phone 202-647-1488 for more information, or write to the U.S. Department of State, Bureau of Consular Affairs, Office of Public Affairs, Room 5807, Washington, D.C. 20520.

Travel Advisories.   Issued by the U.S. Department of State to explain conditions abroad that have serious consequences to physical safety, rights, or health. Obtain them from U.S. embassies and consulates and U.S. Department of Commerce field offices. They're also accessible through your travel agent and the Internet (by subscribing to the mailing list). Send a message to LISTSERV@VTVM2.BITNET; text of your message should read Sheets and Travel Warnings, enter travel-advisories-REQUEST@stolaf.edu.

Travel Health

Infections, Disease and Travel Clinic, Park Nicollet Medical Center, 5000 W. 39th Street, St. Louis Park, MN 55416. Phone: 612-927-3131.

International Traveler's Hotline.   Centers for Disease Control fax service with the latest medical information for destinations around the world. Phone 404-332-4559 for a menu of items and to receive faxed information on a maximum of five topics such as immunization requirements and food/water advisories.

INDEX

ABOUT THE AUTHORS

Roger E. Axtell worked thirty years for The Parker Pen Co., one of the five best-known American brand names in the international marketplace. He retired as Vice President, Worldwide Marketing and since then has written a series of six *Do's and Taboos* books on a range of international subjects such as exporting, protocol, etiquette, travel, hosting, how to communicate effectively, gestures, and body language. A frequent guest on U.S. radio and TV talk shows, Axtell has also appeared on both Canadian and British national television. He has repeatedly appeared on CNN's *International Hour* and ABC's *Good Morning America*. In 1985, *The New Yorker* dubbed him the "international Emily Post."

Tami Briggs is a founder and principal in Transnational Strategies, Inc. (TSI), a cross-cultural business training and consulting company based in Minneapolis, Minnesota. Briggs has helped thousands of women increase their international business effectiveness through programs like "The Role of Gender in International Business," country-specific cross-cultural business management trainings, and relocation and repatriation trainings for women international transferees. She has lived and worked in Switzerland and has taught American culture in Japan. Briggs is a member of the Society for Intercultural Education, Training, and Research (SIETAR), the American Society for Training and Development (ASTD), the Society for Human Resource Management (SHRM), and the Twin Cities Personnel Association (TCPA).

Margaret Corcoran is a consultant in marketing research and cross-cultural business communications and a business writer. She has special expertise in France and is currently co-developing a series of articles for business audiences on French/American communication. In addition to consulting, Corcoran is vice president of marketing for the Alliance Française of Minneapolis–St. Paul and is a member of its Board of Directors. As one of the founders of Transnational Strategies, Inc. (TSI), she successfully trained and consulted for international business executives around the world. Corcoran has lived in France, where she studied European economics and political science. She is a member of the French-American Chamber of Commerce and the Minnesota International Center.

Mary Beth Lamb has helped businesspeople on five continents increase their international business success by developing cross-cultural skills. A consultant, trainer, and public speaker, Lamb is a founder and principal of Transnational Strategies, Inc. (TSI), a cross-cultural business training and consulting company based in Minneapolis, Minnesota. At TSI, Lamb helped thousands of women meet their global business objectives. Lamb was co-owner of an international communications company in Germany and has worked as a television correspondent in Western and Eastern Europe and the United States. She has also served as an international marketing communications consultant to Fortune 500 companies and government agencies. She is a member of the American Society for Training and Development (ASTD), the Society for Human Resource Management (SHRM), the Society for Intercultural Education, Training, and Research (SIETAR), and the Twin Cities Personnel Association (TCPA).